Cloud Computing:
Concepts and Technology

Cloud Computing: Concepts and Technology

Sam Revere

CLANRYE
INTERNATIONAL
www.clanryeinternational.com

Clanrye International,
750 Third Avenue, 9th Floor,
New York, NY 10017, USA

ISBN: 978-1-64726-091-0

Cataloging-in-Publication Data

Cloud computing : concepts and technology / Sam Revere.
    p. cm.
Includes bibliographical references and index.
ISBN 978-1-64726-091-0
1. Cloud computing. 2. Electronic data processing--Distributed processing.
3. Web services. I. Revere, Sam.
QA76.585 .C56 2022
004.678 2--dc23

For information on all Clanrye International publications
visit our website at www.clanryeinternational.com

Contents

Preface VII

Chapter 1   An Introduction to Cloud Computing 1
    a. Characteristics of Cloud Computing   11
    b. Cloud Computing Strategy   13
    c. Cloud Monitoring   20
    d. Mobile Cloud Computing   26
    e. Sustainable Cloud Computing   34

Chapter 2   Cloud Computing: Architecture and Infrastructure 45
    a. Cloud Computing Architecture   45
    b. Cloud Platform   52
    c. Cloud Deployment Models   56
    d. Cloud Computing Networking   61
    e. Cloud Storage   72
    f. Cloud Bursting   75
    g. Microservices Architecture for Cloud Computing   77
    h. Cloud Infrastructure   87
    i. Cloud Server   91
    j. Load Balancing in Cloud Computing   92
    k. Cloud Computing Operation   101

Chapter 3   Web Services Delivered from the Cloud 103
    a. Communications as a Service   103
    b. Infrastructure as a Service   104
    c. Monitoring as a Service   110
    d. Platform as a Service   115
    e. Software as a Service   117

Chapter 4   Cloud Computing: Privacy and Security 123
    a. Secure Distributed Data Storage in Cloud Computing   131
    b. Cloud Computing Security Risks   143
    c. Security as a Service   145

d. Cyber Security in Cloud Computing   147

e. Ways to Reduce Security Breaches in
    Cloud Computing Networks   149

Chapter 5 **Cloud Computing Technologies**... **151**

a. Virtualization in Cloud Computing   151

b. Cloud Computing and IOT   155

c. Cloud Radio Access Networks   156

d. Hybrid Cloud Computing   172

e. Multi-cloud   178

f. Serverless Computing   180

Chapter 6 **Applications of Cloud Computing**... **187**

a. Cloud Applications for Energy Management   187

b. Cloud Computing in the Manufacturing Industry   195

c. Cloud Computing for Intelligent Transportation System   198

d. Application of Cloud Computing in Education   206

e. Business Applications of Cloud Computing   211

f. Cloud Computing Applications for Biomedical Science   215

Permissions

Index

Preface

The on-demand availability of computer system resources without direct active management by the user is known as cloud computing. It is usually used to refer to the data centers, which are available over the Internet to many users. A few major types of clouds are enterprise clouds, public clouds and hybrid cloud. Enterprise clouds, also called private clouds, are usually limited to a single organization while public clouds are available to many organizations. A hybrid cloud is a cloud computing service, which is made up of a fusion of public, private and community cloud services. Cloud computing majorly relies on sharing of resources to achieve economies of scale and coherence. Cloud computing is an upcoming field of science that has undergone rapid development over the past few decades. Different approaches, concepts and technologies related to this field have been included in this book. It will serve as a reference to a broad spectrum of readers.

To facilitate a deeper understanding of the contents of this book a short introduction of every chapter is written below:

Chapter 1- Cloud computing refers to the data centers which provide on-demand availability of computer system resources without direct engagement of the user. Some of its aspects include cloud monitoring, mobile cloud computing, sustainable cloud computing, etc. This is an introductory chapter which will briefly introduce all these aspects of cloud computing.

Chapter 2- The components that are required for cloud computing are termed as cloud architecture. Cloud infrastructure is referred to the hardware and software components required for supporting the cloud computing model. This chapter has been carefully written to provide an easy understanding of cloud architecture and cloud infrastructure.

Chapter 3- Some of the cloud servicing models include communications as a service, infrastructure as a service, monitoring as a service, platform as a service, software as a service, etc. The topics elaborated in this chapter will help in gaining a better perspective about these cloud computing web services.

Chapter 4- Data security and privacy are the two most important factors that are essential for the future development of cloud computing. The security techniques include secure socket layer encryption, intrusion detection system, multi tenancy based access control, etc. This chapter closely examines the aspects and techniques associated with cloud computing privacy and security to provide an extensive understanding of the subject.

Chapter 5- Cloud Computing Technologies refer to the hardware, software and infrastructure which enable the delivery of cloud computing services. Cloud computing and IOT, cloud radio access networks, hybrid cloud computing, multi-cloud, serverless computing, etc. are some technologies that fall under its domain. All these cloud computing technologies have been carefully analyzed in this chapter.

Chapter 6- There are various applications of cloud computing in biomedical sciences, business operations, education, transportation systems, manufacturing industry, etc. This chapter closely examines these key applications of cloud computing to provide an extensive understanding of the subject.

I owe the completion of this book to the never-ending support of my family, who supported me throughout the project.

Sam Revere

An Introduction to Cloud Computing

Cloud computing refers to the data centers which provide on-demand availability of computer system resources without direct engagement of the user. Some of its aspects include cloud monitoring, mobile cloud computing, sustainable cloud computing, etc. This is an introductory chapter which will briefly introduce all these aspects of cloud computing.

Cloud computing is a kind of outsourcing of software, data storage, and processing. Users access applications and files by logging in from any device that has an internet connection. Information and programs are hosted by outside parties and reside on a global network of secure data centers instead of on the user's hard drive. This frees up processing power, facilitates sharing and collaboration, and allows secure mobile access regardless of where the user is or what device is being used.

Cloud computing is a more efficient way of delivering computing resources. With cloud computing, software and service environments are subscription-based — users pay a monthly fee instead of buying licenses. Software and platforms are managed by the providers and are updated continuously for maximum performance and security. Computing power is remote instead of centralized, so users can tap into extra capacity if business spikes. Multiple people can access a shared program or file and collaborate in real time from different locations.

Life before Cloud Computing

Younger workers might find it hard to imagine that there was a time when employees could only access work files, messages, and systems from a terminal at the office that was daisy-chained to other computers in the network via physical cables. Software had to be installed manually on each computer. Company data was stored on large machines in a room or closet that had to be kept well-ventilated to prevent overheating. The loss or failure of a single device could be catastrophic.

Cloud computing has streamlined or eliminated many former office characteristics:

- Large servers: Businesses no longer need to house banks of servers in well-ventilated closets or equipment rooms.

- Dedicated in-house IT support: Tech talent is as prized as ever, but businesses no longer need dedicated in-house workers to troubleshoot their hardware and software systems. Tedious tasks like updating computers one by one have been eliminated.

- Data storage devices: Employees don't have to manually back up data on hard drives, discs, or external devices.

- Limited geographic access: Employees and managers are no longer tethered to the office. They can be just as productive when traveling or working remotely as they can from the business' headquarters. Access to processes and information is not tied to a particular geographic location.

- Outdated off-the-shelf software: Software updates used to require major expenditures every few years to buy the latest version of important programs. Applications had to be manually installed and maintained on every device. Only the largest enterprises could hire developers to create customized software. Bugs and security problems might go unaddressed for years.

- Information loss: Managers used to fear that an emergency or natural disaster could wipe out all of a company's records. Data that is stored locally on office computers is vulnerable to loss or failure, but data stored in the cloud has multiple safeguards.

- Duplicate versions of documents: Employees no longer have to email files back and forth, with one person making changes at a time and different versions of work products stored locally on multiple devices. Cloud-based files with shared access are always up-to-date. Colleagues can be confident that they are all seeing the same thing and working with the same information.

Traditional business applications have always been complicated and expensive. The quantity and variety of hardware and software required to run them were daunting. Organizations needed a whole team of experts to install, configure, test, run, secure, and update them.

When you multiply this effort across dozens or hundreds of apps, it's easy to see why, historically, only the biggest companies with the best IT departments got the customized solutions they needed. Small and midsize businesses didn't stand a chance. Advances in cloud computing have changed that.

Cloud Computing: A Better Way

Cloud computing eliminates the headaches that come with storing your own data, because you're not managing hardware and software — that becomes the responsibility of an experienced vendor. Shared infrastructure works like a utility: You only pay for what you need, upgrades are automatic, and scaling up or down is easy.

Cloud-based apps can be up and running in days or weeks, and they cost less. With a cloud app, you just open a browser, log in, customize the app, and start using it.

Why cloud computing is better:

- Accessible from anywhere: Applications and data are not tied to a device. They are accessible from anywhere, enabling real-time collaboration by remote teams.

- Flexible and scalable: Cloud-based applications are infinitely customizable. It is easy to increase power, storage, and bandwidth as users' needs change.

- Cost-effective: Businesses only pay for what they use, usually on a per-month, per-seat basis. There is no hardware taking up space and using electricity 24/7.

- Hassle-free updates: Web-based software is constantly updated. The vendor handles maintenance, backups, and troubleshooting.

- Fast: Service is delivered on demand through a global network of secure data centers that are constantly upgraded for maximum efficiency and performance.

- Secure: Information is not vulnerable to a flood, fire, natural disaster, or hardware failure in one location. Security protocols and infrastructure are constantly analyzed and updated to address new threats.

Businesses are running all kinds of apps and for many purposes in the cloud, like customer relationship management (CRM), human resources, accounting, and much more.

A word of caution: As cloud computing grows in popularity, thousands of companies are simply rebranding their non-cloud products and services as "cloud computing." Always dig deeper when evaluating cloud offerings and keep in mind that if you have to buy and manage hardware and software, what you're looking at isn't really cloud computing but a false cloud.

Three Types of Cloud Computing

Cloud computing is a way of delivering technology resources to users from remote hubs. There are three main models of cloud computing, based on the type of resources being delivered. Software as a service (SaaS) is the delivery of fully functional products to end users. Infrastructure as a service (IaaS) provides secure network and storage capacity to system administrators. Platform as a service (PaaS) is somewhere in between, giving developers the building blocks to create apps while freeing them from tedious back-end concerns.

Software as a Service (SaaS)

SaaS is the most common type of cloud computing. It delivers complete, user-ready applications over the internet. These typically do not have to be downloaded and installed on each individual user's computer, saving technical staff lots of time. Maintenance and troubleshooting are handled entirely by the vendor.

Software programs perform specific functions and are generally intuitive to use. Examples include Salesforce's suite of customer relationship management tools, Microsoft Office 365 products, Google Apps, QuickBooks, Dropbox, Zendesk, and Slack. These are fully functional productivity tools that can be customized to the users' needs without coding or programming. SaaS provides the greatest amount of customer support.

Infrastructure as a Service (IaaS)

IaaS is the most open-ended type of cloud service for organizations that want to do a lot of customization themselves. The greatest benefit of IaaS is extra capacity, which can be accessed on demand for long-term or short-term needs. IaaS makes it possible for tech-savvy businesses to rent enterprise-grade IT resources and infrastructure to keep pace with growth, without requiring large capital investments.

With IaaS, a third party hosts elements of infrastructure, such as hardware, servers, firewalls, and storage capacity. However, users typically bring their own operating systems and middleware. A business that is developing a new software product might choose to use an IaaS provider to create a testing environment before deploying the program in-house. Clients typically access cloud servers through a dashboard or an API. IaaS is fully self-service.

Platform as a Service (PaaS)

PaaS provides the building blocks for software creation, including development tools, code libraries, servers, programming environments, and preconfigured app components. With PaaS, the vendor takes care of back-end concerns such as security, infrastructure, and data integration so users can focus on building, hosting, and testing apps faster and at lower cost.

With a platform, resources are standardized and consolidated so you don't have to re-invent the wheel each time you build a new app. Multiple developers can work on the same project simultaneously. In many cases, people without coding skills can create problem-solving business applications with drag-and-drop page layouts, point-and-click field creation, and customizable reporting dashboards.

Public, Private and Hybrid Clouds

There are several types of platform services. Every PaaS option is either public, private, or a hybrid mix of the two.

- Public PaaS is hosted in the cloud, and its infrastructure is managed by the provider.

- Private PaaS, on the other hand, is housed in onsite servers or private networks and is maintained by the user.

- Hybrid PaaS uses elements from both public and private, and is capable of executing applications from multiple cloud infrastructures.

PaaS can be further categorized depending on whether it is open or closed source, whether it is mobile compatible (mPaaS), and what business types it caters to. Businesses are taking advantage of new PaaS capabilities to further outsource tasks that would have otherwise relied on local solutions. This is all made possible through advances in cloud computing.

When choosing a PaaS solution, the most important considerations beyond how it is hosted are how well it integrates with existing information systems, which programming languages it supports, what application-building tools it offers, how customizable or configurable it is, and how effectively it is supported by the provider.

Examples of Cloud Computing

Most consumers and businesses are already using the cloud, whether they realize it or not. If you stream music, shop online, have social media accounts, or use mobile banking, you're using the cloud. As digital technologies grow ever more powerful and available, apps and cloud-based platforms are becoming almost universally widespread. Here are some of the ways the cloud has transformed modern life.

- Entertainment: Movies and music that used to take up space in cupboards or on shelves are now accessed from afar through cloud-based streaming services like Netflix or Spotify.

- Social media: The photos and comments you post on Facebook, Instagram, Twitter, and other social platforms are stored remotely in the cloud.

- Documents, spreadsheets, and slide presentations: Files like these used to be maintained exclusively on local hard drives — vulnerable to a crash or power outage if not saved regularly. Now they are commonly kept in the cloud (think of Google Docs and Dropbox), accessible from anywhere and recorded in real time.

- Mobile banking: Banks like Chase, Wells Fargo, and Bank of America all rely on the cloud. Customers can transfer money to co-workers in seconds from their mobile phones or take pictures of checks and deposit them virtually, without ever setting foot in a bank. Transactions are searchable, and statements are stored in the bank's database, accessible on demand, eliminating the need for paper files.

- Customer relationship management: Customer relationship management (CRM) software enables businesses to personalize communications with customers, manage leads, and fine-tune marketing efforts across departments. Intelligent software can send follow-ups such as cart abandonment emails. Every step of the customer journey across all of a business' touchpoints can be linked, coordinated, and analyzed.

- Human resources and payroll: When the cloud is used for human resources functions, businesses see an increase in productivity and cost advantages over businesses utilizing older technology. Recruiting, onboarding, and employee data management are all more efficient. HR teams can easily view resumes, sort candidates, monitor performance, and access records with single-point tracking.

- Accounting: Cloud-based accounting applications do most of the same things as desktop accounting software but they run on remote servers and are accessed via the internet. The benefits include integration across departments, so all stakeholders have access to instantly updated figures and projections. Cloud accounting applications streamline data entry, eliminate redundancy, and reduce the chance of errors.

- Inventory management and logistics: Ordering, stocking, selling, and delivering goods is much more efficient when inventory is managed with cloud-based applications. Products with barcodes can be scanned every step of the way. Vendors, managers, and logistics coordinators can see inventory levels and know where products are in real time. Reordering can be automated.

The Advantages of Cloud Computing

Over the past two decades, cloud computing has become a staple in business and private life. As tech-savvy businesses can attest, there are many benefits of cloud computing. Among the most important, cloud computing is:

Convenient

Cloud computing centralizes information for fast and efficient storage and retrieval. Data is readily accessible to all stakeholders.

Adaptable

Cloud computing allows for adaptable programs and applications that are customizable, while allowing owners control over the core code.

Multitenant

Cloud software provides the opportunity to provide personalized applications and portals to a number of customers or tenants.

Reliable

Because cloud systems are hosted by third parties, businesses and other users have greater assurance of reliability, and when there are problems, easy access to customer support.

Scalable

With the Internet of Things, it is essential that software functions across every device and integrates with other applications. Cloud applications can provide this.

Secure

Cloud computing can also guarantee a more secure environment, thanks to increased resources for security and centralization of data.

Misconceptions about the Cloud

Despite all of the benefits, some business owners are reluctant to move to the cloud because of misconceptions. Here are some common ones.

The cloud is risky and untested: The cloud is often safer for your data than your own computer. Security in the cloud is likely to be tighter than your existing system. Cloud vendors are always working to improve the security of their systems. Through the use of encryption and security protections, the cloud is becoming increasingly safer. Top cloud vendors employ experts in computer science and cyber security to keep their systems updated with the latest encryption technology. This makes the cloud much less vulnerable to a hack than your home or work computer. Another way to look at it is to think of the cloud like a bank. Your money is safer in a bank account than it is if it were stored in a cookie jar in your kitchen. The cloud provides this type of security for your data.

Cloud services are complicated: Cloud vendors design their interfaces to be easy to use and familiar.

The cloud offers features that simplify the use of vendors' services. With intuitive menus, automatic updates, storage flexibility, and the seamless migration of data, the cloud is easy to use.

- The cloud is unreliable: The cloud is more reliable than your computer. The cloud not only stores your data but it backs up your data with additional copies. Many cloud services automatically create backups without you having to prompt them. Cloud vendors use the latest hardware and software to operate their systems in a way that smaller companies cannot. Data stored in the cloud means you can work from anywhere, as long as you have an internet connection. If the power in your building is out and the internet goes down, you can still get access to the cloud by moving to a place with internet access. As long as you have a working computer and an internet connection, you will have access to your data stored in the cloud.

- Stormy weather can affect the cloud: The cloud is not an actual cloud, and it's not located in the sky. The cloud has nothing to do with the weather. Data centers are all inside climate-controlled buildings. The cloud is simply a phrase used to describe a network of computers that operate programs or applications that run on connected servers instead of on a local computer or smartphone.

- Transitioning to the cloud is expensive and time-consuming: Cloud vendors make data migration quick, easy, and cost-effective. The best cloud vendors will provide the proper tools and education needed to migrate your data with ease. Migrating to the cloud is cost-effective since it does not require you to purchase any new hardware or software. This minimizes up-front costs from the start. Cloud services also save money by eliminating the need for your organization to employ IT personnel to manage your servers.

- Cloud services are an all-or-nothing proposition: You choose what you use the cloud for. Many organizations use a hybrid cloud, which combines both a private cloud and a public cloud. Generally, an organization will use its private cloud for critical functions while using a public cloud when its computing needs are in higher demand. The cloud can even be used for backup purposes only. Given the flexibility of the cloud, how you use it is up to you.

- Cloud providers are at fault for most security breaches: Keeping the cloud secure is a full-time endeavor for cloud vendors. The cloud is safer than your own system, given the personnel dedicated to securing your data and preventing breaches. RapidScale claims that 94% of businesses saw an improvement in security after making the switch to the cloud. Most data breaches are due to human error, like having a password that is easy to break, accidentally opening a phishing or malware email, or by simply losing an unsecured laptop. Cloud vendors use two-factor authentication to confirm a user's identity to prevent data breaches.

- Customers don't trust businesses that use the cloud: Customers already trust the cloud, as well as businesses that use the cloud. Popular services like email, social media, and ecommerce sites all use the cloud to store customer data. Photos, credit card information, and personal messages are stored in the cloud.

- There is no customer service or support if something goes wrong: Reliable cloud vendors have dedicated customer service teams ready to help. Cloud vendors provide online help 12 hours a day, 5 days a week. Additional services like 24/7 direct phone access, access to Accelerators (quick, focused work sessions), proprietary apps, on-demand admins, and more are available at an added cost.

- The cloud provider can see all of my data: Cloud vendors isolate and encrypt your data so that only you can see it. Cloud vendors encrypt your data in transit when you send it to the cloud. They also encrypt the data when it's stored on their servers.

- The cloud gives you less control over your data and processes: The cloud is flexible and can be used on a pay-as-you-go basis. It's also accessible anywhere you have an internet connection. The cloud can be used on a pay-as-you-go basis. So you only pay for what you use. This gives you more control and flexibility over the cloud as a resource. You can easily scale your usage based on your data needs. The cloud also makes it easy to migrate your data to and from vendors' servers. So you can easily download all your data whenever you need.

How to have a Best-in-class Cloud

When it comes to cloud computing, best practices for businesses start with screening potential vendors carefully. Your network is only as good as the providers you work with. Good data management, security protocols, and service are crucial.

Choose Cloud Service Providers Wisely

Reputation matters when choosing a provider, but there are tangible assets that will affect how secure and reliable their service is. Top-notch cloud service providers have multiple data centers that are geographically dispersed. This provides defense against natural disasters and geopolitical turmoil. Data centers should also be close to internet backbone connections.

Be sure that you use vendors with the highest security, privacy, and regulatory compliance standards. They should have clear data classification policies and procedures. Most services are on-demand and pay-as-you-go. Vendors should be able to accommodate variable demand or seasonality.

Think about the long-term relationship. You want to choose a company that is fiscally healthy and likely to stay in business. It's important to have migration support, but you also want to avoid vendor lock-in — a situation where proprietary technology is incompatible with other systems and makes it hard to change vendors.

Negotiate the Terms of your Service Level Agreement (SLA)

A cloud service level agreement is a contract, blueprint, and warranty all rolled into one. Take care to define key terms and clearly delineate the roles and responsibilities of all parties. Your agreement should spell out:

- Where your data is located.

- Who owns the data.

- What data controls are in place.

- How your data is protected in transit.

- How your data is protected once it's in the cloud.

- Who in the service provider's organization has access to different types of data.

- What password policies and authentication procedures will be used.

- How accounts are provisioned and deprovisioned.

Your SLA should identify performance measures so you can monitor service. Typical indicators include capacity — the number of users who can access the cloud at any given time — and the response time for processing customer transactions. What log information will be provided, and will it be in a format that you can import into operational analysis software? Your agreement should spell out consequences and penalties. It should also address exit planning.

Optimize your Security

Before entering into a relationship with a cloud service provider, it's important to evaluate your current IT security controls and vulnerabilities. Then review the vendor's security and data protection policies. Look for suppliers with certifications like ISO 27001, ISO 27017, DoD IL4, HIPAA, and the UK's Cyber Essentials.

Most cloud service providers have more cyber security expertise and better controls than traditional IT departments. Monitoring cloud infrastructure is their full-time job, and the success of their service depends on keeping it secure. Data breaches are much more commonly caused by human error than by problems with cloud infrastructure, but no system is infallible. Discuss how and when the cloud service provider is to report failures, outages, or security breaches. Have a risk mitigation plan and measures to prevent downtime.

Protect your Data

Make sure your data is classified by sensitivity with access restricted accordingly. Tiers of data should be handled differently based on how much risk unauthorized disclosure would present to the company and affected users. Know how and where your data is backed up and who can access it. In the unlikely event of a disaster, have a plan for how your data will be recovered and restored.

Monitor your Cloud Services Rigorously

It is important to monitor your cloud services rigorously. Most problems are much easier to solve if caught early. Unusual spikes in activity can alert you to security threats. Similarly, dips in activity could be the result of a glitch and result in lost sales. Any anomalies should be investigated promptly. Most cloud vendors offer lots of service and support.

Accommodating Growth over Time

One of the biggest advantages of cloud computing is its flexibility to scale up or down as needed. As your business grows, you can add bandwidth, add users, add services, or add more cloud service providers. You do not have to make large capital investments in infrastructure to accommodate growth, but it's a good idea to review your architecture from time to time to make sure your systems are working together efficiently.

The Future of Cloud Computing

The future of cloud computing is likely to include exponential advances in processing capability, fueled by quantum computing and artificial intelligence, as well as expansion of cloud adoption. Large and small businesses are likely to create more hybrids of public and private clouds. More enterprises will embrace multicloud strategies to combine services from different providers. Low-code and no-code platforms will continue to democratize technology and empower citizen developers to create apps that solve their own problems, without having to hire programmers.

Expect more wearable technology and internet-connected devices — from fitness trackers, thermostats, and security systems to refrigerators, pet dishes, and washing machines. There will likely be more integration into increased modes of transportation — with self-driving cars and smarter elevators, subways, and aviation. Businesses are already experimenting with using 3D printing to deliver goods on demand.

One thing is for sure: The tech industry will continue to expand its adoption of cloud computing, to the benefit of businesses and consumers alike.

Characteristics of Cloud Computing

As cloud computing services mature both commercially and technologically, it will be easier for companies to maximize the potential benefits. Knowing what cloud computing is and what it does, however, is just as important.

On-demand Self-service

Cloud computing resources can be provisioned without human interaction from the service provider. In other words, a manufacturing organization can provision additional computing resources as needed without going through the cloud service provider. This can be a storage space, virtual machine instances, database instances, and so on.

Manufacturing organizations can use a web self-service portal as an interface to access their cloud accounts to see their cloud services, their usage, and also to provision and de-provision services as they need to.

Broad Network Access

Cloud computing resources are available over the network and can be accessed by diverse customer platforms. It other words, cloud services are available over a network—ideally high broadband communication link—such as the internet, or in the case of a private clouds it could be a local area network (LAN).

Network bandwidth and latency are very important aspects of cloud computing and broad network access, because they relate to the quality of service (QoS) on the network. This is particularly important for serving time sensitive manufacturing applications.

Multi-tenancy and Resource Pooling

Cloud computing resources are designed to support a multi-tenant model. Multi-tenancy allows multiple customers to share the same applications or the same physical infrastructure while retaining privacy and security over their information. It's similar to people living in an apartment building, sharing the same building infrastructure but they still have their own apartments and privacy within that infrastructure. That is how cloud multi-tenancy works.

Resource pooling means that multiple customers are serviced from the same physical resources. Providers' resource pool should be very large and flexible enough to service multiple client requirements and to provide for economy of scale. When it comes to resource pooling, resource allocation must not impact performances of critical manufacturing applications.

Rapid Elasticity and Scalability

One of the great things about cloud computing is the ability to quickly provision resources in the cloud as manufacturing organizations need them. And then to remove them when they don't need them. Cloud computing resources can scale up or down rapidly and, in some cases, automatically, in response to business demands. It is a key feature of cloud computing. The usage, capacity, and therefore cost, can be scaled up or down with no additional contract or penalties.

Elasticity is a landmark of cloud computing and it implies that manufacturing organizations can rapidly provision and de-provision any of the cloud computing resources. Rapid provisioning and de-provisioning might apply to storage or virtual machines or customer applications.

With cloud computing scalability, there is less capital expenditure on the cloud customer side. This is because as the cloud customer needs additional computing resources, they can simply provision them as needed, and they are available right away. Scalability is more planned and gradual. For instance, scalability means that manufacturing organizations are gradually planning for more capacity and of course the cloud can handle that scaling up or scaling down.

Just-in-time (JIT) service is the notion of requiring cloud elasticity either to provision more resources in the cloud or less. For example, if a manufacturing organization all of a sudden needs more computing power to perform some kind of complex calculation, this would be cloud elasticity that would be a just-in-time service. On the other hand, if the manufacturing organization needs to provision human-machine interface (HMI) tags in the database for a manufacturing project, that is not really just-in-time service, it is planned ahead of time. So it is more on the scalability side than elasticity.

Another feature available for rapid elasticity and scalability in the cloud is related to testing of manufacturing applications. If a manufacturing organization needs, for example, a few virtual machines to test a supervisory control and data acquisition (SCADA) system before they roll it out in production, they can have it up and running in minutes instead of physically ordering and waiting for hardware to be shipped.

In terms of the bottom line, when manufacturing organizations need to test something in the cloud, they are paying for what they use as they use it. As long as they remember to de-provision it, they will no longer be paying for it. There is no capital expense here for computer resources. Manufacturing organizations are using the cloud provider's investment in cloud computing resources instead. This is really useful for testing smart manufacturing solutions.

Measured Service

Cloud computing resources usage is metered and manufacturing organizations pay accordingly for what they have used. Resource utilization can be optimized by leveraging charge-per-use capabilities. This means that cloud resource usage—whether virtual server instances that are running or storage in the cloud—gets monitored, measured and reported by the cloud service provider. The cost model is based on "pay for what you use"—the payment is variable based on the actual consumption by the manufacturing organization.

Cloud Computing Strategy

Evaluating how Cloud Computing can Transform your Business

Cloud computing, often referred to as simply "the cloud," is the delivery of dynamically scalable and often virtualized computing resources—everything from applications to data centers—as a service over the Internet (public cloud) or intranet (private cloud) on a flexible pay-for-use basis. From an IT perspective, cloud computing offers an infrastructure management and services delivery approach that leverages:

- Virtualized resources.

- Ability to manage as a single large resource.

- Services delivered with elastic scaling.

"Although cloud is widely recognized as a technology game changer, its potential for driving business innovation remains virtually untapped. Indeed, cloud has the power to fundamentally shift competitive landscapes by providing a new platform for creating and delivering business value".

From this perspective, cloud computing offers a user experience and business model that provides:

- Standardized, self-service offerings that enable efficiency.

- Rapidly provisioned services that create agility.

- Flexible pricing that can enable innovation.

Pacesetters understand that business and IT perspectives on cloud inevitably merge. Yes, cloud can deliver security-rich IT with fewer boundaries. But more importantly, it can enable rapid delivery of product and service innovation.5 As cloud technology matures toward a point of convergence for both business and IT interests, you're presented with a fresh opportunity to evaluate—or re-evaluate—what cloud can mean for your organization.

Considerations for Establishing a Cloud Computing Strategy

Creating a cloud computing strategy will establish a roadmap to achieve your vision for cloud computing. But first, your organization must coalesce around a common definition and perspective for cloud. For example, consider these two definitions:

- Cloud is the industrialization of delivery for IT services. Cloud is a new consumption and delivery model inspired by consumer Internet services enabled by service automation, virtualization and standardization using self-service, economies of scale, flexible pricing models, and workload-based IT resource provisioning.

- Cloud computing is a model for enabling convenient, on-demand network access to a shared pool of configurable resources (e.g., networks, servers, storage, applications and services) that can be rapidly provisioned and released with reduced management effort or service provider interaction.

Each of these definitions reflects an accurate view of cloud, just through a different lens. Your organization's definition of cloud will depend on its unique perspective, and the sheer variability of cloud creates vast opportunities for a customized vision. It's not overreaching to say that with cloud, almost anyone can serve as a developer, virtually any good idea can become an application, practically anyone can influence your business and (security permitting) access your information, and transactions can occur almost anywhere. Given these broad parameters, your organization must determine how cloud's flexibility can serve your business and strategic objectives—and how cloud can even redefine those objectives. Your challenge is to uncover the definition of cloud that is relevant for you.

Once you arrive at consensus on perspective and definition, the next logical step is to examine how opportunities "in the cloud" can increase concrete business value. Discovering those opportunities is like de-fogging a windshield. You can see the road ahead and determine how to best align cloud capabilities with your desired business outcomes. These identified opportunities should be at the heart of a cloud computing strategy that also outlines:

Roles

What role—or roles—should your company assume? For example, if you are the consumer of a private cloud environment, your cloud service supplier is typically part of your organization. If you are a consumer of a public cloud, you will most likely be working with an external provider. Your organization will need to establish an integrator role to manage the performance and interaction with the public cloud provider.

Often, the private versus public cloud question is not an either/ or decision. Organizations are frequently opting for both, or what is called a hybrid cloud environment. Although such an environment enables a company to deploy applications to the most amenable technical infrastructures, it can also result in complex sourcing scenarios.

As a result, the integrator role is of ever-increasing importance, because it holds accountability for cloud services provided by an external party—or parties. This role requires the necessary level of IT literacy to communicate and clearly translate business and technical requirements to service providers. In effect, the integrator is your organization's liaison to all third-party suppliers.

If you own the assets needed to produce and deliver cloud services to the consumer—and those assets can change based on the service layer—then you're considered a cloud service provider (CSP). You have the capability of offering private or public cloud services to your own internal organization, or you could serve as CSP to an external entity. A CSP often works as a critical supplier of services within a hybrid computing model.

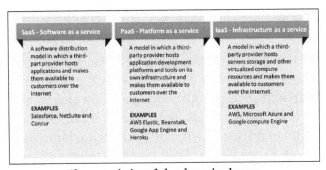

Characteristics of cloud service layers.

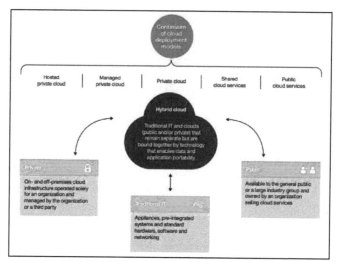

Continuum of cloud deployment models.

Service Types and Deployment Models

You will need to determine the types of services and the deployment models your organization requires. These are familiar concepts by now, but Figures provide a high-level summary.

Sphere of Influence

In developing your cloud framework, you'll need to consider your key stakeholders for cloud services. Are they IT? Employees of certain departments or lines of business (LoBs)? Citizens of extended communities who converge around common business or industry interests?

As you determine this for your own organization, you may initially focus on your IT department. But a recent study shows that business leaders of all stripes—finance, sales, product development and more—are increasingly interested in the business value cloud provides. Respondents were asked how important cloud will be to their organization's overall business success. Currently, 34 percent of LoB respondents and 49 percent of IT respondents say that cloud is extremely important. But by 2016, cloud's strategic importance to business users is expected to double from 34 percent to 72 percent, even surpassing their IT counterparts at 58 percent.

With the merging of LoB and IT interests, these areas will no longer operate in their own silos with competing priorities. Rather, they will collaborate on your organization's overall roadmap and strategy. Although business and IT arrive at cloud for different reasons and with different goals, both roles are unified in their view of cloud's overall value: the ability to deliver IT without boundaries, improve speed and dexterity, and create new business value. Both roles understand that rethinking IT and reinventing the business go hand in hand.

Governance, Controls, Design and Operational Considerations

Governance is a broad concept. It involves control and oversight by your organization over policies, procedures and standards for IT service acquisition, as well as the design, implementation, testing, use and monitoring of deployed services.

Compliance and risk management are governance processes that have always been critical to traditional IT systems, and they are equally vital to cloud-deployed IT solutions. What is different for cloud is an expanded set of criteria. Given that cloud services are often sourced outside the IT organization, lack of controls can put the organization in jeopardy for privacy, security, legal and oversight risks. Cloud "silos" or "cloud clutter" often result when governance is not clearly established.

A robust cloud governance strategy and framework should be part of any cloud computing strategy. Cloud governance includes:

- Establishing stakeholder decision rights, such as determining authority roles for procuring solutions and the required level of stakeholder involvement.

- Developing cloud decision making processes.

- Establishing and enforcing policies to manage cloud providers.

Finally, cloud computing requires design and operational capabilities that many organizations lack today. The requirements list is long and often challenging:

- A "post shared services" governance model.

- Sourcing and procurement processes that engage in "just-in-time" sourcing.

- A services-oriented framework for the delivery of IT services.

- Integrated event, configuration, change, release, capacity and service-level management.

- A service catalog and configuration management database (CMDB) supported by service automation tools.

- Metering, rating billing and subscription support.

- Offering management.

- Virtualized and standardized infrastructure.

- A critical mass of resources that can be pooled to justify the investment in the management infrastructure.

- Software licensing agreements tailored to a cloud consumption mode.

Establishing an effective governance program means considering a wide spectrum of roles, services, deployment models and stakeholders. This range of considerations gives organizations the flexibility to fulfill specific, even unique IT requirements. Yet this same flexibility necessitates a thoughtful approach to assembling an optimum portfolio of IT delivered services.

For example, how do you apply the appropriate level of structure to ensure compliance, achievable service-level agreements (SLAs) and effective security without overloading processes with unneeded complexity? Ironically, achieving the benefits provided by flexibility also requires balancing that flexibility with structure. Cloud computing should be viewed as an expansion of more structured, traditional IT delivery alternatives rather than a replacement for them. Often, the two can complement one another by providing the "checks and balances" of structure and flexibility.

As you develop a governance approach to both existing services and the acquisition of new services, you will need to evaluate each service with a fresh perspective that embraces this new range of delivery possibilities. Solutions that do not fit into a well-developed enterprise architecture can create an expensive and incompatible portfolio of IT services—the exact opposite of the cloud goal of architecting solutions built from standard components integrated for flexibility and lowest cost of delivery.

Determining which Workloads are Best Suited for Cloud Deployment

Once you're ready for cloud, you'll need to evaluate which workloads (meaning a capability or combination of IT capabilities and services that can make up an application) to migrate.

Potential cloud-enabled services tend to originate from three major sources:

- Existing applications can be analyzed for cloud affinities and detractors. In addition, vendor-sourced applications such as Enterprise Resource Planning (ERP), Supply Chain and Customer Relationship Management (CRM) should be vetted based upon the provider's incorporation of cloud-conducive features.

- Future in-house developed applications benefit from an appropriate cloud-aware enterprise architecture and development standards specifically designed for cloud deployment.

- Future vendor-supplied solutions should be evaluated based on vendor-demonstrated capabilities.

At a high level, when comparing candidate workloads and their feasibility for cloud adoption, initial questions revolve around business value. What is the real cost benefit of moving those workloads to the cloud? From there, you will need to evaluate the technical characteristics of the application. Is it technically feasible to move the workload to the cloud? How will that migration impact the ecosystem? And of course, your organization must consider concerns about risk exposure.

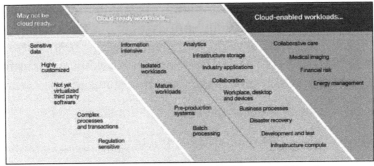

Objectives and criteria for analyzing a portfolio of
applications for cloud suitability.

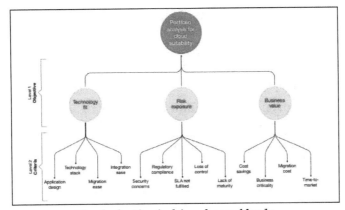

Cloud adoption is driven by workloads.

Even though cloud environments exhibit immense flexibility, not all workloads are suitable for cloud deployment. As well, you will want to explore new workloads that are actually enabled by the cloud. Such workloads by their very nature can greatly enhance business value and innovation for your organization. They can include high-volume, low-cost analytics, collaborative business networks, industry-scale "smart" applications and more.

Utilizing Cloud to Gain Strategic Advantage

Pacesetters experience almost 2 times the revenue growth of their peers, and nearly 2.5 times higher gross profit than their peers. In fact, when research compares Pacesetters to Chasers, defined as organizations that are more cautious about cloud and in early stages of adoption, the Pacesetters' use of cloud diverges dramatically:

- Pacesetters are 136 percent more likely than Chasers to use cloud to reinvent customer relationships.

- Pacesetters are 170 percent more likely than Chasers to use analytics extensively via cloud to derive insights.

- Pacesetters are 79 percent more likely than Chasers to rely on cloud to locate and utilize expertise anywhere in the ecosystem.

Attaining this level of performance means always remembering that cloud is more than just a service delivery platform—it's an entirely new business model. As you define cloud for your organization and develop your cloud strategy, brainstorming around the four objectives below can be a productive exercise, sparking transformative ideas on how cloud can provide strategic advantage for your organization:

- Enable new business models and client relationships.

- Help improve the agility and dexterity of business.

- Deliver security-rich IT with fewer boundaries.

- Enable more rapid delivery of product and service innovation.

Cloud Monitoring

Cloud monitoring is the process of evaluating, monitoring, and managing cloud-based services, applications, and infrastructure. Companies utilize various application monitoring tools to monitor cloud-based applications.

Types of Cloud Services to Monitor

There are multiple types of cloud services to monitor. Cloud monitoring is not just about monitoring servers hosted on AWS or Azure. For enterprises, they also put a lot of importance into monitoring cloud-based services that they consume. Including things like Office 365 and others.

- SaaS: Services like Office 365, Salesforce and others.

- PaaS: Developer friendly services like SQL databases, caching, storage and more.

- IaaS: Servers hosted by cloud providers like Azure, AWS, Digital Ocean, and others.

- FaaS: New serverless applications like AWS Lambda and Azure Functions.

- Application Hosting: Services like Azure App Services, Heroku, etc.

Many of these can be monitored usually traditional application performance monitoring tools. However, cloud monitoring has some unique requirements over basic server monitoring tools. There are also companies like Exoprise who focus on monitoring Office 365, Salesforce and other services.

How it Works

The term cloud refers to a set of web-hosted applications that store and allow access to data over the Internet instead of on a computer's hard drive.

- For consumers, simply using the internet to view web pages, access email accounts on services such as Gmail, and store files in Dropbox are examples of cloud computing for consumers.

- Businesses use it in many of the same ways. They also may use Software as a Service (SaaS) options to subscribe to business applications or rent server space to host proprietary applications to provide services to consumers.

Cloud monitoring works through a set of tools that supervise the servers, resources, and applications running the applications. These tools generally come from two sources:

- In-house tools from the cloud provider: This is a simple option because the tools are part of the service. There is no installation, and integration is seamless.

- Tools from independent SaaS provider: Although the SaaS provider may be different from the cloud service provider, that doesn't mean the two services don't work seamlessly. These providers also have expertise in managing performance and costs.

Cloud monitoring tools look for problems that can prevent or restrict businesses from delivering service to their customers. Generally, these tools offer data on performance, security, and customer behavior:

- Cybersecurity is a necessary part of keeping networks safe from cyber attacks. IT teams can use it to detect breaches and vulnerabilities early and secure the network before the damage gets out of hand.

- By testing at regular intervals, organizations can detect errors quickly and rectify them in order to mitigate any damage to performance and functionality, which improves the customer experience and, as a result, can boost sales and enhance customer retention.

- Speed like functionality and user experience — is a primary driver of customer satisfaction. Speed metrics can be monitored and generate data that helps organizations optimize websites and applications.

If an organization monitors early and often, they can use the data to troubleshoot problems and implement repairs in a timely — if not instantaneous — manner.

Benefits of Cloud Monitoring

The top benefits of leveraging cloud monitoring tools include:

- They already have infrastructure and configurations in place. Installation is quick and easy.

- Dedicated tools are maintained by the host. That includes hardware.

- These solutions are built for organizations of various sizes. So if cloud activity increases, the right monitoring tool can scale seamlessly.

- Subscription-based solutions can keep costs low. They do not require startup or infrastructure expenditures, and maintenance costs are spread among multiple users.

- Because the resources are not part of the organization's servers and workstations, they don't suffer interruptions when local problems disrupt the organization.

- Many tools can be used on multiple types of devices, desktop computers, tablets, and phones. This allows organizations to monitor apps and services from any location with Internet access.

Best Practices

Organizations need to make cloud monitoring a priority and plan for it. The plan should include questions that need to be answered and goals of implementation, such as:

- Identify metrics and events: What activity needs to be monitored? Not everything that can be measured needs to be reported. Monitor the metrics that matter to the bottom line.

- Use one platform to report all the data: Organizations may have their own infrastructures in addition to cloud services to monitor. They need solutions that can report data from different sources on a single platform, which allows for calculating uniform metrics and results in a comprehensive view of performance.

- Monitor cloud service use and fees: The ability to scale is a feature is a key feature of cloud services, but increased use can trigger increased costs. Robust monitoring solutions should track how much organization activity is on the cloud and how much it costs.

- Monitor user experience: Organizations need to know what users experience when using their cloud-based applications. Monitor metrics such as response times and frequency of use to get the complete picture of performance.

- Trigger rules with data: If activity exceeds or falls below defined thresholds, the right solution should be able to add or subtract servers to maintain efficiency and performance.

- Separate and centralize data: Organizations should store monitoring data separately from their apps and services, and it should be centralized for easy access for key stakeholders.

- Try failure: Test your tools to see what happens when there is an outage or data breach and evaluate the alert system when certain thresholds are met.

Cloud Monitoring Tools

Cloud monitoring is a broad category that includes web and cloud applications, infrastructure, networks, platform, application, and microservices. Some cloud monitoring tools do it all, from managing your cloud capacity to tracking your website speed. Other tools are more specialized, helping you track one vital component of your stack at a time.

You should determine the right set of tools by first looking at your needs and budget. If you're happy with the out-of-box monitoring tools from your cloud provider, then maybe you just want a product that helps you monitor application performance. Or maybe you're ready to upgrade to an enterprise-level monitoring solution.

Microsoft Cloud Monitoring

Microsoft gives you a full picture of your web app's performance by providing log analysis, application monitoring, and security alerts. The best part is that these tools are built into Azure, so you don't have to install any new software. Microsoft Cloud Monitoring is perfect for companies who want a simple solution for monitoring their Microsoft stack.

ExoPrise

Exoprise helps businesses stay on top of their cloud apps, specifically Office 365, Skype, Slack, Yammer, Salesforce, and Box. They will monitor your entire Microsoft suite, troubleshoot, detect outages, and make sure your apps are up to SLA compliance. If you need a tool for tracking your cloud tools, ExoPrise might be right for you.

CA Technologies

CA Technologies is an enterprise-level, full-stack monitoring and management solution for businesses with public, private, or hybrid clouds. They have tools to help you do everything from monitor user experiences on your web app, to securing and scaling your operations. If you're a big business looking for a trusted partner in cloud monitoring, check out CA.

Retrace by Stackify

Retrace is an Application Performance Monitoring (APM) tool for apps built in .Net and Java. It combines app performance metrics, errors, logs, and monitoring all into one tool. Retrace is perfect for developers who want code-level insight into how their apps are performing. The affordable price point also makes it accessible to small and medium-sized businesses.

VMware Hyperic

Hyperic provides monitoring for infrastructure, both physical and virtual, as well as monitoring for your OS, middleware, and web apps. Its dashboards and reporting features help ensure that you stay SLA-compliant and that you keep the right people in the loop. It's backed by one of the leading server virtualization companies in VMware, which in turn is owned by Dell.

AppNeta

AppNeta is a SaaS app and network monitoring tool that works across cloud platforms. AppNeta's Performance Manager gives you insight into resource usage, app delivery, and user experience. In 2017 it was given the highest rating for Network Performance Monitoring tools by Gartner.

Rackspace Cloud Monitoring

Rackspace Monitoring is an enterprise-grade monitoring tool for Rackspace OpenStack Cloud users. It offers comprehensive visibility, powerful event processing, and flexible notifications, all in an easy-to-setup package. Rackspace Cloud Monitoring comes free with an Openstack cloud account.

BMC TrueSight Pulse

True sight Pulse from BMC utilizes AIOps technology to monitor your web apps, ensuring a high-quality experience for your end-user. TrueSight integrates with Amazon CloudWatch and Azure Monitoring so you can better visualize data and set additional notifications. Its simple, single-line command line install makes it perfect for Azure and AWS developers who want better data visualization, fast.

SolarWinds

SolarWinds has a tool called Virtualization Manager that makes predictive recommendations to improve the performance of your virtual environment. If you manage virtual infrastructure, you want to check this out. Virtualization Manager also helps with capacity planning and alerts you when things go wrong.

Amazon CloudWatch

Amazon CloudWatch is a must-use tool if you're on AWS. CloudWatch lets you monitor application metrics, log files, and quickly react to changes in your AWS resources. The best part is you don't need to install any additional software.

Redgate

Do you use SQL Server, .NET, or Azure? If so, Redgate is the perfect monitoring tool for you. Redgate specializes in these three areas, providing tons of services to help you make better apps. From SQL Monitor, to .NET Profilers, to their Azure migration services, they are a one-stop shop for Microsoft stacks.

AppRiver

AppRiver helps you monitor and maintain your web apps, specifically Office 365 and email services. AppRiver provides security, web protection, spam guards, and email encryption so your information is safe. AppRiver is perfect for companies who want to keep their communication web apps up-and-running without hassle.

PagerDuty

PagerDuty is an incident reporting and management tool that helps enterprise teams stay on top of cloud maintenance. It integrates with all of your favorite tools, so you're constantly updated on your stack performance. PagerDuty is perfect for enterprise DevOps and IT teams who want to automate incident resolution and get their software running faster.

LogicMonitor

LogicMonitor is an enterprise IT solution that helps businesses monitor their entire stack of infrastructure, apps, and tools. They were named the Best Network Monitoring Tool in 2016 and 2017 by PC magazine.

Unigma

Unigma is a management and monitoring tool for public clouds like AWS, Azure, Google Cloud, and Office 365. It provides simple, beautiful dashboards and automated reporting so you can stay on top of your cloud performance. Unigma also helps you optimize your cloud costs and manage your billing if you're a reseller.

Prometheus

Prometheus is an open source tool used primarily for Docker monitoring. It allows you to slice and dice data into a number of different dimensions using its powerful query language. Then visualize that data with its built-in expression browser. If you're a Docker-using, open source junkie, you will absolutely love Prometheus.

Riverbed

Riverbed created a series of tools designed to help businesses monitor and manage their networks and SaaS applications. They are an enterprise-level solution that can handle your entire cloud stack.

Stackdriver

Google Stackdriver provides monitoring, logging, and logistics for apps on both Google Cloud and AWS. It provides full-stack insights and lets you aggregate all data across cloud platforms. Not surprisingly, it also comes with native integration into Google cloud products.

Mobile Cloud Computing

Mobile Cloud Computing (MCC) is simply cloud computing in which at least some of the devices involved are mobile.

In the case of mobile cloud computing an additional significant benefit is brought to the table. Many mobile devices have significant constraints imposed upon them because of the importance and desirability of smaller sizes, lower weights, longer battery life and other features. This often severely constrains hardware and software development for these devices. Cloud computing allows devices to avoid these constraints by letting the more resource intensive tasks be performed on systems without these constraints and having the results sent to the device. Thus, cloud computing for mobile devices is a very appealing and potentially lucrative trend.

Several methods exist by which this trend can realize itself. First, methods have been proposed which aim to construct general systems for utilizing the cloud to help boost phone performance. This family of solutions can be referred to as general-purpose mobile cloud computing (GPMCC). Second, many individual applications used today with mobile devices such as smartphones employ cloud computing to a greater or lesser extent. There are multiple methods used and proposed by which the cloud can be leveraged. This can be referred to as application-specific cloud computing (ASMCC). Each of these two approaches has advantages and disadvantages and they are not mutually exclusive.

In addition to mobile cloud computing where mobile devices serve as the client and non-mobile devices serve as the server or mainframe, several papers have been written proposing an opposite model. In this model, mobile devices serve as the cloud that can be drawn upon. This paper will outline some work done in this area.

General-purpose MCC Solutions

Cloud computing is a very broad term and can feasibly apply to a wide variety of practices. All that is necessary to gain the label is for a mobile device to utilize the internet in order to use a specific resource in an on-demand manner. There are multiple individual applications which do that today. However, there is also the possibility of a more general-purpose use of these resources in order to help alleviate the limited computational power of mobile devices. It is feasible to develop systems in which tasks that are usually performed locally on the mobile device are outsourced to the cloud as they happen. This can leverage the computing resources of remote computers seamlessly without requiring applications specifically developed for that purpose.

Augmented Execution

Researchers from Berkeley have considered the possibility of increasing the performance of hardware-limited smartphones using cloud computing. Their main method involves creating virtual clones of smartphone execution environments on non-mobile computers and pushing task execution to these virtual devices. Because non-mobile devices often have significantly more computational power, this enables much better performance from smartphones. This could enable a broader spectrum of applications and could ease the burden of software developers to create ultra-efficient software for a more limited platform.

They describe five different types of augmentation they believe could be performed. First, there is primary functionality outsourcing. This takes intensive tasks like speech recognition or video indexing and ports them to the cloud while allowing less intensive tasks to still be executed on the phone itself. Second there is background augmentation. This type of augmentation takes tasks that do not need to be performed immediately, such as virus checking or indexing files and moves them to the cloud. Mainline augmentation allows users to specifically pick an application to be run in an augmented fashion. This preserves the workings of the program but changes the method by which it is executed. Hardware augmentation modifies the virtual clone of the smartphone to modify low level system software. For example, modifying garbage collection to be less aggressive (since less aggressiveness is needed on the clone which has more memory) can speed up execution significantly. Finally, augmentation through multiplicity uses multiple clones of the device to speed up execution. This can help applications which require a great deal of parallel processing.

GPMCC makes it possible to overcome the limits built into mobile devices, and is a promising aspect of MCC.

Application-specific MCC Solutions

In contrast to GPMCC, application-specific MCC involves developing specific applications for mobile devices which use cloud computing. While both can potentially allow a mobile device to perform more intensive operations than it could using only local execution, ASMCC has the added benefit that it allows for uses of cloud computing which require more than simply increased computational power. For example, chat or e-mail clients require ASMCC because the internet is used as a communication resource and not simply for storage or additional computational power (although such applications may leverage these resources as well). Several methods and systems have been proposed which aim to specifically facilitate mobile cloud computing for applications.

Mobile Service Clouds

Researchers have developed a system called Mobile Service Clouds. This system is designed to offer easy and automatic service configuration to create services which can be used by mobile consumers. Given that cloud computing relies heavily on the client-server model, a development like this makes it much easier to create services which can work with applications.

RESTful Services

Jason Christensen has written about strategies for writing MCC applications using RESTful web services. RESTful web services (unlike standard web services) are easy to create, are not processor or time intensive, do not have continuous TCP connections and produce simple XML responses that can be easily parsed. Christensen claims that by leveraging mobile applications that use these services it will be more easily possible to create solid cloud applications.

Elastic Weblets

Researchers have developed a system for elastic applications intended to be used on mobile devices. Their elastic application framework divides a full application into pieces called weblets. These weblets have the important feature of portability. Any given weblet can be switched between both mobile and stationary devices. One significant difficulty with this type of application is the requirement of security for these weblets, which they have a solution for. They believe that some aspects of their system could even be applied to other, non-mobile, cases of cloud computing.

These systems and methods outlined can help developers of MCC applications more easily leverage the resources of the cloud. Since specific cloud-leveraging applications provide many of the unique benefits of MCC these techniques will be of significant importance in the development of MCC.

Mobile Server Cloud Computing

We have only discussed instances of MCC where the mobile device serves as a client and (assumedly) some collection of non-mobile devices act as the server, the provider of resources. It is possible to invert this pattern and let mobile devices serve as the resource rather than the consumer. We will call this mobile server cloud computing (MSCC).

Map Reduce Frameworks for MSCC

MapReduce is an algorithm which dissolves larger problems into smaller pieces that can be solved in parallel with multiple machines. Google created and publicized MapReduce. Given the large number of smart mobile devices connected to the internet, it seems possible to leverage these devices using MapReduce. The limited computational power of an individual device can be compensated for by the relatively small size of many of the tasks.

Researchers have considered this idea. They have created a system for leveraging mobile networked devices to solve problems. In designing this system they had to solve problems in several areas. First, they had to develop a system by which smartphone users could opt in to this program while staying aware of the effects. Second, they had to develop a system by which problems could be split over this device pool and the results could be aggregated. Finally, they had to make sure results could be transmitted to the requesting party and to make sure this could be done fairly quickly (difficult given the sometimes weak reliability of smartphones and their networks).

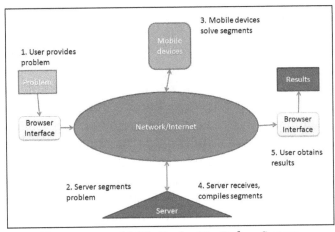

Hetereogenous Mobile Device MapReduce System.

They developed a system consisting of several segments called the heterogeneous mobile device MapReduce system. First, they have a coordinating server which receieves problems, distributes them to nodes, aggregates results and returns the results. Second they have a client for a mobile device which receives, works on and transmits solutions to subproblems. Third, a browser interface which allows the user to submit problems and view results.

After performing tests they concluded that their system could indeed provide significant computational power if enough mobile users participated and recommended that this line of research be continued and possibly developed into a real world application. Thus, it seems likely that MCC is not limited to cases where mobile devices act as the clients.

Mobile Cloud Computing Concerns

Cloud computing as opposed to standard computing has several issues which can cause reluctance or fear in the user base. Some of these issues include concerns about privacy and data ownership and security. Some of these concerns are especially relevant to mobile devices.

Privacy

One significant concern for cloud computing in general is privacy. For applications which employ cloud computing often at least some of the user's data will be stored remotely. This leads to concerns that companies will use or sell this information as well as concerns that the information could be given to government agencies without the user's permission or knowledge.

When it comes to mobile cloud computing, one family of applications specifically raises concerns. Location-aware applications and services perform tasks for users which require knowledge of the user's location. Examples would include an application that finds nearby restaurants for the user or one which allows their friends and family to receive updates regarding their location.

This type of application simultaneously has broad appeal and brings significant concerns. One method sometimes used to alleviate concern is to make data submitted either spatially or temporally imprecise. This is called location cloaking. The cost of location cloaking, of course, is that it can reduce the quality of service delivered by the applications. For example, if a user is attempting to find a nearby restaurant and the request sent to the server by his mobile client is too imprecise he could receive results which are irrelevant or perhaps miss relevant results. Thus, there is an interest in developing location cloaking methods which manage to alleviate privacy concerns and simultaneously reduce the negative effect on location-aware applications.

Researchers have performed some useful work in this area, developing methods and policies for location cloaking which balance the factors discussed. Specifically, they focus their attention on location-based range queries (LRQs), in which a mobile user makes a request for information regarding objects or points of interest within a certain range of their location. They propose a format for an imprecise location-based range query (ILRQ) in which both the location of the user and the location of the returned objects are ambiguous. In addition they present techniques used to prevent trajectory tracking: attempts to infer the future location of users given information about their past locations.

Data Ownership

Another issue that arises from mobile cloud computing relates to the ownership of purchased digital media. With cloud computing it becomes possible to store purchased media files, such as audio, video or e-books remotely rather than locally. This can lead concerns regarding the true ownership of the data. If a user purchases media using a given service and the media itself is stored remotely there is a risk of losing access to the purchased media. The service used could go out of business, for example, or could deny access to the user for some other reason.

As shown by a recent incident, this concern can develop even when the media is not completely stored remotely. In July of 2009 Amazon remotely deleted and refunded copies of George Orwell's 1984 from its users Kindle e-book readers. They did this because they discovered that 1984 was not actually in the public domain and that the publisher of that specific e-book edition of the novel did not have the right to sell or distribute it. This provoked an uproar among Kindle users and commentators. This action was compared to accidentally selling someone stolen property and then later breaking into their home to retrieve it.

This demonstrates that special precautions need to be taken with MCC to assure that incidents like this do not occur. Users should know exactly what rights they have regarding purchased media content. Either systems which imitate as closely as possible the normal processes of content ownership or systems which differ but communicate clearly the extent to which they differ should be used.

Data Access and Security

In addition to issues regarding privacy and data ownership there are the related issues of access and security. If an application relies on remote data storage and internet access in order to function at all then this can significantly affect the user. If, for example a user stores all of their calendar and contact information online, outages can affect their ability to function from day to day.

MCC is particularly vulnerable due to multiple points at which access can be interrupted. Reception and high speed availability can vary greatly for mobile devices. In addition to this, particular services used may have downtime. Finally, there can be issues of data becoming locked in to a particular service.

Concerns like the ones mentioned above have led some analysts to believe that MCC may be a trend which fails. These concerns will definitely have to be considered and dealt with as MCC becomes more prominent.

Cloud Computing as Green Solution

Cloud infrastructure addresses two critical elements of a green IT approach: energy efficiency and resource efficiency. Whether done in a private or public cloud configuration, as-a-service computing will be greener for (at least) the following three reasons.

Resource Virtualization, Enabling Energy and Resource Efficiencies

Virtualization is a foundational technology for deploying cloud-based infrastructure that allows a single physical server to run multiple operating system images concurrently. As an enabler of consolidation, server virtualization reduces the total physical server footprint, which has inherent green benefits.

From a resource-efficiency perspective, less equipment is needed to run workloads, which proactively reduces data center space and the eventual e-waste footprint. From an energy-efficiency perspective, with less physical equipment plugged in, a data center will consume less electricity.

It's worth noting that server virtualization is the most widely adopted green IT project implemented or planned, at 90 percent of IT organizations globally.

Automation Software, Maximizing Consolidation and Utilization to Drive Efficiencies

The presence of virtualization alone doesn't maximize energy and resource efficiencies. To rapidly provision, move, and scale workloads, cloud-based infrastructure relies on automation software.

Combined with the right skills and operational and architectural standards, automation allows IT professionals to make the most of their cloud-based infrastructure investment by pushing the limits of traditional consolidation and utilization ratios.

The higher these ratios are, the less physical infrastructure is needed, which in turn maximizes the energy and resource efficiencies from server virtualization.

Pay-per-use and Self-service, Encouraging more Efficient Behavior and Life-cycle Management

The pay-as-you-go nature of cloud-based infrastructure encourages users to only consume what they need and nothing more. Combined with self-service, life-cycle management will improve, since users can consume infrastructure resources only when they need it -- and "turn off" these resources with set expiration times.

In concert, the pay-per-use and self-service capabilities of cloud-based infrastructure drive energy and resource efficiencies simultaneously, since users only consume the computing resources they need when they need it.

Multitenancy, Delivering Efficiencies of Scale to Benefit many Organizations or Business Units

Multitenancy allows many different organizations (public cloud) or many different business units within the same organization (private cloud) to benefit from a common cloud-based infrastructure.

By combining demand patterns across many organizations and business units, the peaks and troughs of compute requirements flatten out. Combined with automation, the ratio between peak and average loads becomes smaller, which in turn reduces the need for extra infrastructure. The result: massive efficiencies and economies of scale in energy use and infrastructure resources.

So migrating workloads to cloud resources, or developing new workloads in a cloud-native environment, can help an IT organization contribute to energy-efficiency and sustainability goals. But so far, cloud services and their providers are doing little to help their customers on three other facets of a green IT program.

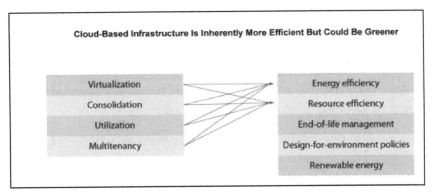

IT buyers that want to maximize the green contribution of cloud computing services should press their suppliers on these dimensions:

- Renewable energy sources: If cloud providers are truly going to position their services as green, they must invest in renewable energy sources. The reality is that even the most energy-efficient data center can have a significant carbon footprint because they are typically getting 70 percent of their electricity from greenhouse-gas-emitting fossil fuels, like coal. Ideally, centralized cloud data centers would be powered by renewable sources of energy, like wind, solar, or hydroelectricity.

  To date, however, cloud providers have prioritized other factors in designing and locating their data centers, including the cost of land, cost of power, property taxes, data privacy regulations, and access to power, bandwidth, local skills, and customers.

- Design-for-environment policies: In 2010, 59 percent of IT buyers included green criteria in their evaluation and selection of IT equipment, up from only 25 percent in 2007. However, energy efficiency trumps all other design-for-environment characteristics, such as recyclability, reduction of toxic chemicals, reduction in packaging, and longevity.

  Moreover, the weight of environmental criteria is used as a tiebreaker, not a deal breaker, and is always subordinate to price, features, and reputation. With that in mind, it's safe to assume that the same mentality is being applied in context to cloud-based infrastructure.

- Environmentally sound end-of-life: By pushing the limits of consolidation and utilization, cloud-based infrastructure minimizes the e-waste footprint upfront by requiring less physical equipment. But what happens when this equipment reaches its end-of-life?

  While all organizations dispose of their end-of-life IT equipment in some shape or form, e-waste policies have long been an afterthought and are the least mature IT asset life-cycle management process. Just because cloud minimizes e-waste upfront, don't assume those managing cloud-based infrastructure have policies to ensure e-waste is redeployed, resold, donated, or recycled.

Cloud computing can be an important facet of an enterprise IT organization's push to be greener. And "the green cloud" (which certainly needs a better marketing label!) can also contribute to meeting critical operational goals:

- Reduce costs. Consolidation means fewer servers, which in turn means lower cooling and space requirements, which means lower energy costs.

- Comply with regulation. By tapping more efficient and therefore lower-emitting resources, cloud computing customers can reduce their carbon emissions and be better-positioned to meet regulatory standards.

- Improve resiliency. Consolidation and improved utilization create more space, more power, and more cooling capacity within the same facility envelope. And tapping into public cloud providers offloads management of those resources from the customer to the service provider.

Sustainable Cloud Computing

Cloud computing can be considered an example of green IT. Jenkin et al. define green ITs as the technologies that directly or indirectly promote environmental sustainability in organizations. The term sustainability refers to the fair resource distribution between present and future generations and between agents in the current generation to maintain a scale of the current economy in relation to the ecological system that supports it. The term environmental sustainability refers to the preservation of the natural environment's ability to support human life. This can be achieved only by making appropriate decisions.

Environmental sustainability has a long history. In 1842, Jean Baptiste Joseph Fourier provided the first reference to greenhouse gases. In 1896, Svante Arrhenius suggested that levels of carbon dioxide in the atmosphere impact global temperatures via the greenhouse effect. The first major conference on environmental sustainability, the Stockholm Conference for the Human Environment, was held in 1972. In 1992, the United Nations Framework Convention on Climate Change (UNFCC) was held in Rio de Janeiro. The Kyoto protocol signed in 1997 legally binds 37 industrialized countries to specific measures.

In order to achieve environmental sustainability, fundamental changes in production must be realized. These changes are parallel to the continuous evolution of technological systems, especially the creation of innovative technological systems. Hekkert et al. specify that the rate of technological change is specified by the competition among existing innovation systems, not only different technologies. In order to understand innovative systems, a definition of technological systems must be provided. Technological systems involve a network of agents that interact in the economic/industrial area under a particular institutional infrastructure and support the generation and production of technology.

Innovative technological systems therefore must be used in order to achieve sustainability. They can be required to be sustainable by using technologies such as those that manage resources in such a way that performance and power are optimized. Additionally, they enable the realization of research with more efficient use of global energy sources. Ce´cile et al. specify that innovative policies for sustainable development should promote technological diversity and long-term innovation capacity with parallel use of clean technologies. Watson et al. mention that it is important to follow a scientific approach in the development of IT for environmental sustainability and to stop using approaches that involve management and policy formation.

Challenges in the use of Cloud Computing as Green Technology

There are a number of challenges associated with the use of green cloud computing. The main challenge is to minimize energy use and satisfy the requirements related to quality of service. However there are a number of issues when cloud computing is considered for environmental applications:

- Energy-aware dynamic resource allocation: In cloud computing, the excessive power cycling of servers could negatively impact their reliability. Furthermore, in the dynamic cloud environment, any interruption of energy can affect the quality of the provided service. Also, a virtual machine (VM) cannot record the timing behavior of a physical machine exactly. This can lead to timekeeping problems and inaccurate time measurements within the VM, which can result in incorrect enforcement of a service-level agreement (SLA).

- Quality of service (QoS)-based resource selection and provisioning: QoS-aware resource selection plays a significant role in cloud computing. Better resource selection and provision can result in energy efficiency.

- Optimization of virtual network topologies: Because of VM migrations or the machines' nonoptimized allocation, communicating VMs may ultimately be hosted on distant physical nodes, and as a result, the cost of data transfer between them may be high.

- Enhancing awareness of environmental issues: The users of green cloud computing technologies should become aware of the use of the technology in the resolution of specific environmental problems, such as the reduction of carbon emissions.

- SLAs: These provide for the replication of one application to multiple servers. Cloud customers should evaluate the range of parameters of SLAs, such as data protection, outage, and price structure, offered by different cloud vendors.

- Cloud data management: Cloud operation is characterized by the accumulation of large amounts of data. Cloud service providers rely on cloud infrastructure providers to achieve full data security. In addition, VMs can migrate from one location to another; therefore, any remote configuration of the cloud by service providers could be insufficient.

- Interoperability: Many public cloud systems are closed and are not designed to interact with each other. Industry standards must be created in order to allow cloud service providers to design interoperable cloud platforms. The Open Grid Forum is an industry group that is working on open cloud computing interface to provide an application program interface (API) for managing different cloud platforms.

- Security: Identity management and authentication are very significant, especially for government data. Governments, specifically the US government, have incorporated cloud computing infrastructures into the work of various departments and agencies. Because the government is a very complex entity, the implementation of cloud computing involves making policy changes, implementing dynamic applications, and securing the dynamic environment.

Cloud Computing and Sustainability

When combined with specific characteristics of other technologies, such as the distributed resource provision of grid computing, the distributed control of digital ecosystems, and the sustainability from green computing, cloud computing can provide a sociotechnical conceptualization for sustainable distributed computing. Grid computing is a form of distributed technology in which a virtual supercomputer includes a cluster of networked computers performing very large tasks. Digital ecosystems are sociotechnical systems characterized by self-organization, scalability, and sustainability. Their purpose is to extend service-oriented architecture (SOA), thus supporting network-based economies. Green computing is the efficient use of computing resources, which respects specific values for societal and organizational success. These values are people, planet, and profit.

Social, economic, and environmental sustainability can also be achieved through the development of a green infrastructure. Weber et al. define green infrastructure as the abundance of landscape features that in combination with ecological processes contributes to human health. Lafortezza et al. identify a green infrastructure framework (GIF) that includes five functions: ecosystem services, biodiversity, social and territorial cohesion, sustainable development, and human well-being. These elements interact with each other.

A number of cloud computing business models have been developed to ensure sustainability. Examples are the cloud cube model that enables collaboration in cloud formations used for specific business needs and the hexagon model, which provides six main criteria (consumers, investors, popularity, valuation, innovation, and get the job done [GTJD]) for business sustainability and shows how cloud computing performs according to these criteria. The cloud can lead to business sustainability through business improvement and the transformation and creation of new business value chains.

Focal companies are responsible for the supply chain; they provide direct contact to the customer. Additionally, they design the product or service offered. Focal companies are also responsible for the environmental and social performance of their suppliers; therefore, there is increased need for sustainable supply chain management. There is a direct linkage between suppliers, focal companies, and customers. The integration of environmental thinking into supply chain management results in green supply chain management. In this case, sustainable information systems can be used to provide sustainable information services in the supply chain. Research on green information systems can be classified to different categories. The first category involves the examination of how the software development life cycle can be modified to reduce the potential negative environmental impacts of systems. The second involves research on environmental reporting, measurement and accounting systems, and the use of knowledge management for environmental sustainability. Some research studies are also related to the consideration of environmental parameters when designing new products. A cloud computing platform can be characterized as a green information system that provides green information services.

The sustainability offered by cloud computing can be shown by the fact that the specific technology allows small business organizations to access large amounts of computing power in a very short time; as a result, they become more competitive with larger organizations. Thirdworld countries can also be significantly benefit by cloud computing technologies because they can use IT services that they previously could not access because they lacked the resources. Cloud computing accelerates the time in the businesses market because it allows quicker access to hardware resources without any upfront investment. In this case, there is no capital expenditure (capex), only operational expenditure (opex). Cloud computing makes possible the realization of new, innovative applications such as real-time, location-, environment-, and context-aware mobile interactive applications; parallel batch processing used for the processing of large amounts of data during very short periods of time; and business analytics for customer behavioral analysis.

Sustainable Applications of Cloud Computing

The architecture, engineering, and construction (AEC) sector is a highly fragmented, project-based industry with very strong data sharing. Beach et al. describe how cloud computing can be used in the AEC sector for better data management and collaboration. In order to create an efficient architecture for a cloud computing prototype, the authors used a building information model (BIM) data representation that is a complete 4-D virtual repository of all the data related to a construction project, such as 3-D models of building structure, construction data management information such as plans and schedules, information about all items within the building, and data about the progress of the construction project. The specific cloud computing platform is based on Comet-Cloud, which is an autonomic computing engine for cloud and grid environments. Specifically, it is useful in the development of clouds with resizable computing capability that both integrates local computational environments and public cloud services and enables the capability to develop a range of programming applications. The CloudBIM prototype was built using CometCloud's master/worker programming model and includes three main elements: client, masters, and workers. The function of CloudBIM is based on the interaction between masters and workers. The workers store data and are responsible for the validation of each query they receive. The client is responsible for the provision of the interface between the users and the local master node. This interface converts users' actions into queries.

Social sustainability can also be achieved through the use of social networks. This type of network can be based on cloud platforms or cloud applications and can be realized in social networks. The creation of social networking sites provides easier and less expensive ways for sustainable development communities to develop a wide variety of new communities. Examples of social networking sites for social sustainability are TakingIT-Global, which supports youth-led action using blogs, online groups and event calendars, UnLtd that supports social entrepreneurship, and People for Earth, a social network that provides advice on how people should live more environmentally friendly lives.

Busan is South Korea's second largest city and the fifth largest container globally. A cloud infrastructure has been provided to Busan based on Cisco Unified Computing System. The developed solution is the Busan Smart+Connected Communities, which aims to deliver social, economic, and environmental sustainability. It connects the Busan metropolitan government, the Busan Mobile Application Centre, and five local universities. During 2014, it is expected that the Busan cloud platform will create 3500 new job opportunities and 300 start-up companies focused on the Mobile Application Center development.

Cloud computing has been also applied to government. The US government has made efforts to introduce cloud computing to the General Services Administration (GSA), the National Aeronautics and Space Administration (NASA), the Department of the Interior, the Department of Health and Human Services (HHS), the Census Bureau, and the White House. Specifically, the GSA can provide cloud-based hosting of the federal government's primary e-government portals—USA.gov—and its Spanish-language companion site, GobiernoUSA.gov. NASA uses the Nebula cloud computing platform, which can provide transparency in the involvement with space efforts. The US Department of the Interior's National Business Center (NBC) has introduced several cloud-based human resources management applications, including Webbased training, staffing, and recruitment programs. The NBC also offers cloud-based financial and procurement software (U.S. Department of the Interior, NBC, 2009). The UK government has also introduced the use of cloud computing through the development of G-cloud, which is a governmentwide cloud computing network. Petrov identified efforts from specific European countries, such as Sweden, France, and Spain, focused on the implementation of cloud computing for economic development, health and education services, and transportation networks.

Cloud computing is currently used for the advancement of scientific research. An example is the Cumulus project, which is an ongoing cloud computing project established at the Steinbuch Centre for Computing of the Karlsruhe Institute of Technology (KIT). The aim of Cumulus is the provision of virtual infrastructures for scientific research. Cloud computing is extremely significant for the European Organization for Nuclear Research (CERN), which realizes a number of experiments (e.g., the ALPHA experiment, the Isotope mass separator on-line facility [ISOLDE] experiment, the large Hadron collider (LHC), the total elastic and diffractive cross-section measurement) and generates amazingly extreme amounts of data (approximately 15 petabytes) useful for simulation and analysis. The CERN Data Centre is responsible for the collection of these data. In 2002, the CERN Data Centre required the use of the worldwide LHC computing grid (WLCG), which is a distributed computing infrastructure in tiers that provides to 8000 physicists real-time access to LHC data. However, CERN is currently focused on the use of cloud technology for better handling these colossal data sets. It is very probable that CERN will adopt the use of the OpenStack cloud computing software in order to update its data management operations. Other examples of the use of cloud computing for scientific research are Red Cloud from Cornell University, Wispy from Purdue University, and the San Diego Supercomputer Center (SDSC) cloud.

Global Forest Watch is an online mapping tool created by Google, the World Resources Institute, and 40 other partners. It is based on the analysis of Landsat7 satellite images that are processed by Google Earth Engine, the company's cloud platform for geodata analysis. The amount of image data that were processed was about 20 tera-pixels, which required 1 million central processing unit (CPU) hours on 10,000 computers operating in parallel for a period of several days. Google estimates that a single computer would need 15 years to perform the tasks realized by Global Forest Watch. The aim of the mapping system is also the enhancement of satellite images with social data, which will document possible forest abuse.

Cloud computing is used to process an inversion process for magnetotellurics, a geophysic technique used for the characterization of geothermal reservoirs and mineral exploration. The entire inversion process is implemented on the Amazon Elastic Compute Cloud (EC2) cloud using available EC2 instances The determination of subsurface electrical conductivity is significant in a range of applications covering tectonic evolution and mineral and geothermal exploration. Mudge et al. describe how a Fortran program was developed in order to abstract logic and process modeling calculations. The program is embedded in a web application. The whole inversion process is implemented on the Amazon EC2 cloud using available EC2 instances. The whole process is further packaged as a MT 3D inversion software product, which is accessible anywhere through a secure login. The magnetotellurics method is used for understanding the processes involved during the Enhanced Geothermal Systems (EGS) fluid system.

Lawrence Berkeley National Laboratory and Northwestern University in the United States created a modeling tool that shows the energy savings from moving local network software and computing to serve cloud farms. The specific tool is called Cloud Energy and Emissions Research Model (CLEER). The aim of the model is the provision of a framework for the assessment of the net energy consumption and greenhouse gas emissions of cloud computing in comparison to traditional systems. Cloud computing saves energy through virtualization, which allows virtual machine consolidation and migration, heat management, and temperature-aware allocation; these are techniques that result in the reduction of power consumption. The large-scale deployment of virtualized server infrastructure can result in the balance of computer and storage loads across physical servers. The optimized design of cloud data centers allows servers to run at optimal temperature and use. Furthermore, cloud computing provides dynamic provisioning of infrastructure capacity and sharing of application instances between client organizations that results to the reduction of peak loads.

Eye on Earth is an environmental information sharing system developed by the European Environment Agency (EEA), which is based on Microsoft Windows Azure cloud platform. Information sharing is important in efficiently and effectively addressing environmental issues. The users of the environment can be policy makers, communities or individuals, environmental organizations, and emergency responders. Different environmental data, such as air and water quality are examined and can be represented in a visual format. For example, an intelligent map allows users to discover environmental information.

The US government has launched the Climate Change Initiative to help organizations and citizens to use public data more efficiently to better prepare for the effects of climate change. Google has donated 50 million hours of cloud computing time on the Google Earth Engine geospatial analysis platform to the project. Google Earth Engine can detect changes on Earth's surface using satellite imagery. Examples of its application are the development of the first global maps of deforestation and a nearly real-time system that identifies deforestation resulting from climate change. The engine will be used to manage the agricultural water supply and model the impacts of sea level rises.

Information and communication technologies (ICTs) play an important role in emergency response systems during natural disasters. Alazawi et al. suggest the use of an intelligent disaster management system based on the use of vehicular ad-hoc networks (VANETs) and mobile and cloud technologies. VANETs are the most advanced technology of intelligent transportation systems (ITS). They are vehicles that are equipped with sensors and wireless communication capability. The main focus of the application of VANETs is safety and transportation efficiency. The cloud-based vehicular emergency response system includes three main layers: the cloud infrastructure, the Intelligence, and the system interface layers. The cloud infrastructure layer is the foundation for the base platform for the emergency system. The intelligence layer provides the necessary computational models to develop optimum emergency response strategies. The system interface layer collects data from the Internet, social media, and even roadside masts. The system was implemented in Ramadi, Iraq.

Suakanto et al. suggest the use of cloud computing infrastructure for detecting environmental disasters early and monitoring environmental conditions. Depending on the type of environmental application in which the system is used, different sensors are used. For example, for air monitoring applications, carbon dioxide or air quality control sensors are used; for water monitoring applications, water pH measurement sensors can be used. A remote terminal unit (RTU) is used in order to collect data from the different types of sensors in analogue and digital form. The units are placed in areas that are prone to disasters. A cloud platform is used for central data storage and processing.

Data collected by the sensors are sent to the listener service of the virtual machines. The main function of this service is to read and process sensor data and store them in the cloud storage repository. When users are online, they can see the stored data by using application services installed on virtual machines.

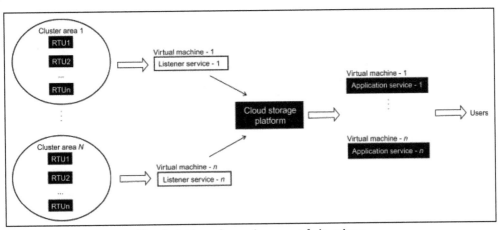

Cloud platform for environmental situations.

Agricultural modernization has great significance for China's growing economy. Even though the country has realized improvements in crop cultivation and animal and plant breeding, agricultural production is a decentralized operation characterized by the use of low-level information technologies. Agricultural modernization involves the use of modern agricultural equipment, modern agricultural planting and breeding technology, and modern forms of production organization and management. Cloud computing can lead to the establishment of an information network services platform and the integration of isolated production facilities, technical equipment, and information services. Applications of cloud computing are the integration and sharing of agricultural information, the real-time monitoring of agricultural production, the provision of agricultural technology services, construction and improvement of agricultural supply chain, and the tracking of the quality of agricultural products.

Technologies Associated with Sustainable Cloud Computing

Some technologies have the same characteristics as cloud computing or are related to cloud computing are:

- Grid computing: This involves a large network of computers used to create large supercomputing resources. In these types of networks, large and complex computing operations can be performed.

- Virtualization: Virtualization allows the consolidation of multiple applications into virtual containers located on a single or multiple servers. Virtualization is the foundation of cloud computing. It enables users to access servers without knowing details of those servers.

- Utility computing: This term defines a "pay-per-use" model for using computing services.

- Autonomic computing: The term autonomic refers to self-management, in this case, of computers. In autonomic computing, computers can correct themselves without human intervention.

- Web services: Web services simplify the application-to-application interaction using a systematic framework based on existing Web protocols and open XML standards. This framework includes three mail elements: communication protocols, service descriptions, and service discovery.

Future Prospects of Sustainable Cloud Computing

The future of cloud computing in relation to its impact to sustainability is excellent. There is huge potential for additional applications of the technology to different industries, such as manufacturing, health care, and education. Examples of this potential are the provision of access to global data resources through cloud computing, the realization of low-cost simulation experiments, provision of massive and flexible computing power for drug discovery, and realtime health monitoring. With its rapid prototyping and collaborative design and the improvement of manufacturing processes, cloud computing can also contribute significantly to supply chain coordination. Furthermore, the technology can be the basis for highly interactive, collaborative learning.

The European Union (EU) envisions the realization of the global cloud ecosystem. It can offer new features to support cloud employment and to improve adoption of cloud computing. It could provide supporting tools that would cover issues related to building and supporting new platforms easily, new programming models, and tools that deal with distribution and control, improved security and data protection, efficient data management, energy efficiency, and easy mash-ups of clouds exposing a single-user interface. The EU can also exploit the capabilities offered by existing cloud systems to enhance the capabilities of products and services offered by European industry. Developing countries, such as India, can seek ways to enhance sustainability through the use of green IT. In fact, India spent 18.2 billion for green IT in 2013. A study by Global e-Sustainability Initiative and Microsoft showed that running services over the cloud can be 95% more efficient than those run in other ways.

Reflections on Sustainable Cloud Computing Applications

Sustainability is a topic of great importance regarding continuous environmental, social, and economic problems. Cloud computing can be applied to all aspects (social, business, environmental) of sustainability. Specific characteristics of the technology, such as sharing data, allow small businesses to have access to huge computing power and as a result, these businesses can become more competitive. Cloud technology can be adjusted to meet requirements of sustainability. It offers dynamic provisioning of resources, multitenancy (the serving of multiple businesses using the same infrastructure), server use, and the power efficiency of data centers. The technology has huge potential in shaping sustainability in different fields. Especially related to environment, it promotes environmental research, development of emergency response systems, and implementation measures to prevent climate change.

However, there are some concerns in relation to the energy efficiency of cloud computing. When files to be transmitted over a network are quite large, the network will be a major contributor to energy consumption. Furthermore, the VM consolidation could reduce the number of active servers but will put an excessive load on few servers whose heat distribution can become a major issue. A green cloud framework that considers these problems can be developed. In such a framework, users submit their cloud service requests through a middleware green broker that manages the selection of the greenest cloud provider to serve the user's request.

A user request can be for software, platform, or infrastructure. The cloud providers register their services in the form of offers to a public directory and the green broker assesses them. These offers include green services, pricing, and time when the service should be assessed for the least carbon emission. The green broker calculates the carbon emission of all cloud providers. It then selects the services that will result in the least carbon emission and buys them on behalf of users. Some additional steps need to be taken: the design of software at various levels (OS, compiler, algorithm, application) that facilitates energy efficiency, the measurement of data center power, and the deployment of the data centers near renewable energy sources.

References

- Cloud-computing, best-practices, platform, products: salesforce.com, Retrieved 30 August, 2019

- Five-characteristics-of-cloud-computing: controleng.com, Retrieved 10 May, 2019

- Cloud-monitoring-tools: stackify.com, Retrieved 14 July, 2019

- 4-reasons-why-cloud-computing-also-green-solution: greenbiz.com, Retrieved 08 June, 2019

- Sustainable-Cloud-Computing-319878404: researchgate.net, Retrieved 26 March, 2019

Cloud Computing: Architecture and Infrastructure

The components that are required for cloud computing are termed as cloud architecture. Cloud infrastructure is referred to the hardware and software components required for supporting the cloud computing model. This chapter has been carefully written to provide an easy understanding of cloud architecture and cloud infrastructure.

Cloud Computing Architecture

A cloud software system mainly requires hardware to power operations, and a way for end users to access the platform. The way this is structured in terms of components and subcomponents is an integral part of planning cloud systems out.

In an enterprise setting, determining which hardware and software components go into building a cloud environment makes up most of cloud architecture. While hardware can be chosen as off-the-shelf pieces, software is a complex part of the equation to solve for.

Many cloud service providers have made a name for themselves in the market by offering extensible hardware solutions and pairing them with easy-to-use and accessible software.

Choosing the right cloud software architecture is an important part of determining the cloud approach of any company. Inefficient cloud architecture planning can lead to over- or underuse of resources and lower cost-effectiveness.

Good planning of cloud software architecture allows for efficient and cost-effective scaling. Cloud architecture is also an integral part of fleshing out any company's architecture and ensuring that all cloud compute needs are taken care of.

What are the Components of Cloud Architecture?

The components of cloud architecture are generally classified into 3 categories: a front-end platform, a backend platform, and cloud-based delivery. The architecture of the system needs the Internet for communication between the front end and the back end.

The delivery system, as the name suggests, is what allows information to be delivered between the front end and the backend. These include Infrastructure-as-a-Service (IaaS), Software-as-a-Service (SaaS), Platform-as-a-Service (PaaS) and more.

Cloud computing architecture also includes many sub disciplines such as cloud-based security, cloud security architecture and multi-cloud architecture.

How is Cloud Computing Architecture Structured?

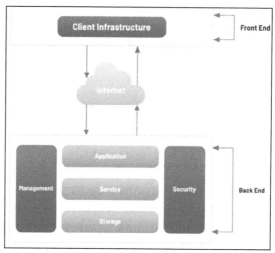

The Structure of Cloud Computing Architecture.

What is Front End Architecture?

Front end architecture is a term used to denote any user-facing part of cloud computing architecture. This is the part that the end user interacts with, and it is comprised of subcomponents that make up the user experience. Front end architecture generally takes the form of a user interface and is an integral part of how the user interacts with cloud computing software.

Most working IT professionals today will mainly interact with front-end cloud software architecture. Examples of front-end architecture include web browsers, local networks and common web apps. Gmail, a popular cloud service used by millions daily, has its front-end architecture in the form of the web application. The interface allows users to access the services offered by the Gmail architecture as a whole.

Front end architecture is made up of three parts:

Software

Front end software architecture includes the software that allows cloud computing software to be run from the user's side. In today's web-powered world, the front-end software architecture generally takes the form of a web browser or client-side application.

User Interface

The user interface is what the end user directly interacts with in order to perform tasks on the cloud. This includes the text editor in services such as Google Docs, or the interface to send and receive emails on Gmail. However, in some cases, the UI and software architecture are rolled into one.

Client Device/Network

The client-side device or network is an integral part of front-end architecture. This includes client-side hardware such as the user's PC and input devices. Generally, in cloud computing, the client device does not require a lot of computing power. This is because most of the "heavy" tasks are processed in the cloud.

What is Back End Architecture?

Back end architecture is the part of the cloud computing architecture that powers the front-end architecture. This includes the core components of the system such as hardware and storage, and is generally located in a server farm in a geographically distant location.

Back end architecture is taken care of by the cloud service provider offering cloud software. Prominent cloud providers such as AWS generally have robust backend architecture to ensure continuous uptime with low latency. In addition to this, powerful front-end cloud architecture plays a role in creating a dependable and easy-to use product.

Back end architecture is made up of many distinct parts, and also includes services such as management and security. The system generally includes components such as:

Application

The application component of the back-end cloud software architecture generally refers to the interface being offered to the end user, except on the side of the server. This layer coordinates the various needs of the consumer with resources in the back end.

Service

This is where all the magic happens. The service is directly responsible for providing the utility in the architecture. This means that any task that is being run on the cloud computing system is taken care of mainly by the service.

Services can perform a wide variety of tasks, and function in a cloud runtime. Some services that are popular among cloud users include storage, application development environments, and web services. It is similar to the heart of the architecture, and is one of the main components in the entire system.

Cloud Runtime

The cloud runtime is where the service runs. It is similar to an operating system in the cloud, with technologies such as virtualization allowing multiple runtimes to exist on the same server.

Runtimes are created with the help of virtualization software, and are commonly referred to as Hypervisors. Software such as VMWare Fusion, Oracle Virtual Box and Oracle VM for x86 are common examples of Hypervisors. It can be compared to the foundation on which the service is built, as it manages the resources and tasks for the service.

Storage

As the name suggests, storage is where all the data required to operate the cloud software resides. Storage varies with cloud service providers today, with all of them having a product dedicated solely to cloud storage. The different kinds of storage offered includes hard drives, solid state drives, and more recently, Intel Optane DC Persistent storage.

In back end architecture, it takes the form of many hard drives in server bays. This is then managed by the management software which partitions the drives into what is needed by the operating system in the cloud to run various services.

Infrastructure

The infrastructure is the engine powering all cloud software services. This includes computing components such as the Central Processing Unit (CPU), Graphics Processing Unit (GPU), motherboard and all the other components required for the system to function smoothly, like network cards and additional specific accelerator cards for special use-cases.

The infrastructure also differs from workload to workload. While lower-powered CPUs and GPUs are available as a cheaper option, enterprise level workloads usually depend on cutting-edge hardware to run. Many cloud service providers also provide accelerators, such as Google's Tensor Processing Unit, available to Google Cloud Platform customers to run AI tasks.

In addition to hardware and software, there are services that are required for the architecture to function smoothly. These include:

Management

In a traditional server setting, many virtual cloud systems, known as runtimes, are on the same physical server. This means that the resources need to be managed according to the needs of the end user. This also has to occur in real-time to ensure seamless use and flexibility for the user.

Management software is in charge of allocating specific resources for certain tasks. While physical resources are abundant in a public cloud solution, ineffective management can cause bottlenecks. This makes management software essential to the 'smooth' functioning of a cloud environment.

Management usually takes the form of what is known as 'middleware', as it interfaces between the back end and front end. Middleware is used to divide system resources and infrastructure in a seamless and dynamic manner.

Security

Cloud security architecture is an important part of cloud software architecture. It is generally built keeping in mind visibility in order to allow for easier debugging in case of an issue with the system.

The way the system is structured should also ensure that mission-critical tasks do not get interrupted. Usually, this is done by duplicating the system virtually, so as to ensure redundancy in the tasks. Storage backups must also be done regularly, and such tasks fall under security.

Cloud security architecture also focuses on securing the server with virtual firewalls, preventing data loss and redundancy mechanisms. These are ways to keep the system running even when it is under potential attack or experiencing system failure owing to malfunctioning hardware.

Such services are integral to ensuring a complete end user experience, as they ensure the smooth functioning of the system. Tasks such as resource management are also critical to ensuring consistency uptime and redundancy for cloud tasks. Security is also an important feature to keep the data contained in the system safe from attackers.

Types of Cloud Deployment (By Models)

Cloud software architecture also varies to some degree according to the deployment model chosen for the system. There are the four main types of cloud deployment models:

Public Cloud Architecture

As the name suggests, a public cloud architecture is open for use by any paying customer. They are termed public clouds as they function as one divided server hosting many different partitions, each of which is available for use.

There is no firewall separating different cloud instances. This means that it is open to the general public to use, with services being provided on a large scale to organizations and individuals.

Common instances of public cloud architecture include the architecture that underpins AWS, Salesforce, Oracle and Microsoft Azure. These service providers offer cloud computing on a pay-per-use basis and allow for scalability on demand.

Advantages

- Easy to use and scale.

- More cost-effective than on-premise solutions.

- Reduced downtime and 24/7 service.

Disadvantages

- Lack of data ownership.

- Centralized control in the hands of service providers.

Private Cloud Architecture

Private cloud architecture is similar to public cloud architecture, except that it is permissioned. This means that only individuals from a certain company or organization can access the server. The service is still provided by a third party, but is protected by various security features to prevent unauthorized access.

Private clouds are partitioned public clouds protected by firewalls, to restrict the entry of non-company personnel to mission-critical systems.

Advantages

- Customizable storage and components.

- Higher degree of security and control.

Disadvantages

- Increased cost of maintenance.

- Training and education costs.

Community Cloud Architecture

Community cloud architecture is similar to private cloud architecture, except that it is shared between multiple companies. This is commonly used in situations wherein multiple companies are working together on a project.

Community clouds are integral to maintaining a common development and working environment across companies. A common environment can enable higher degrees of collaboration between companies. This also means that the requirements for privacy, security and performance will be similar, allowing for consistent performance.

Advantages

- Cost effective, with higher number of participants.

- Customized privacy and security requirements.

- Heightened collaboration between companies.

Disadvantages

- Fixed bandwidth and capacity.

- Lesser capability of scaling.

Hybrid Cloud Architecture

Hybrid cloud architecture is where a public cloud and a private cloud are used together in an overarching architecture. Hybrid cloud architecture is used in scenarios in which companies can make a clear distinction between mission critical data and operations and non-sensitive information that does not need utmost security. This creates an environment in which a public and private cloud can be used in conjunction.

Hybrid clouds are expensive, but they are effective in the right situation. An example would be when an organization works on high-end intellectual property and technology and manages a large number of users at the same time. The former would be stored in a high-security private cloud with limited access, while the latter would be managed by a public cloud with open access.

Types of Cloud Deployment (By Location)

Cloud software architecture deployment can also vary by location, with infrastructure and architecture shifting closer towards the company as required. Various location options allow for greater flexibility both when serving end users and utilizing cloud software for company operations.

On-premise Cloud Deployment

On-premise cloud deployment solutions, more commonly referred to as on-prem solutions, are used when the backend infrastructure is deployed on the premises of the company and not outsourced. On-premise cloud deployment architecture is generally employed by small to medium enterprises. A centralized cloud structure within company premises is created, usually with a limited amount of scalability.

Outsourced Cloud Deployment

Outsourced cloud deployments take place when the physical hardware infrastructure is managed by a third party. Outsourced cloud deployments are more widely used than on-premise solutions, owing to their various benefits. It is important to note that outsourced cloud deployments put sensitive company information in the hands of a third-party.

Owing to the vast infrastructure of cloud providers such as AWS, Azure and Oracle, they can offer easily scalable and easy-to-use systems at an effective cost. This is great for a company that's starting out, as they can take up more computing power as their needs evolve.

Outsourced cloud deployment does have some disadvantages, such as propensity for breaches or public cloud access. However, these can be remedied by a few architectural improvements. These include creating a robust private cloud infrastructure, picking the right service providers, and implementing measures such as intrusion detection and prevention systems.

In a situation where cloud is the obvious next step for deployment in your organization, it is important to think of cloud computing architecture. It is integral towards ensuring a cost-effective and suitable deployment of cloud services. Apart from the scalability offered by dependable cloud computing architecture, the accompanying software and services allow flexible workload optimization.

In case of startups and SMEs, it is better to go with an outsourced public cloud or private cloud, depending on the infrastructural requirements. In the case of larger companies, a case-by-case approach can be adopted. The primary option is still to go with a cloud service provider due to aforementioned reasons, but other architectures can also come in handy, according to the company's requirements.

Beyond a certain scale, cloud software companies offer customized solutions for enterprises. This option offers completely customizable security, access and resources, and is generally a catch-all solution. Certain situations might also require a hybrid architecture, as decided by their data flows. In large-scale enterprises, on-premise solutions, along with a cloud layer, can be implemented for a high level of security and access control.

Cloud Platform

Cloud Platform assumes the responsibility of "Data Centers on the Fly". The reason for this comment is manifested in the elasticity of resources that can be provisioned near-real-time. Literally, you can spin up or down instances in a matter of minutes. Matter of fact you can copy and erect an entire Architecture Stack in hours from one region to another using Cloud Formation without any formal procurement process. However, projecting, predicting and approval of costing from appropriate departments may be necessary.

On any Cloud Hosting Platform resources will be shared amongst many tenants while keeping Security as a prime requirement. This means resources such as: CPU, Memory, Disk Storage, which are hosted on a common Physical Architecture, will be shared in a multi-tenant model. This is clearly depicted in the following diagram.

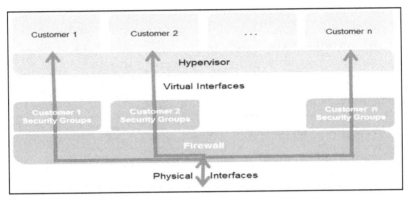

Contrary to a traditional Data Centers where many rudimentary responsibilities are assumed by Data Center Providers, Cloud Providers such as AWS provides them to their customers hassle free. For example, Physical Security, Redundant Power Supply from multiple Power Grids, Availability Zones (think of them as Data Centers) in low flooding zones, Access to a facility with ONLY state-of-the-art technologies and much more.

Additionally, AWS Cloud has augmented many software solutions/packages as pre-packaged services for either free or nominal cost. This provides an efficient way of using these services without the worries of updates on version and security patches. Simple Queue Services (SQS), Docker, Chef are just to name a few services that are ready and available for AWS Cloud Customers.

Shopping Cart Experience

Selection of Cloud Services experience is analogous to experience at a WalMart Store. You shop around at a WalMart store while picking items of your liking and needs and place them in the shopping cart; Cloud allows you a similar experience. You may have many products/services at your disposal on AWS Cloud but you will provision only the services that fulfill your needs to run your infrastructure. Only difference is the checkout for AWS is at the end of the month as a monthly 'Bill Bill' rather than at the end of shopping, as is the case in WalMart on a Point-of-Sale (POS) counter.

You are not limited or bound to use AWS Provided Services, instead you can Bring Your

Own License (BYOL) for software that requires licensing or you can install open source software on an EC2 instances. This helps in bringing the cost down as open source licenses software won't incur any charges. A good example is GoCD Build Server. For your CICD needs, you can use AWS Code Commit, Code Deploy and Code Pipeline. These services will cost you some money (however nominal it may be) but if you are an avid user of GoCD Server, then you can bring this open source CICD software to your AWS environment and configure your entire CICD process using GoCD. Only charge will be your hosted EC2 instance.

To Cloud or not to Cloud?

An important question to ask is "To Cloud or not to Cloud?" While making that decision few things to consider are:

- Is Quick turn-around time on hardware provisioning needed?

- No up-front costing for hardware required?

- I want to pay only the services I use?

- I don't' want a big networking team?

Once you have made up your mind on migrating or setting up your new infrastructure on Cloud, costing should be projected based on:

- Data in/out charges.

- Number of servers required to support your infrastructure.

- Database Nodes required.

Google Cloud Platform (GCP)

Google Cloud Platform is a suite of public cloud computing services offered by Google. The platform includes a range of hosted services for compute, storage and application development that run on Google hardware. Google Cloud Platform services can be accessed by software developers, cloud administrators and other enterprise IT professionals over the public internet or through a dedicated network connection.

Google Cloud Platform offers services for compute, storage, networking, big data, machine learning and the internet of things (IoT), as well as cloud management, security and developer tools. The core cloud computing products in Google Cloud Platform include:

- Google Compute Engine, which is an infrastructure-as-a-service (IaaS) offering that provides users with virtual machine instances for workload hosting.

- Google App Engine, which is a platform-as-a-service (PaaS) offering that gives software developers access to Google's scalable hosting. Developers can also use a software developer kit (SDK) to develop software products that run on App Engine.

- Google Cloud Storage, which is a cloud storage platform designed to store large, unstructured data sets. Google also offers database storage options, including Cloud Datastore for NoSQL nonrelational storage, Cloud SQL for MySQL fully relational storage and Google's native Cloud Bigtable database.

- Google Container Engine, which is a management and orchestration system for Docker containers that runs within Google's public cloud. Google Container Engine is based on the Google Kubernetes container orchestration engine.

Google Cloud Platform offers application development and integration services. For example, Google Cloud Pub/Sub is a managed and real-time messaging service that allows messages to be exchanged between applications. In addition, Google Cloud Endpoints allows developers to create services based on RESTful APIs, and then make those services accessible to Apple iOS, Android and JavaScript clients. Other offerings include Anycast DNS servers, direct network interconnections, load balancing, monitoring and logging services.

Higher-level Services

Google continues to add higher-level services, such as those related to big data and machine learning, to its cloud platform. Google big data services include those for data processing and analytics, such as Google BigQuery for SQL-like queries made against multi-terabyte data sets. In addition, Google Cloud Dataflow is a data processing service intended for analytics; extract, transform and load (ETL); and real-time computational projects. The platform also includes Google Cloud Dataproc, which offers Apache Spark and Hadoop services for big data processing.

For artificial intelligence (AI), Google offers its Cloud Machine Learning Engine, a managed service that enables users to build and train machine learning models. Various APIs are also available for the translation and analysis of speech, text, images and videos.

Google also provides services for IoT, such as Google Cloud IoT Core, which is a series of managed services that enables users to consume and manage data from IoT devices.

The Google Cloud Platform suite of services is always evolving, and Google periodically introduces, changes or discontinues services based on user demand or competitive pressures. Google's main competitors in the public cloud computing market include Amazon Web Services (AWS) and Microsoft Azure.

Google Cloud Platform Services				
COMPUTE	**STORAGE/DA-TABASES**	**NETWORK-ING**	**BIG DATA/loT**	**MACHINE LEARNING**
Compute Engine	Cloud Storage	Virtual Private Cloud (VPC)	BigQuery	Cloud Machine Learning Engine
App Engine	Cloud SQL	Cloud Load Balancing	Cloud Dataflow	Cloud Jobs API
Container Engine	Cloud Bigtable	Cloud CDN	Cloud Dataproc	Cloud Natural Language API
Cloud Function	Cloud Spanner	Cloud CDN	Cloud Datalab	Cloud Speech API
	Cloud Datastore	Cloud Intercon-nect	Cloud Dataprep	Cloud Translation API
	Persistent Disk	Cloud DNS	Cloud Pub/Sub	Cloud Vision API
	Data Transfer		Genomics	Cloud video Intel-ligence
			Google Data Studio	
			Cloud loT Core	

Cloud Deployment Models

A cloud deployment model is a "configuration" of certain cloud environment parameters such as the storage size, accessibility and proprietorship. To choose the most suitable one for you, SaM Solutions recommends companies to make a choice based on their computing, networking, storage requirements, TCO expectations and business goals, as well as available resources.

There are four main cloud deployment models that differ significantly and for which most of the companies opt: a public, private, hybrid and a community one. There are also web-based organization systems that are not so widespread, such as virtual private, inter-cloud and others.

Public Cloud

The name speaks for itself, as public clouds are available to the general public and data are created and stored on third-party servers. As server infrastructure belongs to service providers that manage them and administer pool resources, the need for user companies to buy and maintain their own hardware is eliminated. Provider companies offer resources as a service on a free of charge or pay-per-use basis via the Internet connection. Users can scale them when required.

At the same time, relying on a third party in running their infrastructure deprives users of knowing where their information is kept and who has access to it. Often enough, public clouds experience outages and malfunction, as in the case of the Salesforce CRM disruption in 2016 that caused a 10-hour storage collapse.

The pros of a public cloud are:

- Unsophisticated setup and use.

- Easy access to data.

- Flexibility to add and reduce capacity.

- Cost-effectiveness.

- Continuous operation time.

- 24/7 upkeep.

- Scalability.

- Eliminated need for software.

The cons of a public model:

- Data security and privacy.

- Compromised reliability.

- The lack of individual approach.

The public cloud deployment model is the first choice of businesses that operate within the industries with low privacy concerns. When it comes to popular cloud deployment models, examples are Amazon Elastic Compute, Google AppEngine, IBM's Blue, Microsoft Azure, Salesforce Heroku and others.

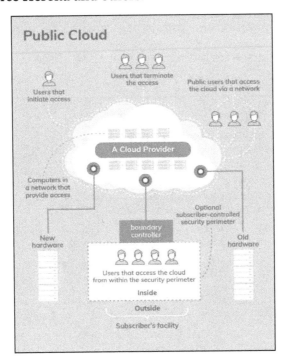

Private Cloud

There is little to no difference between public and private clouds from the technical point of view, as their designs are very similar. However, unlike in the public one, only one specific company owns a private cloud, which is why it is also called internal or corporate. Because these data center architectures reside within the firewall, they provide enhanced security. Even though one organization runs its workloads on a private basis, a third party can also manage it, and the server can be hosted externally or on-premises of the user company.

Only a clearly defined scope of persons have access to the information kept in a private repository, preventing the general public from using it. In light of numerous breaches, a growing number of large corporations decided on a closed private type as it is expected to be less risky.

The advantages of a private model:

- Individual development.

- Storage and network components are customizable.

- High control over the corporate information.

- High security, privacy and reliability.

The major disadvantage of the private cloud deployment model is its cost intensiveness, as it entails considerable expenses on hardware, software and staff training. That is why this secure flexible computing deployment model is not a choice of small to medium companies. Also, it is especially suitable for companies that seek to safeguard their mission-critical operations or for businesses with changing requirements.

Multiple service providers – including Amazon, IBM, Cisco, Dell and Red Hat – also build private solutions.

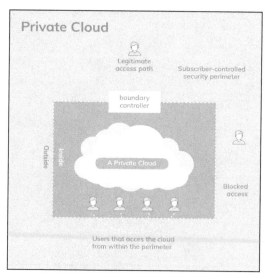

Community Cloud

A community cloud deployment model resembles a private one to a large extent; the only difference is the set of users. While a private type implies that only one company owns the server, in the case of a community one, several organizations with similar backgrounds share the infrastructure and related resources.

As the organizations have uniform security, privacy and performance requirements, this multi-tenant data center architecture helps companies achieve their business-specific objectives. That is why a community model is particularly suited for organizations that work on joint projects. In that case, a centralized cloud facilitates project development, management and implementation. Also, the costs are shared across all users.

The strengths of a community computing type include the following:

- Cost reduction.

- Improved security, privacy and reliability.

- Ease of data sharing and collaboration.

The shortcomings are:

- Higher cost than that of a public one.

- Sharing of fixed storage and bandwidth capacity.

- It is not widespread so far.

Companies can decide on community solutions that Google, Red Hat, IBM, Microsoft or others provide.

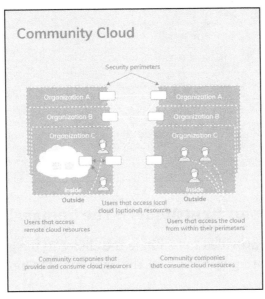

Hybrid Cloud

As it is usually the case with any hybrid phenomenon, a hybrid cloud encompasses the best features of the above-mentioned cloud computing deployment models – a public, private and community ones. It allows companies to mix and match the facets of all three types that best suit their requirements.

As an example, a company can balance its load by locating mission-critical workloads on a secure private cloud and deploying less sensitive ones to a public one. It not only safeguards and controls strategically important assets but does so in the most cost- and resource-effective way possible for each specific case. Also, this approach facilitates data and application portability.

The benefits of a hybrid model are:

- Improved security and privacy.

- Enhanced scalability and flexibility.

- Reasonable price.

However, the hybrid cloud deployment model only makes sense if companies can split their data into mission-critical and non-sensitive.

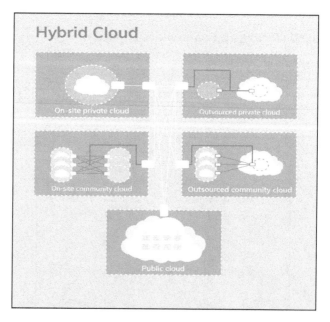

Types of Cloud Deployment Models: The Comparison

Below, a table is being provided to facilitate the choice of the appropriate deployment models of cloud computing by opting for the ones with the most business-critical features.

Table: The comparative analysis of the best cloud deployment models.

Public		Private	Community	Hybrid
Ease of setup and use	Easy	Requires IT proficiency	Requires IT proficiency	Requires IT proficiency
Data security and privacy	Low	High	Comparatively high	High
Data control	Little to none	High	Comparatively high	Comparatively high
Reliability	Vulnerable	High	Comparatively high	High
Scalability and flexibility	High	High	Fixed capacity	High
Cost-effectiveness	The cheapest one	Cost-intensive, the most expensive one	Cost is shared among community members	Cheaper than a private model but more costly than a public one
Demand for in-house hardware	No	Depends	Depends	Depends

Careful consideration of all business and technical requirements, as well as of each model's peculiarity, is a prerequisite for a successful shift to the cloud.

Cloud Computing Networking

Cloud computing technology is still evolving. Various companies, standards bodies, and alliances are addressing several remaining gaps and concerns. Some of these concerns are: What are the challenges behind the virtual networking in IaaS deployment? What are the potential solutions using the existing technologies for the implementation of virtual networks inside IaaS vision? Is there any room to utilize innovative paradigms like Software Defined Networking (SDN) to address virtual networking challenges? When cloud federation (or even cloud bursting) is involved, should the servers in the cloud be on the same Layer 2 network as the servers in the enterprise or, should a Layer 3 topology be involved because the cloud servers are on a network outside the enterprise? In addition, how would this approach work across multiple cloud data centers.

Consider a case where an enterprise uses two separate cloud service providers. Compute and storage resource sharing along with common authentication (or migration of authentication information) are some of the problems with having the clouds "interoperate." For virtualized cloud services, VM migration is another factor to be considered in federation.

Networking in IaaS

Although cloud computing does not necessarily depend on virtualization, several cloud infrastructures are built with virtualized servers. Within a virtualized environment, some of the networking functionalities (e.g., switching, firewall, application-delivery controllers, and load balancers) can reside inside a physical server. Consider the case of the software-based Virtual Switch as shown in Figure. The Virtual switch inside the same physical server can be used to switch the traffic between the VMs and aggregate the traffic for connection to the external physical switch. The Virtual Switch is often implemented as a plug-in to the hypervisor. The VMs have virtual Ethernet adapters that connect to the Virtual Switch, which in turn connects to the physical Ethernet adapter on the server and to the external Ethernet switch. Unlike physical switches, the Virtual Switch does not necessarily have to run network protocols for its operation, nor does it need to treat all its ports the same because it knows that some of them are connected to virtual Ethernet ports. It can function through appropriate configuration from an external management entity.

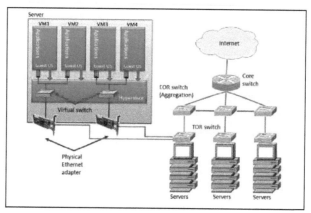

A typical data-center switched network architecture.

Network architecture is one of the key building blocks of cloud computing. A cloud user connects to the network to access the cloud resources. The cloud is accessible through a public network (the Internet) or through a private network infrastructure (e.g., MPLS or dedicated links). The most significant effect of cloud computing on network is in the data center. The data center consists mainly of servers in the racks interconnected through a Top-of-Rack (TOR) Ethernet switch which in turn connects to an aggregation switch, also known as End-of-Rack (EOR) switch. The aggregation switch connects to other aggregation switches and through these switches to other servers in the data center. A core switch connects to the various aggregation switches and provides connectivity to the outside world, typically through Layer 3 (IP). Since most of intra-data center traffic traverses only the TOR and the aggregation switches, a fat-tree topology is proposed to address this anomaly. The presence of virtualized servers adds an extra dimension. Network connections to physical servers will need to involve "bigger pipes" because traffic for multiple Virtual Machines (VMs) will be multiplexed onto the same physical Ethernet connection compared to the case in which the network connection is just used for stand alone server. Data transfer and network bandwidth, WAN acceleration for the cloud, and VM migration are some of the perspectives on cloud computing networking.

IaaS has provided a flexible model, in which customers are billed according to their compute usage, storage consumption, and the duration of usage. However, there is another important factor—data needs to be sent back and forth between the cloud user and cloud service provider. Several IaaS providers charge for the amount of data transferred over the link. These charges can quickly add up if applications are very chatty and require a lot of back-and forth data traffic. Another concern here is the amount of time the initial upload or download can consume.

Some applications and protocols can benefit from WAN acceleration devices that can be used on both ends of a WAN link to cache and locally serve enterprise applications. These appliances are not specific to the cloud—they have been used for several years for application performance improvement when a WAN link is involved. Recently, virtual network appliances for WAN acceleration are also deployed.

VM migration brings its own set of issues. The most common scenario is when a VM is migrated to a different host on the same Layer 2 topology (with the appropriate VLAN configuration). Consider the case where a VM with open TCP connections is migrated. If live migration is used, TCP connections will not see any downtime except for a short hic-cup. However, after the migration, IP and TCP packets destined for the VM will need to be resolved to a different MAC address or the same MAC address but now connected to a different physical switch in the network. Proposed solutions include an unsolicited Address Resolution Protocol (ARP) request from the migrated VM so that the switch tables can be updated, or a pseudo-MAC address for the VM that is externally managed. With VPLS and similar Layer 2 approaches, VM migration can proceed as before—across the same Layer 2 network. Alternatively, the VM can be migrated across either a Layer 2 or Layer 3 network with the TCP connections having to be torn down by the peers. Although lowering down the complexity, this scenario is not desirable from an application availability point of view. VM migration is coupled with the selection of Layer 2 and/or Layer 3 topologies. Another consideration is the amount of data that needs to be moved when a VM is migrated across the network or federated cloud infrastructure. It can potentially be in the range of gigabytes, depending upon the VM and the included operating environment. Live migration implements this transfer in an incremental fashion so that the demand on the network is spread out. However, snap-shot migration (where a VM is suspended and migrated over the network in full) can cause a surge of data on the network, leading to application performance problems for other VMs and physical machines. Shaping the amount of data that can be sent in a specific period of time, bandwidth reservation, proper orchestration and policing at the intermediate network devices is highly desirable in such situations.

Challenges in IaaS

Among various challenges that should be addressed in an IaaS deployment we focus on virtual networking and cloud extension and cloud federation issues and in the sequel we provide innovative opportunities that could be utilized to address these issues.

Existing networking protocols and architectures such as Spanning Tree protocol and Multi-Chassis Link Aggregation (MC-LAG) can limit the scale, latency, throughput and VM migration of enterprise cloud networks. Therefore open standards and proprietary protocols are proposed to address cloud computing networking issues. While existing layer 3 "fat tree" networks provide a proven approach to address the requirements for a highly virtualized cloud data center, there are several industry standards that enhance features of a flattened layer 2 network, using Transparent Interconnection of Lots of Links (TRILL), Shortest Path Bridging (SPB) or have the potential to enhance future systems based on SDN concepts and OpenFlow. The key motivation behind TRILL and SPB and SDN-based approach is the relatively flat nature of the data-center topology and the requirement to forward packets across the shortest path between the endpoints (servers) to reduce latency, rather than a root bridge or priority mechanism normally used in the Spanning Tree Protocol (STP). The IEEE 802.1Qaz, known as Enhanced Transmission Selection (ETS), in line with other efforts, allows low-priority traffic to burst and use the unused bandwidth from the higher-priority traffic queues, thus providing greater flexibility. Vendor proprietary protocols are also developed by major networking equipment manufacturers to address the same issues. For instance Juniper Networks produces switches, using a proprietary multipath L2/L3 encapsulation protocol called QFabric, which allows multiple distributed physical devices in the network to share a common control plane and a separate common management plane. Virtual Cluster Switching (VCS) is a multipath layer 2 encapsulation protocol by Brocade, based on TRILL and Fabric Shortest Path First (FSPF) path selection protocol and a proprietary method to discover neighboring switches. Cisco's FabricPath, is a multipath layer 2 encapsulation based on TRILL, which does not include TRILL's next-hop header, and has a different MAC learning technique. They all address the same issues with different features for scalability, latency, oversubscription, and management. However, none of these solutions have reached the same level of maturity as STP and MAC-LAG.

Layer 2 (switching) and Layer 3 (routing) are two possible options for cloud infrastructure networking. Layer 2 is the simpler option, where the Ethernet MAC address and Virtual LAN (VLAN) information are used for forwarding. The drawback of switching (L2) is scalability. L2 networking flattens the network topology, which is not ideal when there is large number of nodes. Routing (L3) option and subnets provide segmentation for the appropriate functions at the cost of lower forwarding performance and network complexity.

Existing cloud networking architectures follow the "one size fits all" paradigm in meeting the diverse requirements of a cloud. The network topology, forwarding protocols, and security policies are all designed looking at the sum of all requirements preventing the optimal usage and proper management of the network. Some of the challenges in the existing cloud networks are:

- Application performance: Cloud tenants should be able to specify bandwidth requirements for applications hosted in the cloud, ensuring similar performance to onpremise deployments. Many tiered applications require some guaranteed bandwidth between server instances to satisfy user transactions within an acceptable time frame and meet predefined SLAs. Insufficient bandwidth between these servers will impose significant latency on user interactions. Therefore without explicit control, variations in cloud workloads and oversubscription can cause delay and drift of response time beyond acceptable limits, leading to SLA violations for the hosted applications.

- Flexible deployment of appliances: Enterprises deploy a wide variety of security appliances in their data centers, such as Deep Packet Inspection (DPI) or Intrusion Detection Systems (IDS), and firewalls to protect their applications from attacks. These are often employed alongside other appliances that perform load balancing, caching and application acceleration. When deployed in the cloud, an enterprise application should continue to be able to flexibly exploit the functionality of these appliances.

- Policy enforcement complexities: Traffic isolation and access control to the end-users are among the multiple forwarding policies that should be enforced. These policies directly impact the configuration of each router and switch. Changing requirements, different protocols (e.g., OSPF, LAG, VRRP), different flavors of L2 spanning tree protocols, along with vendor specific protocols, make it extremely challenging to build, operate and inter-connect a cloud network at scale.

- Topology dependent complexity: The network topology of data centers is usually tuned to match a pre-defined traffic requirement. For instance, a network topology, which is optimized for east-west traffic (i.e., traffic among servers in a data center), is not the same as the topology for north-south (traffic to/from the Internet). The topology design also depends on how the L2 and/or L3 is utilizing the effective network capacity. For instance adding a simple link and switch in the presence of a spanning tree based L2 forwarding protocol, may not provide additional capacity. Furthermore, evolving the topology based on traffic pattern changes also requires complex configuration of L2 and L3 forwarding rules.

- Application rewriting: Applications should run "out of the box" as much as possible, in particular for IP addresses and for network-dependent failover mechanisms. Applications may need to be rewritten or reconfigured before deployment in the cloud to address several network related limitations. Two key issues are: 1) lack of a broadcast domain abstraction in the cloud network and 2) cloud-assigned IP addresses for virtual servers.

- Location dependency: Network appliances and servers (e.g., hypervisors) are typically tied to a statically configured physical network, which implicitly creates a location dependency constraint. For instance the IP address of a sever is typically determined based on the VLAN or subnet it belongs to. VLAN and subnets are based on physical switch port configuration. Therefore, a VM cannotbe easily and smoothly migrated across the network. Constrained VM migration decreases the level of resource utilization and flexibility. Besides, physical mapping of VLAN or subnet space to the physical ports of a switch often leads to a fragmented IP address pool.

- Multi-layer network complexity: A typical three layer data center network includes TOR layer connecting the servers in a rack, aggregation layer and core layer, which provides connectivity to/from the Internet edge. This multi-layer architecture imposes significant complexities in defining boundaries of L2 domains, L3 forwarding networks and policies, and layer-specific multi-vendor networking equipment.

Providers of cloud computing services are currently operating their own data centers. Connectivity between the data centers to provide the vision of "one cloud" is completely within the control of the cloud service provider. There may be situations where an organization or enterprise needs to be able to work with multiple cloud providers due to locality of access, migration from one cloud service to another, merger of companies working with different cloud providers, cloud providers who provide best-of-class services, and similar cases. Cloud interoperability and the ability to share various types of information between clouds become important in such scenarios. Although cloud service providers might see less immediate need for any interoperability, enterprise customers will see a need to push them in this direction. This broad area of cloud interoperability is sometimes known as cloud federation. Cloud federation manages consistency and access controls when two or more independent cloud computing facilities share either authentication, computing resources, command and control, or access to storage resources. Some of the considerations in cloud federation are as follows:

- An enterprise user wishing to access multiple cloud services would be better served if there were just a single authentication and/or authorization mechanism (i.e., single sign-on scheme). This may be implemented through an authentication server maintained by an enterprise that provides the appropriate credentials to the cloud service providers. Alternatively, a central trusted authentication server could be used to which all cloud services are interfaced. Computing and storage resources may be orchestrated through the individual enterprise or through an interoperability scheme established between the cloud providers. Files may need to be exchanged, services invoked, and computing resources added or removed in a proper and transparent manner. A related area is VM migration and how it can be done transparently.

- Cloud federation has to provide transparent workload orchestration between the clouds on behalf of the enterprise user. Connectivity between clouds includes Layer 2 and/or Layer 3 considerations and tunneling technologies that need to be agreed upon. Consistency and a common understanding are required independent of the technologies. An often ignored concern for cloud federation is charging or billing and reconciliation. Management and billing systems need to work together for cloud federation to be a viable option. This reality is underlined by the fact that clouds rely on per-usage billing. Cloud service providers might need to look closely at telecom service provider business models for peering arrangements as a possible starting point. Cloud federation is a relatively new area in cloud computing. It is likely that standard organizations will first need to agree on a set of requirements before the service interfaces can be defined and subsequently materialized.

Consider an IaaS cloud, to which an enterprise connects to temporarily augment its server capacity. It would be ideal if the additional servers provided by the IaaS cloud were part of the same addressing scheme of the enterprise (e.g., 10.x.x.x). As depicted in Figure, the IaaS cloud service provider has partitioned a portion of its public cloud to materialize a private cloud for enterprise "E". The private cloud is reachable as a LAN extension to the servers in enterprise E's data center. A secure VPN tunnel establishes the site-to-site VPN connection. The VPN gateway on the cloud service provider side (private cloud "C") maintains multiple contexts for each private cloud. Traffic for enterprise "E" is decrypted and forwarded to an Ethernet switch to the private cloud. A server on enterprise "E"'s internal data center sees a server on private cloud "C" to be on the same network. Some evolution scenarios can be considered for this scheme:

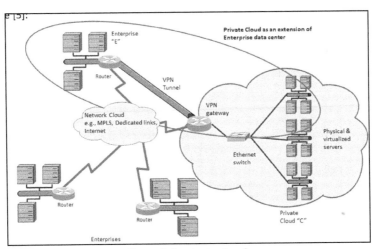

Extended private cloud.

- Automation of the VPN connection between the enterprise and cloud service provider: This automation can be done through a management system responsible for the cloud bursting and server augmentation. The system sets up the VPN tunnels and configures the servers on the cloud service provider end. The management system is set up and operated by the cloud service provider.

- Integration of the VPN functions with the site-to-site VPN network functions from service providers: For instance, service providers offer MPLS Layer 3

VPNs and Layer 2 VPNs (also known as Virtual Private LAN Service, or VPLS) as part of their offerings. Enterprise and cloud service providers could be set up to use these network services.

- Cloud service providers using multiple data centers: In such a situation, a VPLS-like service can be used to bridge the individual data centers, providing complete transparency from the enterprise side about the location of the cloud servers.

Cloud networking is not a trivial task. Modern data centers designed to provide cloud service offerings face similar challenges to build the Internet itself due to their size. At its simplest case (e.g. providing VMs like Amazon's EC2), we are talking about data centers that need to provide as much as 1 million networked devices in a single facility. These requirement means the need for technologies with high performance, scalable, robust, reliable, flexible, easy to monitor, control and manageable.

SDN-based Cloud Computing Networking

SDN is an emerging network architecture where "network control functionality" is decoupled from "forwarding functionality" and is directly programmable. This migration of control, formerly tightly integrated in individual networking equipment, into accessible computing devices (logically centralized) enables the underlying infrastructure to be "abstracted" for applications and network services. Therefore applications can treat the network as a logical or virtual entity. As a result, enterprises and carriers gain unprecedented programmability, automation, and network control, enabling them to build innovative, highly scalable, flexible networks that readily adapt to changing business needs.

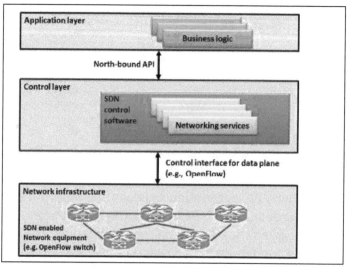

Logical view of SDN architecture.

A logical view of the SDN architecture is depicted in Figure. OpenFlow is the first standard interface designed specifically for SDN, providing high-performance, granular traffic control across multiple vendors' network devices. Network intelligence is logically centralized in SDN control software (e.g. OpenFlow controllers), which maintain a global view of the network. As a result the network, in its ultimate abstracted view, appears as a single logical switch. Adapting SDN architecture, greatly simplifies the design and operation of networks since it removes the need to know and understand the operation details of hundreds of protocols/standards. Enterprises and carriers gain vendor-independent control over the entire network from a single logical point.

In addition to the network abstraction, SDN architecture will provide and support a set of APIs that simplifies the implementation of common network services (e.g., slicing, virtualization, routing, multicast, security, access control, bandwidth management, traffic engineering, QoS, processor and/or storage optimization, energy consumption, and various form of policy management). SDN's promise is to enable the following key features:

- Programmatic approach to dynamically create/deploy virtual networks.

- Decoupled virtual network topology from the actual physical network topology.

- Co-existence of multiple virtual network based on a shared physical network.

- Support isolation ensuring independent operation of virtual networks.

- Enhanced resource utilization of physical networks through network resource pooling.

- Reduced network design and (re) configuration time and complexities.

- Instantiation of flexible virtual networks to meet diverse requirements.

OpenFlow-based SDN has created opportunities to help enterprises build more deterministic, more manageable and more scalable virtual networks that extend beyond enterprise on-premises data centers or private clouds, to public IT resources, while ensuring higher network efficiency to carriers seeking to improve their services profitability by provisioning more services, with fewer, better optimized resources.

Innovation Opportunities

Comparison of Existing Virtual Networking Implementations

Cloud networking infrastructure and server virtualization are more or less the same thing as far as the technology is concerned. Both services have to be scalable, on-demand and orchestrated. In an ideal situation the physical network will provide the transport, and the hypervisors will provide the VM service and the virtual networks will be constructed on top of the transport network. There is a whole range of solutions that can be utilized to implement the virtual networks (segments). The traditional approach is to implement the virtual segments using VLANs, which are limited to 4096 segments (VLANs) and therefore not really scalable. There are some proposals, which suggest to utilize IEEE 802.1ad (Q-in-Q) to address 4K limitation, but there is no orchestration support for Q-in Q currently. On the other extreme, Amazon EC2 is utilizing IP over IP with a rich control plane to provide virtual segments. VMaware networking (Arista VM Tracer), Edge Virtual Bridging (IBM's EVB, IEEE 802.1Qbg), vCloud Director Networking Infrastructure (vCDNI) (VMware, MAC over MAC) or EVB with PBB/SPB, VXLAN (Cisco), Network Virtualization using Generic Routing Encapsulation (NVGRE) (Microsoft) MAC over IP, and Nicira Network Virtualization Platform (NVP) (MAC over IP with a control plane) are other approaches. All of these proposals can be categorized into three architectural groups: a) dumb virtual switch in the hypervisor plus normal physical switch (e.g., traditional VLAN model), b) dumb virtual switch with intelligent physical switch (e.g., VM-aware networking, EVB), and c) Intelligent virtual switch plus a typical (L2/L3) physical switch (e.g.,vCDNI, VXLAN, NVGRE, NVP).

Table: Comparison of virtual networking implementation

Technology	Bridging	All hosts flooding	vNet	VLAN 4K	VM MAC visible	State kept in network
VLANs	Yes	Yes	Yes	Yes	Yes	Yes
VM-aware Networking	Yes	No	Yes	Yes	Yes	Yes
vCDNI	Yes	Yes	Yes	No	No	MAC of hypervisors
VXLAN	Yes	Only to some hosts	Yes	No	No	Multicast groups
Nicira NVP	Yes	No	Some	No	No	No

The first constraint of VLANs is 4K limitation of VLANs. Secondly, all the MAC addresses from all the VMs are visible in the physical switches of the network. This can fill up the MAC table of physical switches, especially if the deployed switches are legacy ones. Typical NICs are able to receive unicast frames for a few MAC addresses. If the number of VMs are more than these limit, then the NIC has to be put in promiscuous mode, which engages the CPU to handle flooded packets. This will waste CPU cycles of hypervisor and bandwidth.

The VM-aware networking (architectural group b) scales a bit better. The whole idea is that the VLAN list on the physical switch to the hypervisor link is dynamically adjusted based on the server need. This can be done with VM-aware TOR switches (Arista, Force 10, Brocade), or VM-Aware network management server (Juniper, Alcatel-Lucent, NEC), which configures the physical switches dynamically, or VM-FEX from Cisco, or EVB from IBM. This approach reduces flooding to the servers and CPU utilization and using proprietary protocols (e.g., Qfabric) it is possible to decrease the flooding in physical switches. However, MAC addresses are still visible in the physical network, the 4K limitations remain intact and the transport in physical network is L2 based with associated flooding problems. This approach could be used for large virtualized data centers but not for IaaS clouds.

The main idea behind vCDNI is that there is a virtual distributed switch which is isolated from the rest of the network and controlled by vCloud director and instead of VLAN, uses a proprietary MAC-in-MAC encapsulation. Therefore the VM MAC addresses are not visible in the physical network. Since there is a longer header in vCDNI protocol, the 4K limitation of VLANs is not intact anymore. Although unicast flooding is not exist in this solution, but multicast flooding indeed exist in this approach. Furthermore it still uses L2 transport.

Conceptually, VXLAN is similar to the vCDNI approach, however instead of having a proprietary protocol on top of L2; it runs on top of UDP and IP. Therefore, inside the hypervisor the port groups are available, which are tight to VXLAN framing, which generates UDP packets, going down through IP stack in the hypervisor and reaches the physical IP network. VXLAN segments are virtual layer 2 segments over L3 transport infrastructure with a 24-bit segment ID to alleviate the traditional VLAN limitation. L2 flooding is emulated using IP multicast. The only issue of VXLAN is that it doesn't have a control plane.

Nicira NVP is very similar to VXLAN with a different encapsulation format, which is pointto- point GRE tunnels; however the MAC-to-IP mapping is downloaded to Open vSwitch using a centralized OpenFlow controller. This controller removes the need for any flooding as it was required in VXLAN (using IP multicast). To be precise, this solution utilizes the MAC over IP with a control plane. The virtual switches, which are used in this approach, are OpenFlow enabled, which means that the virtual switches can be controlled by an external OpenFlow controller (e.g., NOX). These Open vSwitches use point-to-point GRE tunnels that unfortunately cannot be provisioned by OpenFlow. These tunnels have to be provisioned using other mechanisms, because OpenFlow has no Tunnel provisioning message. The Open vSwitch Database Management Protocol (OVSDB), which is a provisioning protocol, is used to construct a full mesh GRE tunnels between the hosts that have VMs from the same tenant. Whenever two hosts have one VM each that belong to the same tenant a GRE tunnel will be established between them. Instead of using dynamic MAC learning and multicast the MAC to IP mapping are downloaded as flow forwarding rules through OpenFlow to the Open vSwitches. This approach scales much better than VXLAN, because there is no state to maintain in the physical network. Furthermore, ARP proxy can be used to stop L2 flooding. This approach requires an OpenFlow and OVSDB controller to work in parallel to automatically provision GRE tunnels.

SDN-based Federation

There are general advantages to be realized by enterprises that adopt Open Flow enabled SDN as the connectivity foundation for private and/or hybrid cloud connectivity. A logically centralized SDN control plane will provide a comprehensive view (abstract view) of data center and cloud resources and access network availability. This will ensure cloud federation (cloud extensions) are directed to adequately resourced data centers, on links providing sufficient bandwidth and service levels. Using the SDN terminologies, a high level description of key building blocks for an SDN-based cloud federation are:

- OpenFlow enabled cloud backbone edge nodes, which connect to the enterprise and cloud provider data center.

- OpenFlow enabled core nodes which efficiently switch traffic between these edge nodes.

- An OpenFlow and/or SDN-based controller to configure the flow forwarding tables in the cloud backbone nodes and providing a WAN network virtualization application (e.g. Optical FlowVisor).

- Hybrid cloud operation and orchestration software to manage the enterprise and provider data center federation, inter-cloud workflow, and resource management of compute/storage and inter-data center network management.

SDN-based federation will facilitate multi-vendor networks between enterprise and service provider data centers, helping enterprise customers to choose best-in-class vendors, while avoiding vendor lock-in; pick a proper access technology from a wider variety (e.g. DWDM, DSL, HFC, LTE, PON, etc.); access dynamic bandwidth for ad-hoc, timely inter-data center workload migration and processing; and eliminate the burden of underutilized, costly high-capacity fixed private leased lines. SDN-enabled bandwidth-on-demand services provide automated and intelligent service provisioning, driven by cloud service orchestration logic and customer requirements.

Cloud Storage

Cloud storage is file storage in the cloud (online). Instead of keeping your files on your local hard drive, external hard drive, or flash drive, you can save them online.

There are multiple reasons to use cloud storage services. Maybe your local hard drives are running low on disk space, in which case you can use the cloud as extra storage. If you want to be able to stream your music collection from anywhere, access your work files at home, easily share vacation videos, etc., you can upload your files online to a cloud storage service. Another reason to use cloud storage is if you want to keep important files secure behind a password and encryption.

In short, cloud storage is helpful not only when it comes to backup but also for security and the ability to easily share files with others or access them yourself from anywhere: your phone, tablet, or another computer.

How Cloud Storage Works

When you upload a file to the internet and that file is there for an extended period of time, it's considered cloud storage. The simplest type of cloud storage is uploading something to a server and having the ability to retrieve it again should you want to.

A reputable cloud storage service protects the files behind encryption and requires you to enter a password in order to be able to access the files. Most of the time, the cloud storage account can be protected behind two-factor authentication, too, so that anyone wanting access to your files has to know not only the password but another code sent to your phone upon the login request.

Most cloud storage services let you upload all types of files: videos, pictures, documents, music, or anything else. However, some are limited to accepting only certain kinds of files, such as only images or music. Cloud storage services are usually fairly clear about what is allowed and what is not.

Different cloud storage services let you upload files to your online account through different methods. Some support in-browser uploads only, meaning that you have to log in to the cloud storage service's website to upload your data, but most have desktop applications that make uploading files easier by a simple drag-and-drop into the service's dedicated folder. Most also support uploading images and videos from your phone.

Less common are torrent cloud storage services that are online torrent clients that not only let you download torrents from your browser but also store your files in your online account to stream or download later.

Once your files are stored online, depending on how the service works, the features you get might include the ability to stream videos and music, access the files from your mobile device, easily share the files with others through a special share link, download the files back to your computer, delete them to free up space in your account, encrypt them so that not even the service can see them, and more.

Cloud Storage versus Cloud Backup

Cloud storage and cloud backup are easily confused. Both work similarly and have a similar end result: the files are stored online. But there are two completely different reasons to use these services, and knowing how they differ is important so that you know which one to choose for your own situation.

Cloud storage is a selective backup procedure where you choose which files to store online, and then you send them to your online account. When you delete a file on your computer that you backed up online, the file is still in your cloud storage account because it isn't actually tied to your computer anymore; it's just a single file that you uploaded online.

Cloud backup is when you install a program on your computer and tell it to keep specific files backed up online. Going a step further than cloud storage, a backup service will also upload any changes you make to the file so that the current version is always stored online. In other words, if you delete a file from your computer, it might also get deleted from your online backup account, and if you change a file on your computer, the online version changes too.

A backup service is great if you want to always keep a huge number of files backed up online. In the event your computer suddenly stops working, you can restore all of those files on a new computer or a different hard drive, and you'll get the same copies you had the last time the backup program stored those files online.

A cloud storage service is less practical as an always-on backup solution and more helpful as a way to back up specific files that you want to have access to from anywhere or share with others. The file versions in the cloud storage account are the same as the versions you uploaded, regardless if you changed them on your computer. Like online backup, you can still download the files again should you need to, like if your computer crashes.

Examples of Personal Cloud Storage Options

Although there are many cloud storage providers, some of the more familiar ones are listed below:

- Amazon Drive offers 5 GB of free cloud storage. If you have an Amazon Prime account, the free plan includes unlimited photo storage and 5 GB for other file types. You can pay for more if you need additional space.

- Google Drive is cloud storage built to work seamlessly with Google products. You get 15 GB of free online storage with Google Drive to keep documents, photos, music, and videos. You can upgrade to Google One for more space, anywhere from 100 GB to 30 TB.

- Microsoft OneDrive is Microsoft's version of cloud storage. Users get 5 GB of free space for any type of file, and like Google Drive, OneDrive works seamlessly with Microsoft products like Outlook Mail.

- Apple iCloud is Apple's cloud storage service that's available to any Apple user, whether you have a Mac, iPhone, iPad, or iPod touch. You can get 5 GB for free, but you can buy more. Much like an online backup service, iCloud can be used to automatically back up your phone's images, emails, and more.

- Dropbox gives its users 2 GB for free and lets you access the files from the web, your desktop, or your mobile device. Dropbox Plus or Professional can be purchased for 1 TB or more of online storage space. There are also Dropbox Business plans.

How to Choose the Right Cloud Storage Provider

Numerous cloud storage providers out there would like your business, so it can be confusing knowing which to choose. Consider several factors before picking any online cloud backup service.

- Security: Your data must be encrypted to keep it private. If you're concerned about the service itself being able to open your files and see all your backed-up data, go with a service that features "zero-knowledge encryption."

- Price: The cost is determined by how much space you anticipate needing. Many services offer either a trial period or free storage to let you try out their features.

- Compatibility: If you want to be able to access your cloud data from your phone, be sure to pick a cloud storage provider that supports it. Similarly, go with a service that can accept the types of files you want to store online, such as a music storage service if you'll be storing your music online.

- Features: Knowing what features your cloud storage service supports is essential in choosing the right one for you. A comparison of the top free cloud storage services can help you decide between a few of the better ones. Beyond that, do some research on the company's websites to see what they offer, like if they support streaming media files from their website or mobile app if that's something you require.

- Ease of use: Uploading and accessing your files on the cloud should be clear and easy to understand. If you want to be able to do this from your desktop, make sure it's simple and won't leave you scratching your head each time you just want to throw some files into your cloud storage account. If it isn't easy to use, look elsewhere.

- Reliability: If a cloud storage service shuts down, you might lose all of your data. Choose a company that you expect would give its users fair warning should they close their doors, or at least offer a way for you to transfer your data elsewhere. Cloud storage services that have been in operation for a long time or that are well known are *probably* more likely to help out should they decide to shut down the business, but you should read the fine print to see their actual policies.

- Bandwidth: If you're a heavy user, you should also think about bandwidth limitations. Some cloud storage services put a cap on how much data can flow in and/or out of your account on a daily or monthly basis. If you plan to have customers, employees, or family or friends download large videos or lots of other files throughout the month, make sure the bandwidth cap isn't prohibitive for you.

Cloud Bursting

Cloud bursting is a term to describe the temporary utilization of cloud resources via a hybrid cloud environment.

Generally speaking, many high performance, non-critical applications can benefit from a cloud bursting strategy. When resource requirements exceed what can be provided by the on-premise or colocated data center, the application will temporarily shift data into a public cloud to free up space in the primary data center.

Public Cloud, Hybrid Cloud and the Value of Cloud Bursting

The public cloud enables companies to utilize the near endless resources of enormous cloud providers such as Amazon Web Services or Microsoft Azure. Through their massive data centers, entire environments can exist and be accessed from these remote and distant locations without equipment on-premise. We no longer need to think of our environments in terms of equipment down the hall.

With such immense capabilities within reach, why only use the public cloud sometimes?

Yes, entire public cloud deployments can be useful solutions for some, but they can give other IT directors pause. While the public cloud does provide ample security, hosting a full IT environment in the cloud may not be the most cost-effective option. Furthermore, this data often travels across the standard internet WAN to reach the organizations end points, so latency can become a concern.

Cloud bursting addresses this dynamic by allowing an environment to only utilize the cloud when and if it is needed with non-essential or non-confidential applications. It provides the best balance of allocating resources and maximizing cost efficiency.

How to Burst into the Cloud

Currently, there are several strategies used for cloud bursting and many are supported by the largest names in the technology industry. Here are just a few:

- Cisco Intercloud Fabric: The intercloud is a term used to describe the cloud of clouds. If a single cloud is a collection of virtualized servers to create a ubiquitous pool of resources, the intercloud is a collection of clouds pooled into one enormous and seamless data center. At the grandest scale, this is still theoretical, but Cisco offers a product called the Cisco Intercloud Fabric which allows hybrid cloud environments to utilize multiple clouds as needed. You can set how much capacity you need and when as well as which provider or providers you require.

- Microsoft Azure: In the past, application developers would have to overprovision their storage and sever resources in order to account for increased demands of their testing environment. The problem was that these developers didn't know how much compute power or storage space they need, so IT directors would purchase far too much hardware just to be safe. Microsoft Azure instead encourages developers to build in the expanse of the cloud. It allows users to pay only for the resources they use and when they use them.

- Equinix: Equinix puts an interesting twist on the public cloud game. Instead of relying on the public WAN to access data in the cloud, Equinix supplies you with a direct VPN connection to your data within the shared environment. With this strategy, IT directors can achieve the best of both worlds in a public cloud environment.

- VMware NSX: NSX is VMware's software defined networking solution. The intelligence is abstracted from the networking equipment using a software overlay. Once the network is virtualized, IT administrators can provision and reprovision networks with the same speed and flexibility as virtual machines.Among other uses, these virtual networks can be drawn to include cloud deployments. Therefore, IT departments can use NSX to move data seamlessly in and out of the cloud as needed.

Cloud Bursting use Cases

As IT environments continue to refine and become more sophisticated, the ability to cloud burst may become a more and more useful option.

- Retail Environments: In the retail industry, the holiday shopping season can create an influx of data beyond the capabilities of their current data centers. Instead of purchasing new equipment to account for a two month swell, bursting into the cloud is a cost effective option.

- Marketing Campaigns: Huge national campaigns can generate a large amount of web traffic in a short amount of time. Bursting into the cloud will help allow for that influx.

- Financial Applications: The end of month, end of quarter, and tax season are brief data intense periods for financial applications and institutions. Cloud bursting helps keep infrastructure low while maintaining capabilities and agility.

- Software Developers: When creating or testing a new web application, the ability to utilize the near endless resources of the cloud proves valuable.

Microservices Architecture for Cloud Computing

Microservices is emerges as a new architecture, in which large and complex software applications are composed of small one or more services. It can be deployed independently of one another. These services are loosely coupled with each other. Each of these microservices fare responsible for completing only one task with efficiently. Microservices are very useful for the applications in cloud computing. Use of microservices in cloud computing allows increasing the popularity of the cloud. Use of microservices offers more choices and options for independent evolve the service. In 2014, it emerges to speed up the process of development in mobile and web applications.

Monolithic

In this architecture, a single code is used for all the components of an application. The entire application is based on a single design and the complete application has to be deployed. Individual components cannot be deployed. But there are some issues with monolithic applications. Some of these are as follows:

- In monolithic application the code is large which makes it difficult to understand.

- Scaling of this architecture is difficult.

- Integration and deployment of the system are more complex and time consuming.

- Due to the large size of code, the Integrated Development Environment (IDE) may be overloaded. This makes the IDE slow and increases in the time for building the application.

- In monolithic architecture, every component is tightly coupled which makes it difficult to change the language, framework or technology.

Besides, above issues of monolithic applications, it also has some challenges. Some of them are: emerging of new technology, uninterrupted release, scaling problem, many teams and addition of new members. These issues challenges can be resolved with the use of microservices architecture.

Microservices

In this technique an individual application can be develop as a group of several small services which are executing on their own process. They communicate with mechanisms with less important such as an HTTP resource API. These small services are constructing around business capabilities and they can deploy independently using deployment system which is entirely automatic. The services are barely managed by a minimum centralized system. These services are written in various programming languages. They use diverse technologies for data storage. In microservice architecture, small services which are autonomous and that work together can be scaled and released independently with potential of various developers using various languages across the globe.

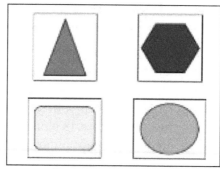

Microservices Architecture.

Characteristics of Microservices

The Microservices architecture has following characteristics:

Autonomous

In this architecture, every service is developed using a suitable tool. There are many developer teams working independently. There is a data storage owned by every microservice.

Modelled around the Business Domain

To offer fast delivery of goals of the business, microservices are aligned vertically that with business potential.

Size

Microservices are smaller in size and it works on the policy of single responsibility principle. It struggles for high cohesion and loose coupling and high cohesion which are the hallmarks of well-designed components.

Standalone

A microservice is a standalone system. It can work and execute autonomously.

Easy Integrations

It allows integrating the microservices using well-known open protocols, interfaces and standards. It offers heterogeneity of technology, therefore, developer teams can use the stack of technology, which is best suited and comfortable to the applications.

Attributes of Microservices

Componentization as a Service

It builds a customized service by using some specific components together.

Organized around Business Capabilities

IT isolates the potentials for some specific areas like interface with user and external integrations.

Development based on Products

The developers use the same software throughout the life-time of the product.

Smart Endpoints and Dumb Pipes

Every microservice is as isolated as possible with the logic of its own domain logic.

Decentralized Control

It allows the developers to select the language of their choice for the development of each component.

Data Management Decentralization

Each microservice is able to label and can handle the data in a different way.

Automation of Infrastructure

It is possible to deploy the pipeline automatically.

Recovery from Failure

It is always prepared to recover from failure.

Migration to Microservices

While changes the architecture and migrating to microservices, it is essential to investigate multiple design features. Also, before adopting the microservices, one should understand the benefits and drawbacks of different approaches.

Divide the Monolith

To migrate towards the microservice, it is necessary to divide the monolith system into smaller parts by identifying the suitable service boundaries (physical as well as logical) among different parts. This boundary selection is the major challenge. Domain Driven Design (DDD) provides a suitable solution to identify the boundary and break the system. One more challenge for dividing the system is how to split the state. Database is the state for most of the applications. In this case, the present database can be divided so that it can denormalize into one source of data per table. Also, one can establish the relationships of foreign key and transactions between two mocroservices.

Communication between Two Services

It is very important to select the appropriate method of communication among the microservices. For asynchronous and synchronous communication, Representatin State Transfer (REST) is a good option over HTTP. For payloads, one can use Binary, eXtensible Markup Language (XML) or JSON (JavaScript Object Notation). Use of binary protocols like Protobuff, Avro or Thrift gives considerable performance for internal services. In HTML, every time the data is modified. Lot of work is required to edit the HTML. XML allows to store and transport data easily. The XML files are used to store the XML data. JSON is a syntax which allows storing and exchanging the text data. It is a format used for text data interchange. It is smaller in size than XML and faster and easier to parse. It supports integration among various languages, and is also readable. Therefore, it is the best choice for both internal and external communication between two services.

Testing

Integration testing is carried out to check the proper working of code to confirm the contracts among the services. But for more number of services, it is difficult to write these test cases. For such cases, it is required to write a test related to users to identify the breakages in contract. To verify the working after the production of results, the test cases are written for fake request.

Deployment

To deploy the services independent of each other, for each service, it is necessary to have a single repository. Apply continuous delivery principles to assure that every modification in the service is fabricated and tested. This also includes integration testing.

Failure Isolation

No service can execute 100% successfully. If there is more number of services, then the chances of failure are more. For example, there are three services which are communicating with each other. Suppose Service A sends a request to Service B. Resulting this, Service B sends request to Service C. If there is some failure at Service C, so it can reply to Service B, results in disruption of service to end users. Use of circuit breaker, timeouts, etc. can avoid the problem of service failure.

Service Discovery

It is the model of separating how processes and services find and communicate with each other. Service discovery problem in microservice is similar to that of the service registry problem in service oriented architecture. In multiple services environment, it is important to know the other services which are required. In this case, Domain Name System (DNS) with a load balancer can be used. But the drawback of DNS is that it cannot scale dynamically or elastically when the nodes are overloaded. Zookeeper is a centralized service for maintaining information related to configuration. These services offer distributed synchronization and group services used by distributed applications. Whenever, the services are executed, most of the effort required for identifying the bugs which are inevitable. Therefore, Zookeeper is a good option as it offers the primitives to construct a service discovery solution. Consul is another solution. It is a service discovery implementation built by Hashicorp. It provides all the required information for service discovery out of the box.

Monitoring

When there are number of services communicating with each other, there is a need of understanding the behavior of the system and issues related to the performance. For this monitoring, some tools are required. To get the unified view of different systems, aggregation is very important. Tools like Splunk or Logstash can be used for this purpose. Splunk tool offers a wide range of log management support for log consolidation and retention. LogStash offers architecture for collecting, parsing and storing logs in microservices architecture. When multiple services are involved, the required visibility is provided by the distributed request tracing.

Documentation

Proper documentation is very important for the widespread use of services. If people do not know the details about the service, then nobody adopts your service.

API Gateway

API Gateway offers a method to handle the issues related to transport security, transport transformations, authentication, load-balancing, dependency resolution and request dispatching. API Gateway can be used to compose one or two microservices. This offers a diverse granularity for users.

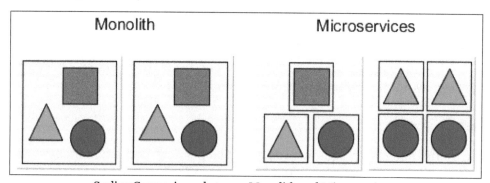

Scaling Comparisons between Monolith and Microservices.

Microservices offer better scalability as compared to monolithic applications. To scale the monolithic application, all the components of an application have to be scaled. To scale a single component of monolithic application, all the components have to be scaled. This is the drawback of monolith architecture, because we have to waste the resources and this also increases the complexity. But in microservices, we can scale only those components of an application which we want to scale instead of all the components. Therefore, scaling in microservices is easier than monolith. Figure illustrates the scaling in monolith and microservices.

Comparison between Microservice and Monolithic Architecture

Microservice architecture is a unique technique for developing applications which have grown up in reputation in last few years. Many application developers adopt it as a first choice for creating their applications. Due to high scalability, this architecture supports a wide variety of devices and platforms. The microservice architecture is most important for developing an application in a cloud environment. In this architecture, the entire application is split into a number of small services which are independent of each other. Each of these small services is liable for executing some specific feature. In a Meta operating system, microservices work as Meta processes. These processes work independently and able to communicate with each other using messages. Also, they can replicate, migrate or suspend to any resources. Number of systems uses microservice concepts for designing and implementation, for example, Netflix.

Microservice architecture can be illustrated by matching it with the approach of monolithic architecture as shown in figure. HTTP request is handled by the monolithic application. It also takes care of retrieve the data, executes the domain logic and updates the data in the database. It selects the HTML views which have to be sent to the browser. In monolithic application, a small change in the design results in to redesign and deploy the entire monolith. Therefore, it is difficult to preserve the design and modular structure of the application. This makes it difficult to modify or change a single module in the entire application.

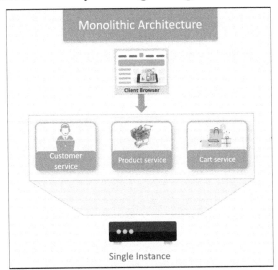

Monolithic Architecture.

In microservice architecture, an application can be divided into multiple parts or components, called microservices. These components are independently scaled. This architecture approach is very useful when the system has very high load with number of reusable modules. Figure illustrates microservice architecture.

The microservice architectures are simple. It focuses on a single component at a time. The systems designed using microservice architecture is loosely coupled as the components of a system work independent of each others. To execute the task, every service is built, selecting the most suitable tool. This architecture allows many teams and developers to work independent of each other using this architecture.

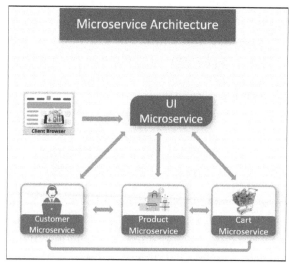

Microservice Architecture.

Benefits of Microservices

It offers many benefits to the developers. Some of the most common benefits are as follows: Code is small and easy to understand, easy to scale, smaller teams, easy to throw away, easy to deploy, capability to employ diverse technology, system resilience.

Drawbacks of Microservices

It also has some drawbacks. Some of them are: communication overhead, documentation overhead, diverse application, maintenance complexity and more initial investment, enlarge communication, gathering the data, security, testing and more monitoring cost.

Communication Mechanisms

The communication prototype in microservice architecture between the application and the client, as well as among different components in the application is different than that of a monolithic application.

API Gateway

In a monolithic, the browsers (client) and applications send HTTP requests using a load balancer to the identical instance of the application. But in a microservice, the set of services replaces the monolith. Suppose the application on the mobile device is a client. This client sends request RESTful HTTP to some specific services as illustrated in figure.

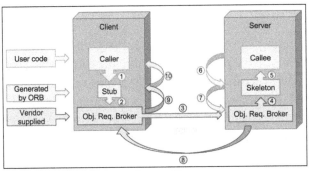

Services Calling.

Above solution looks good but there may be a considerable variance in granularity between the APIs of the service and data requested by the clients. For example, to display a single web page, it is necessary to call number of services (sometime more than 100 services). This so many requests use the bandwidth and lower its performance, and the mobile network may be inefficient, and results in poor performance. So, to avoid this bandwidth consumption, clients should make a small number of requests per page. The approach that supports this is known as API gateway. Figure illustrates this approach. In this approach, the API gateway is installed between the clients and the microservices. API gateway offers a finer grained API to clients using desktop and a coarse grained API to clients using mobile devices. In the following Figure given, the client on desktop sends multiple requests for various services, whereas a client from mobile device makes a request for a single service.

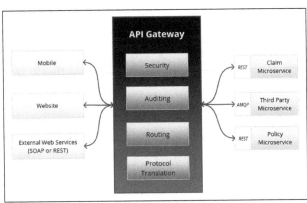

API Gateway.

The API gateway uses LAN with high performance network to handle the requests from clients. It makes the requests to different services available in microservices architecture. It also summarizes the particulars of microservices due to which it develops without affecting the clients. For examples, some microservices may be partitioned into multiple services or multiple microservices may be merged to get one microservice. For these modifications, no changes are required at client ends, only API should be updated. This communication among the microservices is implemented using different mechanisms.

Inter-service Communication Mechanisms

The communication in the microservice architecture depends on the interactions among the various components. In a monolithic application, regular techniques are used to communicate each other by the components. But there are different services, executing in different processes in microservice architecture. As a result, for the communication among the services in microservice architecture, it uses an Inter Process Communication (IPC). Before selecting an inter-service communication mechanism for a service, it is beneficial to know the ways of interactions of the services. Client and services interact with each other by different ways: one-to-one or one-to-many and synchronous or asynchronous. In one-to-one mechanism, every request from client is processed by one instance. In one-to-many mechanism, every request is processed by multiple instances. Another approach is synchronous HTTP or Asynchronous messaging.

Synchronous HTTP

A synchronous communication approach based on HTTP like REST or SOAP is used for IPC. It can work easily across the network, and can be implemented easily. But this approach has some limitations.

REST

Representational State Transfer (REST) is an inter-service communication mechanism which mostly uses HTTP.

Resource is a main notion in REST. This resource signifies an object, like product or customer. HTTP is used by REST for manipulating resources using a Uniform Resource Locator (URL). For example, a 'GET' request sends a resource, which may be an XML document or a JSON object.

Thrift

An alternative to REST is Apache Thrift. It is a framework which allows for writing cross language RPC servers and clients. It offers a C like IDL for defining APIs. User can use the Thrift compiler for creating skeletons for the server side and stubs for the client side. It generates the code for different languages such as Java, C++, PHP, Python, Node.js and Ruby.

Asynchronous Messaging

Another approach for communication is an asynchronous approach. It is based on message such as an AMQP-based message broker. It has number of advantages. Some of these are as follows:

- It decouples producers from consumers of the message. The messages are stored with the message broker until the message consumer is ready to process the messages. Therefore, message producers do not have the complete information regarding the message consumers. The message producer has only to talk with the broker. It is not necessary to use a service discovery mechanism.

- It also supports publish-subscribe and one-way requests communication patterns. The drawback of this system is the complexity of the system is more due to use of a message broker.

Asynchronous Message-based Communication

In asynchronous message-based communication, processes communicate with each other by asynchronously exchanging the messages. A request by a client to a service is done by sending a message. If the reply is expected, then the service sends a separate message to the client. As asynchronous communication method is used without waiting for the reply from the server, client continues his message transmission assuming that the reply will come later on. Channels are used for the exchange of messages. There may be any numbers of message senders and receivers who can use the same channel. A message consists of headers and a message body. Channels are of two types: publish subscribe and point-to-point.

A publish subscribe channel distributes every message to all relevant receivers. These types of channels are used for one-to-many communications by the services. A point-to-point channel distributes a message to only one receiver in the channel. These types of channels are used for one-to-one communications by the services. Figure illustrates the working of publish-subscribe channels.

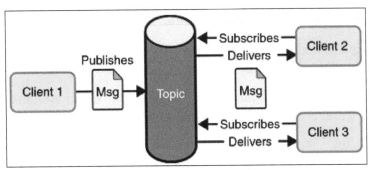

Publish-subscribe Channels.

Cloud Infrastructure

Cloud infrastructure is the layer of software and hardware between your internal systems and the public cloud. Incorporating many different tools and solutions, this infrastructure is the essential system for a successful cloud computing deployment.

This layer of cloud infrastructure has grown as public cloud has changed the structure of the data center and its hardware. Up until now, IT equipment and data center systems adopted the circled wagon approach. Everything was behind a firewall and facing inward. The only users were inside the company and inside the firewall, as were the apps.

The cloud – and to some extent mobile – forces a break in that circle. Now businesses need to face outward, to AWS, Azure, Google Cloud, or other cloud companies. Businesses need to create a secure data flow in their firewall to connect securely to the public cloud and keep intruders out, while at the same time maintaining acceptable levels of performance.

The Internal Cloud Meets Cloud Infrastructure

As the cloud has grown, many enterprises have adopted an internal cloud model, often known as a private cloud. These private clouds don't have the compute capacity of an Amazon or IBM, but they do have the flexibility to spin up virtual instances and keep them in-house.

The goal is to simplify the combination of the private cloud and pubic cloud, often known as a hybrid cloud. To help with this process, companies use technologies such as hyper-converged infrastructure (HCI), where a vendor provides everything needed to install a turnkey cloud environment. This allows businesses to turn their traditional on-premises data center into cloud-like infrastructure that can managed from a single dashboard.

All services are delivered through the Infrastructure as a Service (IaaS) model. As such, everything is virtualized, so the cloud-based infrastructure can be set up easily, duplicated, replaced, and shut down.

Cloud Infrastructure Building Blocks

The components of cloud infrastructure are typically broken down into three main categories: compute, networking, and storage:

- Compute: Performs the basic computing for the cloud systems. This is almost always virtualized so the instance can be moved around.

- Networking: Usually commodity hardware running some kind of software-defined networking (SDN) software to manage cloud connections (see below for more information about networking).

- Storage: Usually a combination hard disks and flash storage designed to move data back and forth between the public and private clouds.

Storage is where cloud infrastructure parts ways from the traditional data center infrastructure. Cloud infrastructure usually uses locally attached storage instead of shared disk arrays on a storage area network. Cloud providers like AWS, Azure and Google charge more for SSD storage than they do for hard disk storage.

Cloud storage also uses a distributed file system designed for different kinds of storage scenarios, such as object, big data, or block. The type of storage used depends on the tasks you need handled. Key point: cloud storage can scale up or down as needed.

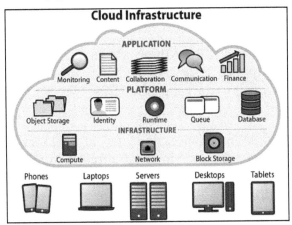

Cloud infrastructure is the foundation upon which sits platform and any application. Connected devices like a laptop, phone or server transfer data in and out of this larger cloud system.

IaaS Benefits

IaaS is the foundation on which cloud infrastructure is built. Cloud infrastructure is the bricks and mortar, IaaS is the store. IaaS makes it possible to rent those cloud infrastructure components – compute, storage and networking – over the Internet from a public cloud provider.

The benefits of IaaS are numerous:

- Cuts upfront costs: IaaS eliminates the upfront capital expense of buying new server hardware, waiting several weeks for it to be delivered, more time for it to be installed and deployed and then provisioned. You can log into your AWS control panel and spin up a virtual instance in 15 minutes.

- Scalable capacity: If you need more capacity, you can buy more just as quickly, and you can scale down if you find you don't need as much as allocated. And instead of the up-front capital expense of buying new equipment, IaaS follows a usage-based consumption model where you pay-per-use.

- Discounts: IaaS vendors also provide discounts for sustained usage, or if you make a large up-front purchase. The savings can be high, too, as much as 75%.

The next step up from IaaS is platform as a service (PaaS), which is built on the same IaaS platforms and hardware. But PaaS is expanded to offer more services, such as a complete development environment, including a Web server, tools, programming language, and database.

Why use a Cloud Infrastructure?

In a traditional IT infrastructure, everything is tied to a server. Your storage is on a specific storage array. Apps run on dedicated physical servers. If anything goes down, your work comes to a halt.

In a cloud infrastructure, because everything is virtualized, nothing is tied to a particular physical server. This applies to services as well as apps. Do you think when you log onto Gmail you are logging into the same physical server every time? No, it's a virtualized server at any one of dozens of Google data centers.

The same applies to your AWS instances and your internal services, should you deploy a cloud infrastructure model for your internal infrastructure. By virtualizing storage, compute and networking components, you can build from whatever services are available and not heavily utilized. For example, you can launch an application on a virtual server on hardware with low utilization. Or you can deploy a network connection on a switch with low traffic.

With cloud infrastructure, DevOps teams can build their apps so they can deploy an app programmatically. They can tell an app to look for a low utilization server or to deploy as close to the data store as possible. You can't do that in a traditional IT environment.

Big Networking Changes

Network technology has created a major change the relationship between cloud infrastructure and traditional IT. The current standard in WAN communication technology, Multiprotocol Label Switching (MPLS), is designed for use internally in your data center. It does not handle high bandwidth apps very well and is easily overloaded. Plus, the data is transmitted unencrypted, which raises obvious problems when transmitting over the public Internet.

SD-WAN is made for the public Internet and lets you use a VPN to encrypt traffic. It uses intelligent routing to manage traffic to avoid bottlenecks, and most of the SD-WAN vendors have built their own private networks to supplement the public Internet, so you do not have to compete with Netflix traffic.

Because it is built for the public Internet, one of the biggest advantages to SD-WAN is security. SD-WAN offers end-to-end encryption across the entire network, including the Internet, and all devices and endpoints are completely authenticated, thanks to software-defined security.

Cloud Infrastructure Challenges

Cloud infrastructure in the public cloud is not a flawless solution. There can be issues, and typically these issues are serious. Note, these are issues unique to the public cloud and should not impact any private cloud infrastructure you deploy internally.

Noisy Neighbors

The first problem is the issue of the noisy neighbor. When you are running a virtual instance, your VM is running on an AWS/Azure/IBM/Google server in a data center. That physical server is likely a two-socket rack mount with two Intel Xeons and a lot of memory. If you allocate four cores on a 28-core Xeon, the other 24 are going to be rented out to someone else, and you have no way of knowing their identity.

The result could be an app that impacts your performance, be it compute, in memory or the network. A common practice among cloud users is to spin up a bunch of virtual machines, run benchmarks to see which perform best, and shut down the ones they do not need.

The solution to this is what is called bare metal cloud. In a bare metal environment, the CPU is not virtualized. That 28-core Xeon is all yours. No noisy neighbors. No OS, either. Bare metal solutions mean you bring everything, from the OS stack on up.

The bare metal solution is designed for specific environments where performance is critical, or if you want access to custom chips. For example, in a virtualized environment, you cannot access the networking chip. In bare metal you can, so you can do custom networking, like packet inspection.

Latency

The other issue is latency. Public cloud performance is not consistent, except perhaps at night when usage plummets. If you have an application that is sensitive to issues of latency, you might have a costly problem.

One solution is to change the location of your app. You might be connecting to a data center on the other side of the country. You can request a data center that is physically closer to you, to reduce the lag. Of course, that might cost you more, so you have to weigh the benefits.

You can connect directly to the cloud provider, AWS as AWS Direct Connect, for example. Yet that is an even pricier solution since you are now using the provider's own network.

Cloud Server

A cloud server is a virtual server (rather than a physical server) running in a cloud computing environment. It is built, hosted and delivered via a cloud computing platform via the internet, and can be accessed remotely. They are also known as virtual servers. Cloud servers have all the software they require to run and can function as independent units.

What is the Cloud?

The cloud is commonly used to refer to several servers connected to the internet that can be leased as part of a software or application service. Cloud-based services can include web hosting, data hosting and sharing, and software or application use.

'The cloud' can also refer to cloud computing, where several servers are linked together to share the load. This means that instead of using one single powerful machine, complex processes can be distributed across multiple smaller computers.

One of the advantages of cloud storage is that there are many distributed resources acting as one – often called federated storage clouds. This makes the cloud very tolerant of faults, due to the distribution of data. Use of the cloud tends to reduce the creation of different versions of files, due to shared access to documents, files and data.

What are the Benefits of a Cloud Server?

- A cloud server gives the business user stability and security because any software problems are isolated from your environment. Other cloud servers won't impact on your cloud server and vice versa. If another user overloads their cloud server, this will have no impact on your cloud server, unlike with physical servers.

- Cloud servers are stable, fast and secure. They avoid the hardware issues seen with physical servers, and they are likely to be the most stable option for businesses wanting to keep their IT budget down.

- Cloud servers provide a faster service for your money. You'll get more resources and a faster service than you would for a similar price of physical server. A cloud-hosted website will run faster.

- You get scalability with cloud servers. It is very easy and quick to upgrade by adding memory and disk space, as well as being more affordable.

Load Balancing in Cloud Computing

A website or a web-application can be accessed by a plenty of users at any point of time. It becomes difficult for a web application to manage all these user requests at one time. It may even result in system breakdowns. For a website owner, whose entire work is dependent on his portal, the sinking feeling of website being down or not accessible also brings lost potential customers.

Here, the load balancer plays an important role.

Cloud Load balancing is the process of distributing workloads and computing resources across one or more servers. This kind of distribution ensures maximum throughput in minimum response time. The workload is segregated among two or more servers, hard drives, network interfaces or other computing resources, enabling better resource utilization and system response time. Thus, for a high traffic website, effective use of cloud load balancing can ensure business continuity. The common objectives of using load balancers are:

- To maintain system firmness.

- To improve system performance.

- To protect against system failures.

Cloud providers like Amazon Web Services (AWS), Microsoft Azure and Google offer cloud load balancing to facilitate easy distribution of workloads. For ex: AWS offers Elastic Load balancing (ELB) technology to distribute traffic among EC2 instances. Most of the AWS powered applications have ELBs installed as key architectural component.

Similarly, Azure's Traffic Manager allocates its cloud servers' traffic across multiple datacenters.

How does Load Balancing Work?

Here, load refers to not only the website traffic but also includes CPU load, network load and memory capacity of each server. A load balancing technique makes sure that each system in the network has same amount of work at any instant of time. This means neither any of them is excessively over-loaded, nor under-utilized.

The load balancer distributes data depending upon how busy each server or node is. In the absence of a load balancer, the client must wait while his process gets processed, which might be too tiring and demotivating for him.

Various information like jobs waiting in queue, CPU processing rate, job arrival rate etc. are exchanged between the processors during the load balancing process. Failure in the right application of load balancers can lead to serious consequences, data getting lost being one of them.

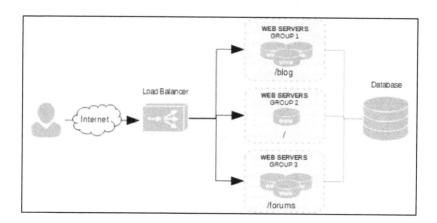

Different companies may use different load balancers and multiple load balancing algorithms like static and dynamic load balancing. One of the most commonly used methods is Round-robin load balancing.

It forwards client request to each connected server in turn. On reaching the end, the load balancer loops back and repeats the list again. The major benefit is its ease of implementation. The load balancers check the system heartbeats during set time intervals to verify whether each node is performing well or not.

What are the Advantages of Cloud Load Balancing?

High Performing Applications

Cloud load balancing techniques, unlike their traditional on-premise counterparts, are less expensive and simple to implement. Enterprises can make their client applications work faster and deliver better performances, that too at potentially lower costs.

Increased Scalability

Cloud balancing takes help of cloud's scalability and agility to maintain website traffic. By using efficient load balancers, you can easily match up the increased user traffic and distribute it among various servers or network devices. It is especially important for ecommerce websites, who deals with thousands of website visitors every second. During sale or other promotional offers they need such effective load balancers to distribute workloads.

Ability to Handle Sudden Traffic Spikes

A normally running University site can completely go down during any result declaration. This is because too many requests can arrive at the same time. If they are using cloud load balancers, they do not need to worry about such traffic surges. No matter how large the request is, it can be wisely distributed among different servers for generating maximum results in less response time.

Business Continuity with Complete Flexibility

The basic objective of using a load balancer is to save or protect a website from sudden outages. When the workload is distributed among various servers or network units, even if one node fails the burden can be shifted to another active node.

Thus, with increased redundancy, scalability and other features load balancing easily handles website or application traffic.

Cloud Load Balancer

If you are targeting large audience or expecting high traffic to your website/web application globally, then you got to use LB (load balancer). The load balancer can help you in many ways:

- High availability.

- Scaling the application.

- No or minimum downtime.

- Security.

- Better geographical user experience.

- SSL offloading.

Traditional LB hardware cost around $5,000 so most of the medium, start up or low-budget project doesn't think of getting one.

But not anymore, you can use cloud load balancer for as low as $20 per month with all the great features you get in traditional LB.

If you are designing high-availability application for better performance & security then the following cloud LB will help you.

Each has some advantage or additional features than others so choose what works for you.

AWS ELB

Amazon Web Services (AWS) Elastic Load Balancer (ELB) is no doubt, one of the best load balancing solution available in the cloud.

AWS got two types of load balancers:

- Application load balancer – preferred for application layer (HTTP/HTTPS).

- Classic load balancer – preferred for transport layer (TCP).

If you are building web based applications and use HTTP or HTTPS protocol, then application load balancer is the best choice.

ELB distribute the incoming requests to backend configured EC2 instances based on the routing algorithm.

Some of the following features of AWS Application Load Balancer:

- It support HTTP/2, IPv6, WebSockets.

- You can offload SSL/TLS.

- AWS WAF integration supported.

- You can enable sticky session (cookies).

- Forward request to the backend based on context URI/path.

- Add health check.

Elastic LB provides the following monitoring metrics by default:

- Average latency.

- Requests Summary.

- New/active connection count.

- Processed bytes.

- And much more.

Google Cloud Load Balancing

Google provides global single anycast IP to front-end all your backend servers for better high-availability and scalable application environment.

Google provides three types of load balancing solutions:

- HTTP(S) – layer 7, suitable for web applications.

- TCP – layer 4, suitable for TCP/SSL protocol based balancing.

- UDP – layer 4, useful for UDP protocol based balancing.

Google Cloud is built on the same infrastructure as Gmail, YouTube so doubting on performance is out of a question.

Google Cloud LB supports more than 1 million requests per second and you can auto-scale your applications based on the demand without any manual intervention.

Autoscaling let you be prepared for a spike in traffic without slowing down the website performance.

Some of the worth mentioning Google Cloud HTTP (S) LB features:

- Affinity.

- One-click Google CDN integration.

- SSL termination.

- Health checks.

- You can create content-based balancing.

- Global forwarding rules.

LB monitoring is integrated with Stackdriver, full-stack monitoring powered by Google. You get almost everything metrics you need to monitor from your LB.

The good thing is you can use Stackdriver not just for Google Cloud but also AWS resources.

If you need Websockets support then, you got to use TCP load balancing as application LB doesn't support it yet.

NodeBalancers

Are you hosting your website with Linode?

NodeBalancers by Linode provide all the essential features of LB at only $20 per month. Configuration is quite straightforward and comes with some of the basic features as the following:

- It support IPv4, IPv6.

- Throttle the connection for suspicious traffic to prevent the resources abuse.

- Can have multi-port balancing.

- you can terminate SSL handshake.

- Session persistence so your request always goes to the same backend server.

- Health checks to ensure request goes to healthy server.

- You can choose routing algorithm from round robin, least connection or source IP.

NodeBalancers >> balancer101 >> Port 80						
Nodes						
Label	Address	Weight	Mode	Status	Last Status Change	
backend	192.168.1.1.80	100	Accept	UP	201-07-11 11:37:09.0	
Backend2	192.168.1.2.80	100	Accept	Unknown		

NodeBalancers can be used to balance any TCP based traffic including HTTP, MySQL, SSH, etc.

Rackspace Cloud Load Balancers

Rackspace is one of the leading in cloud hosting solution providers offer cloud LB to manage the online traffic by distributing the request to the multiple backend servers.

It supports multiple routing algorithms like round-robin, weighted, least connection & random. You can balance almost any type of services protocol including:

- TCP.

- SMTP/IMAP.

- HTTP/HTPS.

- LDAP/LDPAS.

- MySQL.

- FTP/SFTP.

- UDP.

Some of the Rackspace cloud LB features:

- SSL acceleration for improved throughput.

- You can terminate SSL so less CPU overload on your web server.

- Session persistence to forward request to one server.

- 10Gb/second network throughput.

- Manage LB through API.

- Protection malicious traffic by throttling the connection.

Rackspace LB is capable of handling 20,000 concurrent connections, and in a case of the spike, it can extend up to 100,000 connections.

You get logs for all traffic in Apache-style access logs for better log management.

Azure Load Balancer

Load balance the internal or internet facing applications using Microsoft Azure LB. With the help of you Azure LB, you can build high-available and scalable web applications.

It supports TCP/UDP protocol including HTTP/HTTPS, SMTP, real-time voice, video messaging applications. If you are hosting your application already on Azure, then you can forward your request from LB to the virtual servers.

Some notable features of Azure LB:

- Native IPv6 support.

- You can have NAT rules for better security.

- Hash-based traffic distribution.

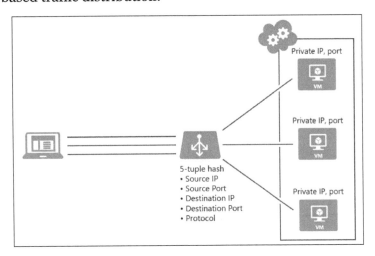

There are three types of load balancing solution provide by Azure.

- Application Gateway: Layer 7, terminate the client connection and forward the request to the backend servers/services.

- Azure load balancer: Layer 4, distribute TCP traffic across Azure instances.

- Traffic manager: DNS level distribution.

SSL offloading, Path forwarding is supported only in "Application Gateway."

DigitalOcean Load Balancer

Similar to Linode, you can control DigitalOcean's load balancer either through a control panel or API. If you are hosting your web application with DO and looking for HA solution, then this would be probably the best one at a lower cost.

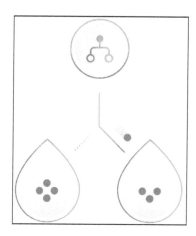

It supports HTTP, HTTPS & TCP protocol with round robin and least connection routing algorithm. DO let you terminate SSL, configure the sticky session, health checks, forwarding rules, etc. for $20 per month.

Incapsula Load Balancer

Incapsula provides load balancer as a service for three main availability scenarios.

Local load balancer: Request is forwarded to most suites servers based on routing algorithm within the same data center.

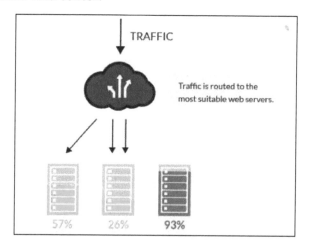

Global server load balancer (GSLB): Perfect for a large organization or hybrid cloud infrastructure where you can forward the requests to multiple data center for high availability and better performance.

GSLB support geo-targeting which means you can forward the traffic based on visitor geolocation to the regional page or nearest data center.

Auto site failover: Automate and accelerate disaster recovery based on the health checks without manual intervention. Traffic are instantly rerouted to another data center.

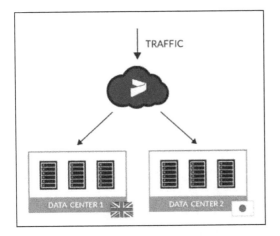
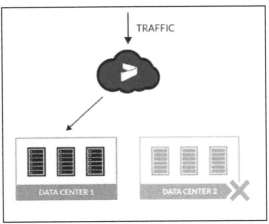

Incapsula provides real-time dashboard, active/passive health checks & option to create the redirect/rewrite rules.

Cloud Computing Operation

Cloud computing operation refers to delivering superior cloud service. Today, cloud computing operations have become very popular and widely employed by many of the organizations just because it allows to perform all business operations over the Inter-net.

These operations can be performed using a web application or mobile based applications. There are a number of operations performed in cloud. Some of them are shown in the following diagram:

Managing Cloud Operations

There are several ways to manage day-to-day cloud operations, as shown in the following diagram:

- Always employ right tools and resources to perform any function in the cloud.

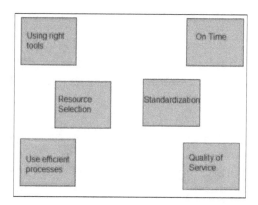

- Things should be done at right time and at right cost.

- Selecting an appropriate resource is mandatory for operation management.

- The process should be standardized and automated to manage repetitive tasks.

- Using efficient process will eliminate the waste of efforts and redundancy.

- One should maintain the quality of service to avoid re-work later.

References

- What-is-cloud-computing-architecture-front-end-back-end-explained: it.toolbox.com, Retrieved 29 April, 2019

- What-is-cloud-platform: quickstart.com, Retrieved 11 January, 2019

- Four-best-cloud-deployment-models-you-need-to-know: sam-solutions.com, Retrieved 31 March, 2019

- Cloud-Computing-Networking-Challenges-and-Opportunities-for-Innovations-249325475: researchgate.net, Retrieved 11 May, 2019

- What-is-cloud-infrastructure, cloud-computing: datamation.com, Retrieved 08 July, 2019

- What-is-load-balancing-in-cloud-computing-and-its-advantages: znetlive.com, Retrieved 11 April, 2019

Web Services Delivered from the Cloud

Some of the cloud servicing models include communications as a service, infrastructure as a service, monitoring as a service, platform as a service, software as a service, etc. The topics elaborated in this chapter will help in gaining a better perspective about these cloud computing web services.

Communications as a Service

Communication as a Service (CaaS) is a method of delivering communication services in a method akin to Software as a Service delivery, but with some special considerations relating specifically to communications applications and the integration with proprietary communications systems.

CaaS can include a range of communications services, including voice over IP (VoIP), instant messaging, message routing, call recording and video conferencing.

Who is CaaS for?

Many people are familiar with consumer CaaS solutions such as Skype, FaceTime and instant messaging tools such as Facebook Messenger. However, mainstream adoption of communications over the public internet has been relatively slow.

It is worth noting here that VoIP isn't necessarily a public-internet solution; it could just as easily be used over dedicated circuits or LAN/WAN. Business users have benefitted from the cost advantages of VoIP largely by deploying on-site IP-based PBX systems. These offer significant cost advantages by enabling the business to run the corporate telephony system on the same network as is used for data; thereby eliminating the need to install and operate separate networks for voice and data. However, these systems are expensive to purchase, configure and manage – putting them out of reach of most small-to-medium-sized businesses (SMBs).

By eliminating the need for businesses to purchase and maintain such expensive communications hardware, CaaS puts much greater options for communication management in the hands of SMBs.

Advantages of CaaS

The continued convergence of communications has blurred the line between software applications and communications applications. CaaS offers the potential to manage multiple services – voice, video, data – over multiple devices – landline telephone, mobile or smartphone, PC – in a controlled environment.

It offers greatest potential for small businesses – enabling the utilisation of VoIP, VPNs, PBX and unified communications without the need for to invest in the upfront costs of the hardware or the need to employ the skilled professionals required to manage and maintain the systems.

Some argue "VoIP is an upgrade for your business whether you need to open a new office on the other side of the country, adjust your business hours on the fly, or prioritise calls from your most important contacts, online telephony makes it possible to adjust how you work as you work."

Are there any Risks Involved in CaaS?

The quality and the reliability of these solutions is of primary concern, given the mission critical nature of telephony and other communications services.

What do I Need to do before Implementing Communications as a Service?

It is important to ensure the administrative tools are in place to manage and monitor the system. Because communications applications are mission-critical applications, even greater effort must be made to ensure that the appropriate service level agreements (SLAs) and associated penalties in case of service breach are put in place both in terms of service uptime and security.

Infrastructure as a Service

Infrastructure as a service (IaaS) is a form of cloud computing that provides virtualized computing resources over the internet. IaaS is one of the three main categories of cloud computing services, alongside software as a service (SaaS) and platform as a service (PaaS).

IaaS Architecture and how it works

In an IaaS model, a cloud provider hosts the infrastructure components traditionally present in an on-premises data center, including servers, storage and networking hardware, as well as the virtualization or hypervisor layer.

The IaaS provider also supplies a range of services to accompany those infrastructure components. These can include detailed billing, monitoring, log access, security, load balancing and clustering, as well as storage resiliency, such as backup, replication and recovery. These services are increasingly policy-driven, enabling IaaS users to implement greater levels of automation and orchestration for important infrastructure tasks. For example, a user can implement policies to drive load balancing to maintain application availability and performance.

IaaS customers access resources and services through a wide area network (WAN), such as the internet, and can use the cloud provider's services to install the remaining elements of an application stack. For example, the user can log in to the IaaS platform to create virtual machines (VMs); install operating systems in each VM; deploy middleware, such as databases; create storage buckets for workloads and backups; and install the enterprise workload into that VM. Customers can then use the provider's services to track costs, monitor performance, balance network traffic, troubleshoot application issues, manage disaster recovery and more.

Any cloud computing model requires the participation of a provider. The provider is often a third-party organization that specializes in selling IaaS. Amazon Web Services (AWS) and Google Cloud Platform (GCP) are examples of independent IaaS providers. A business might also opt to deploy a private cloud, becoming its own provider of infrastructure services.

IaaS Advantages and Disadvantages

Organizations choose IaaS because it is often easier, faster and more cost-efficient to operate a workload without having to buy, manage and support the underlying infrastructure. With IaaS, a business can simply rent or lease that infrastructure from another business.

IaaS is an effective model for workloads that are temporary, experimental or that change unexpectedly. For example, if a business is developing a new software product, it might be more cost-effective to host and test the application using an IaaS provider. Once the new software is tested and refined, the business can remove it from the IaaS environment for a more traditional, in-house deployment. Conversely, the business could commit that piece of software to a long-term IaaS deployment, where the costs of a long-term commitment may be less.

In general, IaaS customers pay on a per use basis, typically by the hour, week or month. Some IaaS providers also charge customers based on the amount of virtual machine space they use. This pay-as-you-go model eliminates the capital expense of deploying in-house hardware and software.

When a business cannot use third-party providers, a private cloud built on premises can still offer the control and scalability of IaaS, though the cost benefits no longer apply.

Despite its flexible, pay-as-you-go model, IaaS billing can be a problem for some businesses. Cloud billing is extremely granular, and it is broken out to reflect the precise usage of services. It is common for users to experience sticker shock -- or finding costs to be higher than expected -- when reviewing the bills for every resource and service involved in an application deployment. Users should monitor their IaaS environments and bills closely to understand how IaaS is being used, and to avoid being charged for unauthorized services.

Insight is another common problem for IaaS users. Because IaaS providers own the infrastructure, the details of their infrastructure configuration and performance are rarely transparent to IaaS users. This lack of transparency can make systems management and monitoring more difficult for users.

IaaS users are also concerned about service resilience. The workload's availability and performance is highly dependent on the provider. If an IaaS provider experiences network bottlenecks or any form of internal or external downtime, the users' workloads will be affected. In addition, because IaaS is a multi-tenant architecture, the noisy neighbor issue can negatively impact users' workloads.

IaaS versus SaaS versus PaaS

IaaS is only one of several cloud computing models, and it is complemented by alternative models that include PaaS and SaaS.

PaaS builds on the IaaS model because, in addition to the underlying infrastructure components, providers host, manage and offer operating systems, middleware and other runtimes for cloud users. While PaaS simplifies workload deployment, it also restricts a business's flexibility to create the environment that they want.

With SaaS, providers host, manage and offer the entire infrastructure, as well as applications, for users. A SaaS user does not need to install anything; he or she simply logs in and uses the provider's application, which runs on the provider's infrastructure. Users have some ability to configure the way that the application works and which users are authorized to use it, but the SaaS provider is responsible for everything else.

Major IaaS Vendors and Products

There are many examples of IaaS vendors and products. AWS offers storage services such as Simple Storage Services (S3) and Glacier, as well as compute services, including its Elastic Compute Cloud (EC2). GCP offers storage and compute services through Google Compute Engine (GCE), as does Microsoft Azure.

These are just a tiny sample of the broad range of services offered by major IaaS providers. Services can include serverless functions, such as AWS Lambda, Azure Functions or Google Cloud Functions; database access; big data compute environments; monitoring; logging; and more.

There are also many other smaller, or more niche players in the IaaS marketplace, including Rackspace Managed Cloud, CenturyLink Cloud, DigitalOcean and more.

Users will need to carefully consider the services, reliability and costs before choosing a provider -- and be ready to select an alternate provider and to redeploy to the alternate infrastructure if necessary.

cPouta

cPouta is an Infrastructure as a Service (IaaS) cloud. In IaaS cloud environments, users can quickly setup virtual machines with a set amount of resources, attach various types of storage to the machines and connect them using virtual networks. The user does not need to buy hardware, network it and install operating systems, as this has already been handled by the cloud administrators.

- Comparing the cloud to traditional hosted services.

- Comparing the cloud to traditional HPC environments.

- cPouta related terms and concepts.

    o OpenStack.

    o Platform-as-a-Service (PaaS).

    o Software-as-a-Service (SaaS).

    o Virtual machine.

    o Virtual network.

    o Virtual machine image.

Comparing the Cloud to Traditional Hosted Services

Traditional hosted services typically rely on a set of fixed resources. Users get access to physical servers, firewalls, storage and so on, or a virtualized representation of the same. Storage in hosted services is provided by onboard disks, disk arrays or a Storage Area Network (SAN) depending on performance, multi-tenancy or backup requirements. Quite often hosted services utilize proprietary software for specialized tasks such as live migration or live backups, and resiliency is provided by duplicating or clustering each element so the service can do failover to the remaining healthy ones when disaster strikes. Often this simply means physical level redundancy: A new box will claim the responsibility of the old one. This happens in addition to the redundancy on other levels e.g. multiple disks, multiple network links and so on. In other words everything from individual elements of the hosting infrastructure to the hosts that end users are running are considered - if not irreplaceable - at least precious. In terms of scaling the end user application or service, growth in utilization is typically projected for longer periods of time such as months or years, and extensions in capacity are planned based on these projections.

In contrast, applications or services running on top of cloud IaaS are almost designed from the very premise that any or all of the hosts can fail at any time. If this occurs, new hosts are simply built on demand to replace the old ones, drawing from what can be considered a semi-infinite pool of resources. Every possible element of the cloud service is typically virtualized so dependencies to bare-metal components are minimized. The storage backend of a cloud service needs to provide a good amount of I/O per second (IOPS), resiliency against failures, as well as good scalability whenever there is a sudden increase in demand. Traditional storage solutions may not meet these requirements so new types of Open Source Storage solutions are increasingly used for cloud storage, allowing use of commodity hardware and a mix between various hardware vendors. Features such as live migration support are often directly built in to these open solutions.

Cloud services also utilize many forms of Configuration Management (CM). Of course, CM can also be used with traditional hosted services, but operating a cloud service almost mandates that the underlying system configurations are stored and utilized in a consistent manner. This goes for any application or service that the user is operating, too. Once a configuration of any part of the service is written down with a CM tool of choice, that configuration can be replicated to any number of additional nodes or promptly used when rebuilding a faulty one. Furthermore, this decouples the replaceable from the irreplaceable very effectively. Frontend servers, application servers, caches and so on can always be rebuilt utilizing CM, but databases and other elements where state and data are stored can't. So while working in a cloud mindset it certainly becomes easier to recover a system by rebuilding most parts of it, any element holding irreplaceable information should still be backed up to external systems and protected against failure.

In terms of scaling, a good way to operate services in the cloud is to set a baseline capacity (X load balancers, Y web servers, Z database servers...) and increase it based on trending demand. This goes for scaling the system down, too. Whenever cloud resources are not required, the proper thing to do is to destroy them, freeing resources to the pool. In this way scaling a user application or service in the cloud is much different than with traditional hosted services, but it also adds to the benefit of the user since by terminating idle instances they are consuming less Billing Units for idle cycles.

Comparing the Cloud to Traditional HPC Environments

A comparison against the traditional HPC (High-Performance Computing) services that CSC also provides is presented in the following table.

	Traditional HPC environment	Cloud environment virtual machine
Operating system	Same for all: CSC's cluster OS	Chosen by the user

Software installation	Done by cluster administrators, customers can only install software to their own directories, no administrative rights	Installed by the user, the user has admin rights
User accounts	Managed by CSC's user administrator	Managed by the user
Security e.g. software patches	CSC administrators manage the common software and the OS	User has more responsibility: e.g. patching of running machines
Running jobs	Jobs need to be sent via the cluster's Batch Scheduling System (BSS)	The user is free to use or not use a BSS
Environment changes	Changes to SW (libraries, compilers) happen.	The user can decide on versions.
Snapshot of the environment	Not possible	Can save as a Virtual Machine image
Performance	Performs well for a variety of tasks	Very small virtualization overhead for most tasks, heavily I/O bound and MPI tasks affected more

cPouta Related Terms and Concepts

OpenStack

OpenStack is the free open source software that has been used to build the cPouta cloud environment. It offers components for managing virtual machines (Nova), networks (Neutron), identity (Keystone), virtual machine images (Glance) and persistent volume storage (Cinder). There is also a web interface for managing most of the other components (Horizon).

Infrastructure-as-a-Service (IaaS)

IaaS provides users with virtualised servers, storage and networks through a self-service interface. Users have flexibility to choose many aspects of their environment, but they must also support the operating system, middleware, software and data themselves.

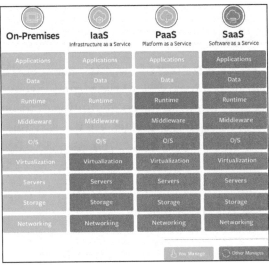

Industry standard definition IaaS and the other cloud terms.

Platform-as-a-Service (PaaS)

PaaS provides a higher level service to users, but with less choice about the underlying platform. CSC's regular HPC service (i.e. Sisu and Taito) is in some ways PaaS when considered with Scientists User Interface (SUI), although HPC applications typically use a very wide mixture of interfaces, non-standard API's and command line tools. Mainstream PaaS providers offer a framework which provides a documented common API for all aspects of the service.

Software-as-a-Service (SaaS)

In SaaS applications are delivered over the Internet. There are many examples of this in common use including web based email and cloud file storage. An example of SaaS from CSC would be the Chipster analysis software for high-throughput data. Chipster is an easy to use graphical interface that contains over 240 analysis tools for next generation sequencing (NGS), microarray and proteomics data.

Virtual Machine

A virtual machine is a computer simulated in software that runs as a process on a host machine. It exposes a part of the resources of the underlying machine to a guest operating system. This approach is more flexible compared to using just physical servers, as a single large physical server can be partitioned into isolated smaller virtual machines.

Virtual Network

One or more virtual networks can run on the same physical network. This helps prevent users from seeing each others' network traffic in a shared infrastructure. In IaaS services virtual networks are assigned to specific users or groups of users to provide security and ensure fair use of shared network links.

Virtual Machine Image

A large file containing a complete state of a virtual machine. The majority of a virtual machine image is the simulated hard disk of the virtual machine. As such virtual machine images vary in size depending on the configuration of the virtual machine and the installed applications. Virtual machine images are the starting point for creating new virtual machines and they can be easily cloned, snapshotted, backed up and managed.

Monitoring as a Service

Monitoring as a Service (MaaS) in the Cloud is a concept that combines the benefits of cloud computing technology and traditional on-premise IT infrastructure monitoring solutions. MaaS is a new delivery model that is suited for organizations looking to adopt a monitoring framework quickly with minimal investments.

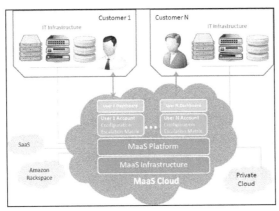

Traditional On-premise Monitoring Framework

On premise monitoring is the traditional deployment model for monitoring private networks (internal IT infrastructure). This has been a very effective model over the years and works well for organization that can afford to implement this monitoring framework. On-premise monitoring involves purchase of software tools and investing in monitoring infrastructure and skilled IT personnel.

On-Premise monitoring provides the following benefits:

- In-House Monitoring Infrastructure: Customers can own the in-house infrastructure for monitoring. This implies more control over the infrastructure with regards to upgrades, maintenance and management.

- Higher Levels of Security: Since the monitoring infrastructure is located in-house, customer gets better security where the monitoring tool does not need to cross firewall domains and connect over the open internet.

- Inherent Connectivity to Internal Assets: Monitoring infrastructure is already a part of the internal network (LAN and MPLS). Hence connecting to all the infrastructure assets is easy.

- Real Time Monitoring Data: On-premise monitoring provides real-time data where alerts are generated and shown to the customer immediately. The monitoring dashboard and email servers are all within the customer premise and hence there are no delays.

- Customization and Extensions: On-premise monitoring solutions can be heavily customized to meet the exact needs of a specific customer environment. This could be in the form of monitoring of custom applications or personalized dashboards and escalation matrices.

When to use On-premise Monitoring

On-Premise monitoring is suitable for following situations:

- Customer wants to own the monitoring infrastructure: In scenarios where customer is willing to invest in the monitoring infrastructure, some customers prefer to own the monitoring infrastructure. On-Premise monitoring is the only option in such cases.

- Customer has the expertise and IT personnel: Customers may already have the expertise in setting up and managing a monitoring framework in-house. If the customer has the IT personnel to manage the monitoring framework, then on-premise monitoring is a good option.

- Customer is sensitive about data: For customers in data sensitive sectors such as Banking, Finance, Government and Healthcare, access to data is restricted due to regulations such as HIPAA, PCI DSS and FIPS. In those scenarios, on-premise monitoring is the only option since no data is transferred outside the organization.

- There are many custom applications running: To monitor customized applications, even the monitoring tool must be customized. It is easy to customize an On-Premise monitoring solution as compared to a hosted monitoring solution.

The Adoption of Cloud and Software as a Service Delivery Models

Cloud computing has been evolving into different technology areas such as Infrastructure as a Service (IaaS), Platform as a Service (PaaS) and Software as a Service (SaaS). These technology areas are finding increasing adoption in the marketplace.

A recent report published by IDC has indicated that the Cloud Computing market is expected to cross $100 billion by end of 2014.

The economic drivers for adoption of Cloud Technologies have been well understood in the market.

- Lower investments: Cloud offerings typically have very low upfront costs. All SaaS product offerings are charged on a pay per use monthly subscription basis, which implies lower cost of ownership.

- No infrastructure costs: Cloud service offerings use cloud based infrastructures such as Amazon or Rackspace or a private cloud. Hence the customer does not have to bear the cost of the infrastructure setup with cloud services.

- Outsourced technology expertise: With cloud offerings, customers get a ready to use product that can be immediately consumed by the end user. Customer does not need to invest in an in-house IT team having that particular technology expertise.

- Simplified management: With offerings in the cloud, the service provider deals with on-going management, maintenance and upgrades of technology. The customer can focus on his core business needs.

Monitoring as a Service Offering

The Monitoring as a Service (MaaS) offering provides a monitoring solution based on a monitoring infrastructure in the cloud. The MaaS vendor invests in the monitoring framework including the hardware, monitoring software and specialized IT personnel on behalf of the customer. The customer just needs to pay for the service he wants to use – on a subscription model similar to any SaaS product offering.

Benefits of Monitoring as a Service (MaaS)

The following are the benefits of a Monitoring as a Service (MaaS) product:

- Ready to use monitoring tool login: The vendor takes care of setting up the hardware infrastructure, monitoring tool, configuration and alert settings on behalf of the customer. The customer gets a ready to use login to the monitoring dashboard that is accessible using an internet browser. A mobile client is also available for the MaaS dashboard for IT administrators.

- Inherently available 24×7×365: Since MaaS is deployed in the cloud, the monitoring dashboard itself is available 24×7×365 that can be accessed anytime from anywhere. There are no downtimes associated with the monitoring tool.

- Easy integration with business processes: MaaS can generate alert based on specific business conditions. MaaS also supports multiple levels of escalation so that different user groups can get different levels of alerts.

- Cloud aware and cloud ready: Since MaaS is already in the cloud, MaaS works well with other cloud based products such as PaaS and SaaS. MaaS can monitor Amazon and Rackspace cloud infrastructure. MaaS can monitor any private cloud deployments that a customer might have.

- Zero maintenance overheads: As a MaaS, customer, you don't need to invest in a network operations centre. Neither do you need to invest an in-house team of qualified IT engineers to run the monitoring desk since the MaaS vendor is doing that on behalf of the customer.

When to use Monitoring as a Service (MaaS)?

Monitoring as a Service (MaaS) is an attractive choice for the following scenarios:

- Price sensitive customers: For small and medium enterprises, MaaS provides cost effective pay per use pricing model. Customers don't need to make any heavy investments neither in capital expenditures (capex) nor in operating expenditures (opex).

- Cloud based SaaS and PaaS offering add-on: MaaS provides a better technology fit for monitoring cloud based SaaS and PaaS offerings. MaaS can be provided as an add-on product offering along with SaaS and PaaS.

- Distributed infrastructure assets: In scenarios where the IT infrastructure assets are distributed across different locations and branch offices, MaaS is a good option since the monitoring infrastructure is centralized in the cloud and can easily monitor all distributed infrastructure assets.

- Mixture of cloud and On-Premise infrastructure: MaaS is already in the cloud. Hence in deployments where customer has a mix of on-premise and cloud infrastructure, MaaS provides good monitoring options for the hybrid environment.

- Multitenant monitoring requirements: For vendors offering multi-tenant functionality on their hosted services, MaaS provides a strong backend framework for monitoring the multi-tenant services and their availability.

Infrastructure Assets that can be Monitored using MaaS

MaaS is capable of monitoring all aspects of IT infrastructure assets:

- Servers and systems monitoring: Server Monitoring provides insights into the reliability of the server hardware such as Uptime, CPU, Memory and Storage. Server monitoring is an essential tool in determining functional and performance failures in the infrastructure assets.

- Database monitoring: Database monitoring on a proactive basis is necessary to ensure that databases are available for supporting business processes and functions. Database monitoring also provides performance analysis and trends which in turn can be used for fine tuning the database architecture and queries, thereby optimizing the database for your business requirements.

- Network monitoring: Network availability and network performance are two critical parameters that determine the successful utilization of any network – be it a LAN, MAN or WAN network. Disruptions in the network affect business productivity adversely and can bring regular operations to a standstill. Network monitoring provides pro-active information about network performance bottlenecks and source of network disruption.

- Storage monitoring: A reliable storage solution in your network ensures anytime availability of business critical data. Storage monitoring for SAN, NAS and RAID storage devices ensures that your storage solution are performing at the highest levels. Storage monitoring reduces downtime of storage devices and hence improves availability of business data.

- Applications monitoring: Applications Monitoring provides insight into resource usage, application availability and critical process usage for different Windows, Linux and other open source operating systems based applications. Applications Monitoring is essential for mission critical applications that cannot afford to have even a few minutes of downtime. With Application Monitoring, you can prevent application failures before they occur and ensure smooth operations.

- Cloud monitoring: Cloud Monitoring for any cloud infrastructure such as Amazon or Rackspace gives information about resource utilization and performance in the cloud. While cloud infrastructure is expected to have higher reliability than on-premise infrastructure, quite often resource utilization and performance metrics are not well understood in the cloud. Cloud monitoring provides insight into exact resource usage and performance metrics that can be used for optimizing the cloud infrastructure.

- Virtual infrastructure monitoring: Virtual Infrastructure based on common hypervisors such as ESX, Xen or Hyper-V provides flexibility to the infrastructure deployment and provides increased reliability against hardware failures. Monitoring virtual machines and related infrastructure gives information around resource usage such as memory, processor and storage.

Platform as a Service

Platform as a Service (PaaS) is an abstracted and integrated cloud-based computing environment that supports the development, running, and management of applications. Application components may exist in a cloud environment or may integrate with applications managed in private clouds or in data centers.

A primary value of a PaaS environment is that developers don't have to be concerned with some of the lower-level details of the environment. You can look at a software stack as a pyramid:

- Infrastructure as a Service (IaaS) is at the foundational level and includes capabilities such as operating systems, networks, virtual machines, and storage.

- In the middle is the PaaS environment, which includes services for developing and deploying applications.

- Software as a Service (SaaS) is at the top of the pyramid representing the actual applications offered to end users.

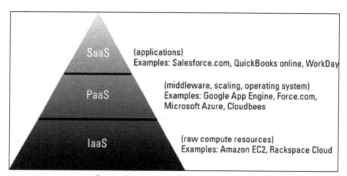

The software stack as a pyramid.

PaaS vendors create a managed environment that brings together a combination of components that would have been managed separately in a traditional development environment. Services integrated in PaaS include middleware, operating systems, and development and deployment services to support software development and delivery organizations.

The goal of the PaaS provider is to create an abstracted environment that supports an efficient, cost-effective, and repeatable process for the creation and deployment of high-quality applications. These applications are designed to be implemented in public or private cloud environments.

PaaS enables an organization to do the following:

- Leverage key middleware services without having to deal with the complexities of managing individual hardware and software elements.

- Access a complete stack of development and deployment tools via a web browser, a middleware environment where APIs can be used to plug into selected development and deployment tools. A developer might also leverage a full desktop development environment.

- Overcome the challenges of managing lots of individual development and deployment tools by providing a suite of integrated and standardized tools — operating systems, security products, and the like — that meet company requirements.

Platform as a Service (PaaS) can be viewed as having two fundamental parts: the platform and the service. The PaaS vendor doesn't just deliver the software making up the platform; it also continuously services the software. As new updates and new configurations become available, the PaaS vendor can immediately push them to its customers.

One of the decisions you need to make when beginning to use a PaaS is whether you want to maintain the software or if you want the vendor to be the administrator.

- If you choose to maintain the software yourself, you must set up, configure, maintain, and administer the PaaS yourself (either on a public or private cloud).

- Alternatively, you can have the vendor to provide these services. The result is reduced friction between the development and deployment teams. There will, of course, be situations in which it's critical for the internal team to control and manage a complex software environment.

Software as a Service

SaaS is a model of software deployment where an application is hosted as a service provided to customers across the Internet. SaaS is generally used to refer to business software rather than consumer software, which falls under Web 2.0. By removing the need to install and run an application on a user's own computer it is seen as a way for businesses to get the same benefits as commercial software with smaller cost outlay. SaaS can alleviate the burden of software maintenance and support but users relinquish control over software versions and requirements. Other terms that are used in this sphere include Platform as a Service (PaaS) and Infrastructure as a Service (IaaS). A public cloud sells services to anyone on the Internet. A private cloud is a proprietary network or a data center that supplies hosted services to a limited number of people. All the major companies have come up with their own code based or non-code based cloud computing frameworks. Some of the most prominent code-based frame works are:

- Java Google web Toolkit (Google App Engine).

- Python Djangno (Google App Engine).

- Ruby on Rails.

- Microsoft.NET (Azura Service Platform).

When a service provider uses public cloud resources to create their private cloud, the result is called a virtual private cloud. Private or public, the goal of cloud computing is to provide easy, scalable access to computing resources and IT services. SaaS is one of the methodologies of Cloud Computing, which is based on a "one-to-many" model whereby an application is shared across multiple clients. The exact definition of software as a service (SaaS) is open to debate, and asking different people would probably result in different definitions. Everyone believe that SaaS is going to have a major impact on the software industry, because software as a service will change the way people build, sell, buy, and use software. For this to happen, though, software vendors need resources and information about developing SaaS applications effectively. Still, most experts would probably agree on a few fundamental principles that distinguish SaaS from traditional packaged software on the one hand, and simple websites on the other.

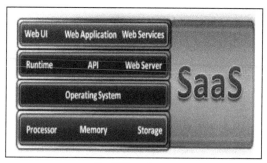

SaaS Structure.

Expressed most simply, software as a service can be characterized as "Software deployed as a hosted service and accessed over the Internet." Software as a service (or SaaS) is a way of delivering applications over the Internet-as a service. Instead of installing and maintaining software, you simply access it via the Internet, freeing yourself from complex software and hardware management. SaaS applications are sometimes called Web-based software, ondemand software, or hosted software. Whatever the name, SaaS applications run on a SaaS provider's servers. The provider manages access to the application, including security, availability, and performance. SaaS customers have no hardware or software to buy, install, maintain, or update. Access to applications is easy: you just need an Internet connection. This types of cloud computing delivers a single application through the browser to thousands of customers using a multitenant architecture. On the customer side, it means no upfront investment in servers or software licensing; on the provider side, with just one app to maintain, costs are low compared to conventional hosting.Salesforce.com is by far the best-known example among enterprise applications which provide CRM solutions as SaaS, but SaaS is also common for HR apps and has even worked its way up the food chain to ERP, with players such as Workday. Beside these, some of the desktop applications like Google Apps and Zoho Office had made their mark in the market.

The Application Architecture

Much like any other software, Software as a Service can also take advantage of Service Oriented Architecture to enable software applications to communicate with each other.

Each software service can act as a service provider, exposing its functionality to other applications via public brokers, and can also act as a service requester, incorporating data and functionality from other services. It is important to understand that the SaaS methodology requires system architecture capable of supporting peak usage demands and the ability to process large numbers of transactions in a secure and reliable environment.

The software would need to meet certain criteria's to work on a model such as this. The application would need to be well architected to sustain and provide the scalability, ease of use of the traditional desktop applications. There are three key points which would differentiate a successful SaaS application from an un-successful SaaS application:

- Scalability: Scaling the application means maximizing concurrency and using application resources more efficiently-for example, optimizing locking duration, statelessness, sharing pooled resources such as threads and network connections, caching reference data, and partitioning large databases.

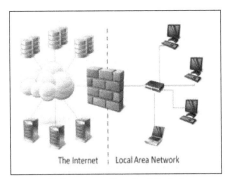

Software as Service Model.

- Multi-tenant efficient: Multi-tenancy may be the most significant paradigm shift that an architect accustomed to designing isolated, single-tenant applications has to make. For example, when a user at one company accesses customer information by using a CRM application service, the application instance that the user connects to may be accommodating users from dozens, or even hundreds, of other companies-all completely abstracted to any of the users. This requires an architecture that maximizes the sharing of resources across tenants, but that is still able to differentiate data belonging to different customers.

- Configurable: If a single application instance on a single server has to accommodate users from several different companies at once, you can't simply write custom code to customize the end-user experience-anything you do to customize the application for one customer will change the application for other customers as well. Instead of customizing the application in the traditional sense, then, each customer uses metadata to configure the way the application appears and behaves for its users. The challenge for the SaaS architect is to ensure that the task of configuring applications is simple and easy for the customers, without incurring extra development or operation costs for each configuration There can be four ways of hosting an application on the SaaS architecture. These are also called as the maturity models of SaaS.

- Ad-hoc/Custom: It is similar to the traditional application service provider (ASP) model of software delivery, dating back to the 1990s. Each customer has its own customized version of the hosted application, and runs its own instance of the application on the host's servers.

- Configurable: The vendor hosts a separate instance of the application for each customer (or tenant). Unlike the previous one, each instance is individually customized for the tenant, at this level, all instances use the same code implementation, and the vendor meets customers' needs by providing detailed configuration options that allow the customer to change how the application looks and behaves to its users. Despite being identical to one another at the code level, each instance remains wholly isolated from all the others.

- Configurable, multi-tenant-efficient: The vendor runs a single instance that serves every customer, with configurable metadata providing a unique user experience and feature set for each one. Authorization and security policies ensure that each customer's data is kept separate from that of other customers; and, from the end user's perspective, there is no indication that the application instance is being shared among multiple tenants. This approach eliminates the need to provide server space for as many instances as the vendor has customers, allowing for much more efficient use of computing resources than the second level, which translates directly to lower costs. A significant disadvantage of this approach is that the scalability of the application is limited.

- Scalable, configurable, multi-tenant-efficient: The vendor hosts multiple customers on a load-balanced farm of identical instances, with each customer's data kept separate, and with configurable metadata providing a unique user experience and feature set for each customer. Although the basic definition of cloud computing could also be used in Software as a Service, there are basic differences SaaS have when compared to other forms of cloud computing.

- Network or online access: SaaS is an online application or at least, a network based application. Users will never need any installation in their local gadgets which is connected to the local network or the internet. Usually, the application is launched through a browser which could provide access not only to the application but additional services from the vendor.

- Centralized management: control, monitoring and update could be done in a single location. The businesses that maintain the application will never need to manually make some changes in the local gadget but would provide improvement instead on the online application.

- Powerful communication features: Software as a Service is not only based on the fact that it provides functions for online processing, it also has powerful communication features. The mere fact that SaaS is often used online provides a strong backbone for Instant Messaging (Chat) or even voice calls (VOIP).

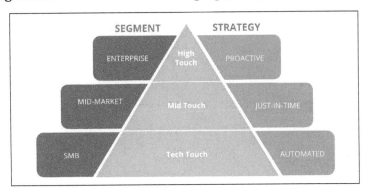

Advantages/Disadvantages of SaaS

Software as a Service is geared towards specific type of business. Although they can easily work in most enterprise settings, there are certain requirements SaaS would have that make it undesirable for some businesses.

- Powerful internet connection required: Although connection online is available almost everywhere, the rate of connection is never the same. Some areas can't provide strong internet connection and SaaS (as an online application) will have to load everything in the browser. The expected function might not even move forward without strong internet connectivity.

- Increased security risk: Attacks are highly likely if everything is launched online. This is probably the most challenging part in SaaS and in Cloud Computing industry. SaaS has increase security concerns compared to other platforms because of its consistent interaction with different users.

- Load balancing feature: One of the challenges the business would face in cloud computing and all SaaS applications is load balancing. Although industry giants offer load balancing, it will still require consistent monitoring from businesses.

API & MASH-UPS in SaaS

SaaS is getting better and better as new trends in the industry are slowly being implemented. Among the trends in cloud computing is the powerful integration of API or Application Programming Interface. Although SaaS could provide the functionality the business needs, upgrades are important to keep up with the demands. Instead of changing the application, businesses will just add an API in their application. The integration is easy and maximum efficiency of the additional function is expected.

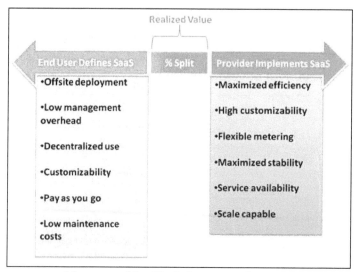

Advantage of SaaS in Software Development.

References

- Communications-as-a-service, cloud-computing: comparethecloud.net, Retrieved 14 August, 2019

- Infrastructure-as-a-Service-IaaS: searchcloudcomputing.techtarget.com, Retrieved 09 August, 2019

- Pouta-concepts: research.csc.fi, Retrieved 30 April, 2019

- Monitoring-as-a-service-maas-does-it-work, white-paper, resources: altnix.com, Retrieved 27 May, 2019

- What-is-platform-as-a-service-paas-in-cloud-computing, hybrid-cloud, cloud-computing, programming: dummies.com, Retrieved 10 March, 2019

Cloud Computing: Privacy and Security

Data security and privacy are the two most important factors that are essential for the future development of cloud computing. The security techniques include secure socket layer encryption, intrusion detection system, multi tenancy based access control, etc. This chapter closely examines the aspects and techniques associated with cloud computing privacy and security to provide an extensive understanding of the subject.

Cloud computing is very promising for the IT applications; however, there are still some problems to be solved for personal users and enterprises to store data and deploy applications in the cloud computing environment. One of the most significant barriers to adoption is data security, which is accompanied by issues including compliance, privacy, trust, and legal matters. The role of institutions and institutional evolution is close to privacy and security in cloud computing.

Data security has consistently been a major issue in IT. Data security becomes particularly serious in the cloud computing environment, because data are scattered in different machines and storage devices including servers, PCs, and various mobile devices such as wireless sensor networks and smart phones. Data security in the cloud computing is more complicated than data security in the traditional information systems.

To make the cloud computing be adopted by users and enterprise, the security concerns of users should be rectified first to make cloud environment trustworthy. The trustworthy environment is the basic prerequisite to win confidence of users to adopt such a technology.

Comparative studies on data security and privacy could help to enhance the user's trust by securing data in the cloud computing environment.

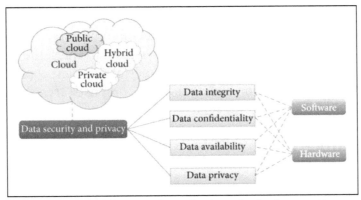

Organization of data security and privacy in cloud computing.

Data Integrity

Data integrity is one of the most critical elements in any information system. Generally, data integrity means protecting data from unauthorized deletion, modification, or fabrication. Managing entity's admittance and rights to specific enterprise resources ensures that valuable data and services are not abused, misappropriated, or stolen.

Data integrity is easily achieved in a standalone system with a single database. Data integrity in the standalone system is maintained via database constraints and transactions, which is usually finished by a database management system (DBMS). Transactions should follow ACID (atomicity, consistency, isolation, and durability) properties to ensure data integrity. Most databases support ACID transactions and can preserve data integrity.

Authorization is used to control the access of data. It is the mechanism by which a system determines what level of access a particular authenticated user should have to secure resources controlled by the system.

Data integrity in the cloud system means preserving information integrity. The data should not be lost or modified by unauthorized users. Data integrity is the basis to provide cloud computing service such as SaaS, PaaS, and IaaS. Besides data storage of large-scaled data, cloud computing environment usually provides data processing service. Data integrity can be obtained by techniques such as RAID-like strategies and digital signature.

Owing to the large quantity of entities and access points in a cloud environment, authorization is crucial in assuring that only authorized entities can interact with data. By avoiding the unauthorized access, organizations can achieve greater confidence in data integrity. The monitoring mechanisms offer the greater visibility into determining who or what may have altered data or system information, potentially affecting their integrity. Cloud computing providers are trusted to maintain data integrity and accuracy. However, it is necessary to build the third party supervision mechanism besides users and cloud service providers.

Verifying the integrity of data in the cloud remotely is the perquisite to deploy applications. Bowers et al. proposed a theoretical framework "Proofs of Retrievability" to realize the remote data integrity checking by combining error correction code and spot-checking. The HAIL system uses POR mechanism to check the storage of data in different clouds, and it can ensure the redundancy of different copies and realize the availability and integrity checking. Schiffman et al. proposed trusted platform module (TPM) remote checking to check the data integrity remotely.

Data Confidentiality

Data confidentiality is important for users to store their private or confidential data in the cloud. Authentication and access control strategies are used to ensure data confidentiality.

The data confidentiality, authentication, and access control issues in cloud computing could be addressed by increasing the cloud reliability and trustworthiness.

Because the users do not trust the cloud providers and cloud storage service providers are virtually impossible to eliminate potential insider threat, it is very dangerous for users to store their sensitive data in cloud storage directly. Simple encryption is faced with the key management problem and cannot support complex requirements such as query, parallel modification, and fine-grained authorization.

Homomorphic Encryption

Encryption is usually used to ensure the confidentiality of data. Homomorphic encryption is a kind of encryption system proposed by Rivest et al. It ensures that the cipher text algebraic operation results are consistent with the clear operation after encryption results; besides, the whole process does not need to decrypt the data. The implementation of this technique could well solve the confidentiality of data and data operations in the cloud.

Gentry firstly proposed the fully homomorphic encryption method, which can do any operation that can be performed in clear text without decrypting. It is an important breakthrough in the homomorphic encryption technology. However, the encryption system involves very complicated calculation, and the cost of computing and storage is very high. This leads to the fact that the fully homomorphic encryption is still far from real applications.

A cryptographic algorithm named Diffie-Hellman is proposed for secure communication, which is quite dissimilar to the key distribution management mechanism.

For more flexibility and enhanced security, a hybrid technique that combines multiple encryption algorithms such as RSA, 3DES, and random number generator has been proposed. RSA is useful for establishing secure communication connection through digital signature based authentication while 3DES is particularly useful for encryption of block data.

Encrypted Search and Database

Because the homomorphic encryption algorithm is inefficient, researchers turn to study the applications of limited homomorphic encryption algorithm in the cloud environment. Encrypted search is a common operation.

Manivannan and Sujarani have proposed a lightweight mechanism for database encryption known as transposition, substitution, folding, and shifting (TSFS) algorithm. However, as the numbers of keys are increased, the amount of computations and processing also increases.

In-Memory Database encryption technique is proposed for the privacy and security of sensitive data in untrusted cloud environment. A synchronizer exists between the owner and the client for seeking access to the data. Client would require a key from the synchronizer to decrypt the encrypted shared data it receives from the owner. The synchronizer is utilized to store the correlated shared data and the keys separately. A shortcoming of this technique is that the delays occur due to the additional communication with the central synchronizer. However, this limitation can be mitigated by adopting group encryption and through minimizing communication between nodes and synchronizer.

Huang and Tso proposed an asymmetric encryption mechanism for databases in the cloud. In the proposed mechanism, the commutative encryption is applied on data more than once and the order of public/private key used for encryption/decryption does not matter. Reencryption mechanism is also used in the proposed scheme which shows that the cipher-text data is encrypted once again for duality. Such schemes are very useful in the cloud applications where privacy is a key concern.

A privacy-preserving multikeyword ranked search approach over encrypted cloud data was proposed, which can search the encrypted cloud data and rank the search results without leakage of the user's privacy.

Distributive Storage

Distributive storage of data is also a promising approach in the cloud environment. Al-Zain et al. discussed the security issues related to data privacy in the cloud computing including integrity of data, intrusion, and availability of service in the cloud. To ensure the data integrity, one option could be to store data in multiple clouds or cloud databases. The data to be protected from internal or external unauthorized access are divided into chunks and Shamir's secret algorithm is used to generate a polynomial function against each chunk. Ram and Sreenivaasan have proposed a technique known as security as a service for securing cloud data. The proposed technique can achieve maximum security by dividing the user's data into pieces. These data chunks are then encrypted and stored in separated databases which follow the concept of data distribution over cloud. Because each segment of data is encrypted and separately distributed in databases over cloud, this provides enhanced security against different types of attacks.

Arfeen et al. describe the distribution of resources for cloud computing based on the tailored active measurement. The tailored measurement technique is based on the network design and the specific routes for the incoming and outgoing traffic and gradually changing the resources according to the user needs. Tailored measurement depends on the computing resources and storage resources. Because of the variable nature of networks, the allocation of resources at a particular time based on the tailored active method does not remain optimal. The resources may increase or decrease, so the system has to optimize changes in the user requirement either offline or on-line and the resource connectivity.

Hybrid Technique

A hybrid technique is proposed for data confidentiality and integrity, which uses both key sharing and authentication techniques. The connectivity between the user and the cloud service provider can be made more secure by utilizing powerful key sharing and authentication processes. RSA public key algorithm can be used for secure distribution of the keys between the user and cloud service providers.

A three-layered data security technique is proposed: The first layer is used for authenticity of the cloud user either by one factor or by two factor authentications; the second layer encrypts the user's data for ensuring protection and privacy; and the third layer does fast recovery of data through a speedy decryption process.

An event-based isolation of critical data in the cloud approach is proposed, TrustDraw, a transparent security extension for the cloud which combines virtual machine introspection (VMI) and trusted computing (TC).

Data Concealment

Data concealment could also be used to keep the data confidentiality in the cloud. Delettre et al. introduced a concealment concept for databases security. Data concealment approaches merge real data with the visual fake data to falsify the real data's volume. However, authorized users can easily differentiate and separate the fake data from the real data. Data concealment techniques increase the overall volume of real data but provide enhanced security for the private data. The objective of data concealment is to make the real data safe and secure from malicious users and attackers. Watermarking method can serve as a key for the real data. Only the authorized users have key of watermarking, so the authentication of users is the key to ensure the true data to be accessible for right users.

Deletion Confirmation

Deletion confirmation means that data could not be recovered when users delete their data after the deletion confirmation. The problem is very serious, because more than one copy exists in the cloud for the security and convenience of data recovery. When users delete their data with confirmation, all the copies of data should be deleted at the same time. However, there are some data recovery technologies that could recover the data deleted by users from the hard disks. So the cloud storage providers should ensure that the deleted data of users could not be recovered and used by other unauthenticated users.

To avoid the data be recovered and unauthenticatedly used, a possible approach is to encrypt the data before uploading to the cloud storage space. FADE system is based on technologies such as Ephemerizer. In the system, data are encrypted before they are uploaded to the cloud storage. When users decide to delete their data, the system just to apply the specific strategy to all the storage space could be covered with new data for replacing the deletion operation.

Data Availability

Data availability means the following: when accidents such as hard disk damage, IDC fire, and network failures occur, the extent that user's data can be used or recovered and how the users verify their data by techniques rather than depending on the credit guarantee by the cloud service provider alone.

The issue of storing data over the transboarder servers is a serious concern of clients because the cloud vendors are governed by the local laws and, therefore, the cloud clients should be cognizant of those laws. Moreover, the cloud service provider should ensure the data security, particularly data confidentiality and integrity. The cloud provider should share all such concerns with the client and build trust relationship in this connection. The cloud vendor should provide guarantees of data safety and explain jurisdiction of local laws to the clients.

Locating data can help users to increase their trust on the cloud. Cloud storage provides the transparent storage service for users, which can decrease the complexity of cloud, but it also decreases the control ability on data storage of users. Benson et al. studied the proofs of geographic replication and succeeded in locating the data stored in Amazon cloud.

Reliable Storage Agreement

The most common abnormal behavior of untrusted storage is that the cloud service providers may discard part of the user's update data, which is hard to be checked by only depending on the simple data encryption. Additionally, a good storage agreement needs to support concurrent modification by multiple users.

Mahajan et al. proposed Depot which can guarantee Fork-Join-Causal-Consistency and eventual consistency. It can effectively resist attacks such as discarding and it can support the implementation of other safety protections in the trusted cloud storage environment (such as Amazon S3).

Feldman et al. proposed SPORC, which can implement the safe and reliable real-time interaction and collaboration for multiple users with the help of the trusted cloud environment, and untrusted cloud servers can only access the encrypted data.

However, operation types supported by reliable storage protocol support are limited, and most of the calculations can only occur in the client.

Reliability of Hard-drive

Hard-drive is currently the main storage media in the cloud environment. Reliability of hard disks formulates the foundation of cloud storage. Pinheiro et al. studied the error rate of hard-drives based on the historical data of hard-drive. They found that the error rate of hard-drives is not closely relevant to the temperature and the frequency to be used, while the error rate of hard-drives has the strong clustering characteristics. Current SMART mechanism could not predict the error rate of hard disks. Tsai et al.

studied the correlation between the soft error and hard error of hard disks, and they also found that the soft error could not predict the hard errors of hard-drives precisely, only about 1/3 probability that hard errors follow the soft errors.

Data Privacy

Privacy is the ability of an individual or group to seclude themselves or information about themselves and thereby reveal them selectively. Privacy has the following elements:

- When: A subject may be more concerned about the current or future information being revealed than information from the past.

- How: A user may be comfortable if his/her friends can manually request his/her information, but the user may not like alerts to be sent automatically and frequently.

- Extent: A user may rather have his/her information reported as an ambiguous region rather than a precise point.

In commerce, consumer's context and privacy need to be protected and used appropriately. In organizations, privacy entails the application of laws, mechanisms, standards, and processes by which personally identifiable information is managed.

In the cloud, the privacy means when users visit the sensitive data, the cloud services can prevent potential adversary from inferring the user's behavior by the user's visit model (not direct data leakage). Researchers have focused on Oblivious RAM (ORAM) technology. ORAM technology visits several copies of data to hide the real visiting aims of users. ORAM has been widely used in software protection and has been used in protecting the privacy in the cloud as a promising technology. Stefanov et al. proposed that a path ORAM algorithm is state-of-the-art implementation.

The privacy issues differ according to different cloud scenarios and can be divided into four subcategories as follows:

- How to enable users to have control over their data when the data are stored and processed in cloud and avoid theft, nefarious use, and unauthorized resale.

- How to guarantee data replications in a jurisdiction and consistent state, where replicating user data to multiple suitable locations is an usual choice, and avoid data loss, leakage, and unauthorized modification or fabrication.

- Which party is responsible for ensuring legal requirements for personal information.

- To what extent cloud subcontractors are involved in processing which can be properly identified, checked, and ascertained.

Service Abuse

Service abuse means that attackers can abuse the cloud service and acquire extra data or destroy the interests of other users.

User data may be abused by other users. Deduplication technology has been widely used in the cloud storage, which means that the same data often were stored once but shared by multiple different users. This will reduce the storage space and cut down the cost of cloud service providers, but attackers can access the data by knowing the hash code of the stored files. Then, it is possible to leak the sensitive data in the cloud. So proof of ownership approach has been proposed to check the authentication of cloud users.

Attackers may lead to the cost increase of cloud service. Fraudulent resource consumption is a kind of attack on the payment for cloud service. Attackers can consume the specific data to increase the cost for cloud service payment. Idziorek et al. proposed this question and researched on the detection and identification of fraud resource consumption.

Averting Attacks

The cloud computing facilitates huge amount of shared resources on the Internet. Cloud systems should be capable of averting Denial of Service (DoS) attacks.

Shen et al. analyzed requirement of security services in cloud computing. The authors suggest integrating cloud services for trusted computing platform (TCP) and trusted platform support services (TSS). The trusted model should bear characteristics of confidentiality, dynamically building trust domains and dynamic of the services. Cloud infrastructures require that user transfers their data into cloud merely based on trust. Neisse et al. analyzed indifferent attacks scenarios on Xen cloud platform to evaluate cloud services based on trust. Security of data and trust in cloud computing is the key point for its broader adoption.

Yeluri et al. focused on the cloud services from security point of view and explored security challenges in cloud when deploying the services. Identity management, data recovery and management, security in cloud confidentiality, trust, visibility, and application architecture are the key points for ensuring security in cloud computing.

Identity Management

Cloud computing provides a podium to use wide range of Internet-based services. But besides its advantages, it also increases the security threat when a trusted third party is involved. By involving a trusted third party, there is a chance of heterogeneity of users which affects security in the cloud. A possible solution to this problem could be to use a trusted third party independent approach for Identity Management to use identity data on untrusted hosts.

Squicciarini et al. focused on problems of data leakage and loss of privacy in cloud computing. Different levels of protections can be used to prevent data leakage and privacy loss in the cloud. Cloud computing provides new business services that are based on demand. Cloud networks have been built through dynamic virtualization of hardware, software, and datasets. Cloud security infrastructure and the trust reputation management play a vital role to upgrade the cloud services. The Internet access security, server access security, program access security, and database security are the main security issues in the cloud.

Secure Distributed Data Storage in Cloud Computing

Technologies for Data Security in Cloud Computing

- Database outsourcing and query integrity assurance: Researchers have pointed out that storing data into and fetching data from devices and machines behind a cloud are essentially a novel form of database outsourcing.

- Data integrity in untrustworthy storage: One of the main challenges that prevent end users from adopting cloud storage services is the fear of losing data or data corruption. It is critical to relieve the users' fear by providing technologies that enable users to check the integrity of their data.

- Web-application-based security: Once the dataset is stored remotely, a Web browser is one of the most convenient approaches that end users can use to access their data on remote services. In the era of cloud computing, Web security plays a more important role than ever.

- Multimedia data security: With the development of high-speed network technologies and large bandwidth connections, more and more multimedia data are being stored and shared in cyber space. The security requirements for video, audio, pictures, or images are different from other applications.

Database Outsourcing and Query Integrity Assurance

In recent years, database outsourcing has become an important component of cloud computing. Due to the rapid advancements in network technology, the cost of transmitting a terabyte of data over long distances has decreased significantly in the past decade. In addition, the total cost of data management is five to ten times higher than the initial acquisition costs. As a result, there is a growing interest in outsourcing database management tasks to third parties that can provide these tasks for a much lower cost due to the economy of scale. This new outsourcing model has the benefits of reducing the costs for running Database Management Systems (DBMS) independently and enabling enterprises to concentrate on their main businesses. Figure demonstrates the general architecture of a database outsourcing environment with clients. The database owner outsources its data management tasks, and clients send queries to the untrusted service provider. Let T denote the data to be outsourced. The data T are is preprocessed, encrypted, and stored at the service provider. For evaluating queries, a user rewrites a set of queries Q against T to queries against the encrypted database.

The outsourcing of databases to a third-party service provider was first introduced by Hacigümüs et al. Generally, there are two security concerns in database outsourcing. These are data privacy and query integrity.

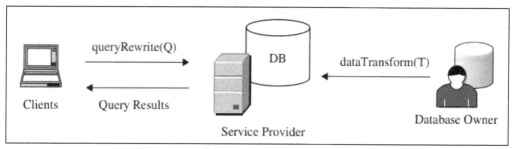

The system architecture of database outsourcing.

Data Privacy Protection: Hacigümüs et al. proposed a method to execute SQL queries over encrypted databases. Their strategy is to process as much of a query as possible by the service providers, without having to decrypt the data. Decryption and the remainder of the query processing are performed at the client side. Agrawal et al. proposed an order-preserving encryption scheme for numeric values that allows any comparison operation to be directly applied on encrypted data. Their technique is able to handle updates, and new values can be added without requiring changes in the encryption of other values. Generally, existing methods enable direct execution of encrypted queries on encrypted datasets and allow users to ask identity queries over data of different encryptions. The ultimate goal of this research direction is to make queries in encrypted databases as efficient as possible while preventing adversaries from learning any useful knowledge about the data. However, researches in this field did not consider the problem of query integrity.

Query Integrity Assuranc: In addition to data privacy, an important security concern in the database outsourcing paradigm is query integrity. Query integrity examines the trustworthiness of the hosting environment. When a client receives a query result from the service provider, it wants to be assured that the result is both correct and complete, where correct means that the result must originate in the owner's data and not has been tampered with, and complete means that the result includes all records satisfying the query. Devanbu et al. authenticate data records using the Merkle hash tree, which is based on the idea of using a signature on the root of the Merkle hash tree to generate a proof of correctness. Mykletun et al. studied and compared several signature methods that can be utilized in data authentication, and they identified the problem of completeness but did not provide a solution. Pang et al. utilized an aggregated signature to sign each record with the information from neighboring records by assuming that all the records are sorted with a certain order. The method ensures the completeness of a selection query by checking the aggregated signature. But it has difficulties in handling multipoint selection query of which the result tuples occupy a noncontinuous region of the ordered sequence.

The work in Li et al. utilizes Merkle hash tree-based methods to audit the completeness of query results, but since the Merkle hash tree also applies the signature of the root Merkle tree node, a similar difficulty exists. Besides, the network and CPU overhead on the client side can be prohibitively high for some types of queries. In some extreme cases, the overhead could be as high as processing these queries locally, which can undermine the benefits of database outsourcing. Sion proposed a mechanism called the challenge token and uses it as a probabilistic proof that the server has executed the query over the entire database. It can handle arbitrary types of queries including joins and does not assume that the underlying data is ordered. However, the approach is not applied to the adversary model where an adversary can first compute the complete query result and then delete the tuples specifically corresponding to the challenge tokens. Besides, all the aforementioned methods must modify the DBMS kernel in order to provide proof of integrity.

Recently, Wang et al. proposed a solution named dual encryption to ensure query integrity without requiring the database engine to perform any special function beyond query processing. Dual encryption enables cross-examination of the outsourced data, which consist of (a) the original data stored under a certain encryption scheme and (b) another small percentage of the original data stored under a different encryption scheme. Users generate queries against the additional piece of data and analyze their results to obtain integrity assurance.

For auditing spatial queries, Yang et al proposed the MR-tree, which is an authenticated data structure suitable for verifying queries executed on outsourced spatial databases. The authors also designed a caching technique to reduce the information sent to the client for verification purposes. Four spatial transformation mechanisms are presented in Yiu et al. for protecting the privacy of outsourced private spatial data. The data owner selects transformation keys that are shared with trusted clients, and it is infeasible to reconstruct the exact original data points from the transformed points without the key. However, both aforementioned researches did not consider data privacy protection and query integrity auditing jointly in their design. The state-of-the-art technique that can ensure both privacy and integrity for outsourced spatial data is proposed in Ku et al. In particular, the solution first employs a one-way spatial transformation method based on Hilbert curves, which encrypts the spatial data before outsourcing and hence ensures its privacy. Next, by probabilistically replicating a portion of the data and encrypting it with a different encryption key, the authors devise a mechanism for the client to audit the trustworthiness of the query results.

Data Integrity in Untrustworthy Storage

While the transparent cloud provides flexible utility of network-based resources, the fear of loss of control on their data is one of the major concerns that prevent end users from migrating to cloud storage services. Actually it is a potential risk that the storage infrastructure providers become self-interested, untrustworthy, or even malicious. There are different motivations whereby a storage service provider could become untrustworthy—for instance, to cover the consequence of a mistake in operation, or deny the vulnerability in the system after the data have been stolen by an adversary.

Actually, before the term "cloud computing" appears as an IT term, there are several remote data storage checking protocols that have been suggested. Later research has summarized that in practice a remote data possession checking protocol has to satisfy the following five requirements. Note that the verifier could be either the data owner or a trusted third party, and the prover could be the storage service provider or storage medium owner or system administrator.

- Requirement 1: It should not be a pre-requirement that the verifier has to possess a complete copy of the data to be checked. And in practice, it does not make sense for a verifier to keep a duplicated copy of the content to be verified. As long as it serves the purpose well, storing a more concise contents digest of the data at the verifier should be enough.

- Requirement 2: The protocol has to be very robust considering the untrustworthy prover. A malicious prover is motivated to hide the violation of data integrity. The protocol should be robust enough that such a prover ought to fail in convincing the verifier.

- Requirement 3: The amount of information exchanged during the verification operation should not lead to high communication overhead.

- Requirement 4: The protocol should be computationally efficient.

- Requirement 5: It ought to be possible to run the verification an unlimited number of times.

A PDP-Based Integrity Checking Protocol: Ateniese et al. proposed a protocol based on the provable data procession (PDP) technology, which allows users to obtain a probabilistic proof from the storage service providers. Such a proof will be used as evidence that their data have been stored there. One of the advantages of this protocol is that the proof could be generated by the storage service provider by accessing only a small portion of the whole dataset. At the same time, the amount of the metadata that end users are required to store is also small—that is, $O(1)$. Additionally, such a small amount data exchanging procedure lowers the overhead in the communication channels too.

Figure below presents the flowcharts of the protocol for provable data possession. The data owner, the client in the figure, executes the protocol to verify that a dataset is stored in an outsourced storage machine as a collection of n blocks. Before uploading the data into the remote storage, the data owner pre-processes the dataset and a piece of metadata is generated. The metadata are stored at the data owner's side, and the dataset will be transmitted to the storage server. The cloud storage service stores the dataset and sends the data to the user in responding to queries from the data owner in the future.

As part of pre-processing procedure, the data owner (client) may conduct operations on the data such as expanding the data or generating additional metadata to be stored at the cloud server side. The data owner could execute the PDP protocol before the local copy is deleted to ensure that the uploaded copy has been stored at the server machines successfully. Actually, the data owner may encrypt a dataset before transferring them to the storage machines. During the time that data are stored in the cloud, the data owner can generate a "challenge" and send it to the service provider to ensure that the storage server has stored the dataset. The data owner requests that the storage server generate a metadata based on the stored data and then send it back. Using the previously stored local metadata, the owner verifies the response.

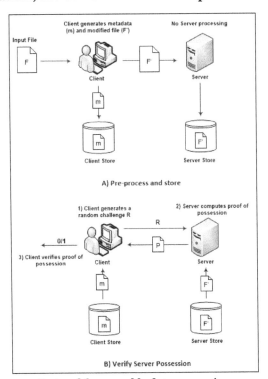

Protocol for provable data possession.

On the behalf of the cloud service provider's side, the server may receive multiple challenges from different users at the same time. For the sake of availability, it is highly desired to minimize not only the computational overhead of each individual calculation, but also the number of data blocks to be accessed. In addition, considering the pressure on the communication networks, minimal bandwidth consumption also implies that there are a limited amount of metadata included in the response generated by the server. In the protocol shown in Figure, the PDP scheme only randomly accesses one subdata block when the sample the stored dataset. Hence, the PDP scheme probabilistically guarantees the data integrity. It is mandatory to access the whole dataset if a deterministic guarantee is required by the user.

An Enhanced Data Possession Checking Protocol: Sebe et al. pointed out that the above PDP-based protocol does not satisfy Requirement #2 with 100% probability. An enhanced protocol has been proposed based on the idea of the Diffie-Hellman scheme. It is claimed that this protocol satisfies all five requirements and is computationally more efficient than the PDP-based protocol. The verification time has been shortened at the setup stage by taking advantage of the trade-offs between the computation times required by the prover and the storage required at the verifier. The setup stage sets the following parameters:

- p and q: two primary factors chosen by the verifier.

- N = pq: a public RSA modulus created by the verifier.

- $\theta(N) = (p-1)(q-1)$: the private key of the verifier, which is the secret only known by the verifier.

- l: an integer that is chosen depending on the trade-offs between the computation time required at the prover and the storage required at the verifier.

- t: a security parameter.

- PRNG: a pseudorandom number generator, which generates t-bit integer values.

The protocol is presented as follows:

At first, the verifier generates the digest of data m:

- Break the data m into n pieces, each is l-bit. Let $m_1, m_2 ..., m_n$ $(n = \lceil |m|/l \rceil)$ be the integer values corresponding to fragments of m.

- For each fragment m_i, compute and store $M_i = m_i \bmod \theta(N)$.

The challengeresponse verification protocol is as follows:

The verifier:

- Generates a random seed S and a random element $\alpha \in Z_N \setminus \{1, N-1\}$.

- Sends the challenge (α, S) to the prover.

Upon receiving the challenge, the prover:

- Generates n pseudorandom values $c_i \in [1, 2^t]$ for i = 1 to n, using PRNG seeded by S.

- Calculates $r = \sum_{i=1}^{n} c_i m_i$ and $R = \alpha^r \mod N$.
- Sends R to the verifier.

The verifier:

- Regenerates the n pseudorandom values $c_i \in [1, 2^t]$ for i = 1 to n, using PRNG seeded by S.
- Calculates $r' \sum_{i=1}^{n} c_i m_i \mod \Phi(N)$ R' = $\alpha^{r'} \mod N$.
- Checks whether R = R'.

Due to the space constraints, this section only introduces the basic principles and the working flows of the protocols for data integrity checking in untrustworthy storages. The proof of the correctness, security analysis, and the performance analysis of the protocols are left for the interested readers to explore deeper.

Web-application-based Security

In cloud computing environments, resources are provided as a service over the Internet in a dynamic, virtualized, and scalable way [29, 30]. Through cloud computing services, users access business applications on-line from a Web browser, while the software and data are stored on the servers. Therefore, in the era of cloud computing, Web security plays a more important role than ever. The Web site server is the first gate that guards the vast cloud resources. Since the cloud may operate continuously to process millions of dollars' worth of daily on-line transactions, the impact of any Web security vulnerability will be amplified at the level of the whole cloud.

Web attack techniques are often referred as the class of attack. When any Web security vulnerability is identified, attacker will employ those techniques to take advantage of the security vulnerability. The types of attack can be categorized in Authentication, Authorization, Client-Side Attacks, Command Execution, Information Disclosure, and Logical Attacks.

Authentication: Authentication is the process of verifying a claim that a subject made to act on behalf of a given principal. Authentication attacks target a Web site's method of validating the identity of a user, service, or application, including Brute Force, Insufficient Authentication, and Weak Password Recovery Validation. Brute Force attack employs an automated process to guess a person's username and password by trial and error. In the Insufficient Authentication case, some sensitive content or functionality are protected by "hiding" the specific location in obscure string but still remains accessible directly through a specific URL. The attacker could discover those URLs through a Brute Force probing of files and directories. Many Web sites provide password recovery service. This service will automatically recover the user name or password to the user if she or he can answer some questions defined as part of the user registration process.

If the recovery questions are either easily guessed or can be skipped, this Web site is considered to be Weak Password Recovery Validation.

Authorization: Authorization is used to verify if an authenticated subject can perform a certain operation. Authentication must precede authorization. For example, only certain users are allowed to access specific content or functionality.

Authorization attacks use various techniques to gain access to protected areas beyond their privileges. One typical authorization attack is caused by Insufficient Authorization. When a user is authenticated to a Web site, it does not necessarily mean that she should have access to certain content that has been granted arbitrarily. Insufficient authorization occurs when a Web site does not protect sensitive content or functionality with proper access control restrictions. Other authorization attacks are involved with session. Those attacks include Credential/Session Prediction, Insufficient Session Expiration, and Session Fixation.

In many Web sites, after a user successfully authenticates with the Web site for the first time, the Web site creates a session and generate a unique "session ID" to identify this session. This session ID is attached to subsequent requests to the Web site as "Proof" of the authenticated session.

Credential/Session Prediction attack deduces or guesses the unique value of a session to hijack or impersonate a user.

Insufficient Session Expiration occurs when an attacker is allowed to reuse old session credentials or session IDs for authorization. For example, in a shared computer, after a user accesses a Web site and then leaves, with Insufficient Session Expiration, an attacker can use the browser's back button to access Web pages previously accessed by the victim.

Session Fixation forces a user's session ID to an arbitrary value via CrossSite Scripting or peppering the Web site with previously made HTTP requests. Once the victim logs in, the attacker uses the predefined session ID value to impersonate the victim's identity.

Client-Side Attacks: The Client-Side Attacks lure victims to click a link in a malicious Web page and then leverage the trust relationship expectations of the victim for the real Web site. In Content Spoofing, the malicious Web page can trick a user into typing user name and password and will then use this information to impersonate the user.

Cross-Site Scripting (XSS) launches attacker-supplied executable code in the victim's browser. The code is usually written in browser-supported scripting languages such as JavaScript, VBScript, ActiveX, Java, or Flash. Since the code will run within the security context of the hosting Web site, the code has the ability to read, modify, and transmit any sensitive data, such as cookies, accessible by the browser.

Cross-Site Request Forgery (CSRF) is a serve security attack to a vulnerable site that does not take the checking of CSRF for the HTTP/HTTPS request. Assuming that the attacker knows the URLs of the vulnerable site which are not protected by CSRF checking and the victim's browser stores credentials such as cookies of the vulnerable site, after luring the victim to click a link in a malicious Web page, the attacker can forge the victim's identity and access the vulnerable Web site on victim's behalf.

Command Execution: The Command Execution attacks exploit server-side vulnerabilities to execute remote commands on the Web site. Usually, users supply inputs to the Web-site to request services. If a Web application does not properly sanitize user-supplied input before using it within application code, an attacker could alter command execution on the server. For example, if the length of input is not checked before use, buffer overflow could happen and result in denial of service. Or if the Web application uses user input to construct statements such as SQL, XPath, C/C11 Format String, OS system command, LDAP, or dynamic HTML, an attacker may inject arbitrary executable code into the server if the user input is not properly filtered.

Information Disclosure: The Information Disclosure attacks acquire sensitive information about a web site revealed by developer comments, error messages, or well-know file name conventions. For example, a Web server may return a list of files within a requested directory if the default file is not present. This will supply an attacker with necessary information to launch further attacks against the system. Other types of Information Disclosure includes using special paths such as "." and ".." for Path Traversal, or uncovering hidden URLs via Predictable Resource Location.

Logical Attacks: Logical Attacks involve the exploitation of a Web application's logic flow. Usually, a user's action is completed in a multi-step process. The procedural workflow of the process is called application logic. A common Logical Attack is Denial of Service (DoS). DoS attacks will attempt to consume all available resources in the Web server such as CPU, memory, disk space, and so on, by abusing the functionality provided by the Web site. When any one of any system resource reaches some utilization threshold, the Web site will no long be responsive to normal users. DoS attacks are often caused by Insufficient Anti-automation where an attacker is permitted to automate a process repeatedly. An automated script could be executed thousands of times a minute, causing potential loss of performance or service.

Multimedia Data Security Storage

With the rapid developments of multimedia technologies, more and more multimedia contents are being stored and delivered over many kinds of devices, databases, and networks. Multimedia Data Security plays an important role in the data storage to protect multimedia data. Recently, how storage multimedia contents are delivered by both different providers and users has attracted much attentions and many applications.

Protection from Unauthorized Replication: Contents replication is required to generate and keep multiple copies of certain multimedia contents. For example, content distribution networks (CDNs) have been used to manage content distribution to large numbers of users, by keeping the replicas of the same contents on a group of geographically distributed surrogates. Although the replication can improve the system performance, the unauthorized replication causes some problems such as contents copyright, waste of replication cost, and extra control overheads.

Protection from Unauthorized Replacement: As the storage capacity is limited, a replacement process must be carried out when the capacity exceeds its limit. It means the situation that a currently stored content must be removed from the storage space in order to make space for the new coming content. However, how to decide which content should be removed is very important. If an unauthorized replacement happens, the content which the user doesn't want to delete will be removed resulting in an accident of the data loss. Furthermore, if the important content such as system data is removed by unauthorized replacement, the result will be more serious.

Protection from Unauthorized Pre-fetching: The Pre-fetching is widely deployed in Multimedia Storage Network Systems between server databases and end users' storage disks. That is to say, If a content can be predicted to be requested by the user in future requests, this content will be fetched from the server database to the end user before this user requests it, in order to decrease user response time. Although the Pre-fetching shows its efficiency, the unauthorized pre-fetching should be avoided to make the system to fetch the necessary content.

Open Questions and Challenges

Almost all the current commercial cloud service providers claim that their platforms are secure and robust. On one hand, they adopt robust cipher algorithms for confidentiality of stored data; on the other hand, they depend on network communication security protocols such as SSL, IPSec, or others to protect data in transmission in the network. For the service availability and high performance, they choose virtualization technologies and apply strong authentication and authorization schemes in their cloud domains. However, as a new infrastructure/platform leading to new application/service models of the future's IT industry, the requirement for a security cloud computing is different from the traditional security problems.

Encryption, digital signatures, network security, firewalls, and the isolation of virtual environments all are important for cloud computing security, but these alone won't make cloud computing reliable for consumers.

Concerns at Different Levels

The cloud computing environment consists of three levels of abstractions:

- The cloud infrastructure providers: Which is at the back end, own and manage the network infrastructure and resources including hardware devices and system software.

- The cloud service providers: Which offer services such as on-demand computing, utility computing, data processing, software services, and platforms for developing application software.

- The cloud consumers: Which is at the front end of the cloud computing environment and consists of two major categories of users: (a) application developers, who take advantage of the hardware infrastructure and the software platforms to construct application software for ultimate end users; and (b) end users, who carry out their daily works using the ondemand computing, software services, and utility services.

Regarding data/information security, the users at different levels have variant expectations and concerns due to the roles they play in the data's life cycle.

From the perspective of cloud consumers, normally who are the data owners, the concerns are essentially raised from the loss of control when the data are in a cloud. As the dataset is stored in unknown third-party infrastructure, the owner loses not only the advantages of endpoint restrictions and management, but also the fine-grained credential quality control. The uncertainty about the privacy and the doubt about the vulnerability are also resulted from the disappearing physical and logical network boundaries.

The main security concerns of the end users include confidentiality, loss of control of data, and the undisclosed security profiles of the cloud service and infrastructure providers. The users' data are transmitted between the local machine and cloud service provider for variant operations, and they are also persistently stored in the cloud infrastructure provider's facilities. During this procedure, data might not be adequately protected while they are being moved within the systems or across multiple sites owned by these providers. The data owner also cannot check the security assurances before using the service from the cloud, because the actual security capabilities associated with the providers are transparent to the user/owner.

The problem becomes more complicated when the service and infrastructure providers are not the same, and this implies additional communication links in the chain. Involving a third party in the services also introduces an additional vector of attack. Actually, in practice there are more challenging scenarios. For instance, consider that multiple end users have different sets of security requirements while using the same service offered by an individual cloud service provider. To handle such kind of complexity, one single set of security provisions does not fit all in cloud computing. The scenarios also imply that the back-end infrastructure and/or service providers must be capable of supporting multiple levels requirements of security similar to those guaranteed by front-end service provider.

From the perspective of the cloud service providers, the main concern with regard to protecting users' data is the transfer of data from devices and servers within the control of the users to its own devices and subsequently to those of the cloud infrastructure, where the data is stored. The data are stored in cloud service provider's devices on multiple machines across the entire virtual layer. The data are also hosted on devices that belong to infrastructure provider. The cloud service provider needs to ensure users that the security of their data is being adequately addressed between the partners, that their virtual environments are isolated with sufficient protection, and that the cleanup of outdated images is being suitably managed at its site and cloud infrastructure provider's storage machines.

Undoubtedly, the cloud infrastructure providers' security concerns are not less than those of end users or cloud service providers. The infrastructure provider knows that a single point of failure in its infrastructure security mechanisms would allow hackers to take out thousands of data bytes owned by the clients, and most likely data owned by other enterprises. The cloud infrastructure providers need to ask the following questions:

- How are the data stored in its physical devices protected?

- How does the cloud infrastructure manage the backup of data, and the destruction of outdated data, at its site?

- How can the cloud infrastructure control access to its physical devices and the images stored on those devices?

Technical and Nontechnical Challenges

The above analysis has shown that besides technical challenges, the cloud computing platform (infrastructure and service) providers are also required to meet a couple of nontechnical issues—for example, the lack of legal requirements on data security to service providers. More specifically, the following technical challenges need to be addressed in order to make cloud computing acceptable for common consumers:

- Open security profiling of services that is available to end users and verifiable automatically. Service providers need to disclose in detail the levels of specific security properties rather than providing blanket assurances of "secure" services.

- The cloud service/infrastructure providers are required to enable end users to remotely control their virtual working platforms in the cloud and monitor others' access to their data. This includes the capability of finegrained accessing controls on their own data, no matter where the data files are stored and processed. In addition, it is ideal to possess the capability of restricting any unauthorized third parties from manipulating users' data, including the cloud service provider, as well as cloud infrastructure providers.

- Security compliance with existing standards could be useful to enhance cloud security. There must be consistency between the security requirements and/or policies of service consumers and the security assurances of cloud providers.

- It is mandatory for the providers to ensure that software is as secure as they claim. These assurances may include certification of the security of the systems in question. A certificate—issued after rigorous testing according to agreed criteria (e.g., ISO/IEC 15408)—can ensure the degree of reliability of software in different configurations and environments as claimed by the cloud providers.

Regarding the above technical issues, actually they have been and will be addressed by constant development of new technologies. However, some special efforts are needed to meet the nontechnical challenges. For instance, one of the most difficult issue to be solved in cloud computing is the users' fear of losing control over their data. Because end users feel that they do not clearly know where and how their data are handled, or when the users realize that their data are processed, transmitted, and stored by devices under the control of some strangers, it is reasonable for them to be concerned about things happening in the cloud. In traditional work environments, in order to keep a dataset secure, the operator just keeps it away from the threat. In cloud computing, however, it seems that datasets are moved closer to their threats; that is, they are transmitted to, stored in, and manipulated by remote devices controlled by third parties, not by the owner of the data set. It is recognized that this is partly a psychological issue; but until end users have enough information and insight that make them believe cloud computing security and its dynamics, the fear is unlikely to go away.

End-user license agreements (EULAs) and vendor privacy policies are not enough to solve this psychological issue. Service-level agreements (SLAs) need to specify the preferred security assurances of consumers in detail. Proper business models and risk assessments related to cloud computing security need to be defined. In this new security-sensitive design paradigm, the ability to change one's mind is crucial, because consumers are more security-aware than ever before. They not only make the service-consuming decision on cost and service, they also want to see real, credible security measures from cloud providers.

Cloud Computing Security Risks

Loss or Theft of Intellectual Property

Companies increasingly store sensitive data in the cloud. An analysis by Skyhigh found that 21% of files uploaded to cloud-based file sharing services contain sensitive data including intellectual property. When a cloud service is breached, cyber criminals can gain access to this sensitive data. Absent a breach, certain services can even pose a risk if their terms and conditions claim ownership of the data uploaded to them.

Compliance Violations and Regulatory Actions

These days, most companies operate under some sort of regulatory control of their information, whether it's HIPAA for private health information, FERPA for confidential student records, or one of many other government and industry regulations. Under these mandates, companies must know where their data is, who is able to access it, and how it is being protected. BYOC often violates every one of these tenets, putting the organization in a state of non-compliance, which can have serious repercussions.

Loss of Control over End User Actions

When companies are in the dark about workers using cloud services, those employees can be doing just about anything and no one would know—until it's too late. For instance, a salesperson who is about to resign from the company could download a report of all customer contacts, upload the data to a personal cloud storage service, and then access that information once she is employed by a competitor. The preceding example is actually one of the more common insider threats today.

Malware Infections that Unleash a Targeted Attack

Cloud services can be used as a vector of data exfiltration. Skyhigh uncovered a novel data exfiltration technique whereby attackers encoded sensitive data into video files and uploaded them to YouTube. We've also detected malware that exfiltrates sensitive data via a private Twitter account 140 characters at a time. In the case of the Dyre malware variant, cyber criminals used file sharing services to deliver the malware to targets using phishing attacks.

Contractual Breaches with Customers or Business Partners

Contracts among business parties often restrict how data is used and who is authorized to access it. When employees move restricted data into the cloud without authorization, the business contracts may be violated and legal action could ensue. Consider the example of a cloud service that maintains the right to share all data uploaded to the service with third parties in its terms and conditions, thereby breaching a confidentiality agreement the company made with a business partner.

Diminished Customer Trust

Data breaches inevitably result in diminished trust by customers. In one of the larges breaches of payment card data ever, cyber criminals stole over 40 million customer credit and debit card numbers from Target. The breach led customers to stay away from Target stores, and led to a loss of business for the company, which ultimately impacted the company's revenue.

Data Breach Requiring Disclosure and Notification to Victims

If sensitive or regulated data is put in the cloud and a breach occurs, the company may be required to disclose the breach and send notifications to potential victims. Certain regulations such as HIPAA and HITECH in the healthcare industry and the EU Data Protection Directive require these disclosures. Following legally-mandated breach disclosures, regulators can levy fines against a company and it's not uncommon for consumers whose data was compromised to file lawsuits.

Increased Customer Churn

If customers even suspect that their data is not fully protected by enterprise-grade security controls, they may take their business elsewhere to a company they can trust. A growing chorus of critics are instructing consumers to avoid cloud companies who do not protect customer privacy.

Revenue Losses

News of the Target data breach made headlines and many consumers stayed away from Target stores over the busy holiday season, leading to a 46% drop in the company's quarterly profit. The company estimated the breach ultimate cost $148 million. As a result, the CIO and CEO resigned and many are now calling for increased oversight by the board of directors over cyber security programs.

Security as a Service

Security as a Service (SECaaS) can most easily be described as a cloud delivered model for outsourcing cybersecurity services. Much like Software as a Service, SECaaS provides security services on a subscription basis hosted by cloud providers. Security as a Service solutions have become increasingly popular for corporate infrastructures as a way to ease the in-house security team's responsibilities, scale security needs as the business grows, and avoid the costs and maintenance of on-premise alternatives.

Benefits of Security as a Service

Cost Savings

One of the biggest benefits of a Security as a Service model is that it saves a business money. A cloud delivered service is often available in subscription tiers with several upgrade options so a business only pays for what they need, when they need. It also eliminates the need for expertise.

The Latest Security Tools and Updates

When you implement SECaaS, you get to work with the latest security tools and re-sources. For anti-virus and other security tools to be effective, they must be kept up to date with the latest patches and virus definitions. By deploying SECaaS throughout your organization, these updates are managed for you on every server, PC and mobile device.

Faster Provisioning and Greater Agility

One of the best things about as-a-service solutions is that your users can be given access to these tools immediately. SECaaS solutions can be scaled up or down as required and are provided on demand where and when you need them. That means no more uncertainty when it comes to deployment or updates as everything is managed for you by your SECaaS provider and visible to you through a web-enabled dashboard.

Free Up Resources

When security provisions are managed externally, your IT teams can focus on what is important to your organization. SECaaS frees up resources, gives you total visibility through management dashboards and the confidence that your IT security is being managed competently by a team of outsourced security specialists. You can also choose for your IT teams to take control of security processes if you prefer and manage all policy and system changes through a web interface.

Security as a Service Examples

The range of SECaaS services currently available is vast and offers protection at the most granular level. Some examples include:

- Continuous Monitoring.

- Data Loss Prevention (DLP).

- Business Continuity and Disaster Recovery (BC/DR or BCDR).

- Email Security.

- Antivirus Management.

- Spam Filtering.

- Identity and Access Management (IAM).

- Intrusion Protection.

- Security Assessment.

- Network Security.

- Security Information and Event Management (SIEM).

- Web Security.

- Vulnerability Scanning.

How to Choose a Security as a Service Provider

Handing over the security of your most critical and sensitive business assets is a massive undertaking. Choosing a SECaaS provider takes careful consideration and evaluation. Here are some of the most important considerations when selecting a provider:

- Availability: Your network must be available 24 hours a day and so should your SECaaS provider. Vet out the vendor's SLA to make sure they can provide the uptime your business needs and to know how outages are handled.

- Fast response times: Fast response times are just as important as availability. Look for providers that offer guaranteed response times for incidents, queries and system updates.

- Disaster recovery planning: Your provider should work closely with you to understand the vulnerabilities of your infrastructure and the external threats that are most likely to cause the most damage. From vandalism to weather disasters, your provider should ensure your business can recover quickly from these disruptive events.

- Vendor partnerships: A SECaaS provider is only ever as good as the vendors that have forged partnerships with. Look for providers that work with best in class security solution vendors and who also have the expertise to support these solutions.

Whether it is saving money, improving efficiencies or protecting your infrastructure from the latest security threats, managed services like SECaaS can provide great value to your organization by strengthening your defenses and improving your bottom line.

Cyber Security in Cloud Computing

There is a technology that has made life easier for users and businesses. It is known as cloud computing.

Nowadays it is impossible to understand the digital transformation of businesses and organisations without cloud computing.

It is estimated that 50% of businesses around the world will have adopted at least one cloud service. This data reflects that businesses bet on cloud computing to reduce their investment in servers and infrastructures to store data.

When it comes to talking about security, it is safer to use the cloud than other providers. However, not all cloud computing services are the same, so you have to analyze the protection offered by each one of them.

How should Cyber Security be in a Cloud Service?

Cloud services must comply with cyber security standards that guarantee the integrity of the data of the users and companies that contract the services.

To begin with, cloud computing must offer secure navigation. The access to the web or application must be endowed with an SLL (Secure Sockets Layer) certificate where the identity of the owners of the site is indicated. You can verify it by clicking on the padlock located in the bar where the URL is typed. If the padlock is green and closed, then you are navigating in a safe place.

Another important aspect is the verification of who the person is trying to access the cloud service.

For this, it is recommended that the cloud has multi-factorial authentication, which means that after user and password credentials, there must be a second or more credentials that discriminates and verifies access.

At this point, it's worth remembering that security also resides in the user. So, securing access with a strong password will prevent brute force attacks from succeeding.

Firewalls and secure user groups are also keys to working securely with a cloud service. Secure user groups can be created and thus discriminate access to resources according to the level of privileges.

Data encryption is also important to prevent data reading by third parties. Some services in the cloud integrate it. However, there are applications such as Boxcryptor that maintain the privacy of the files with endpoint encryption such as Dropbox, Google Drive or OneDrive, among others.

Finally, it is highly recommended to read the privacy policies of the cloud services that you subscribe to. Many are offered for free, but they access the data that users send to the cloud for selling it to third parties, or simply for getting some kind of benefit of it.

Ways to Reduce Security Breaches in Cloud Computing Networks

Cloud security has to be a part of your company's overall security strategy. Reducing security breaches in cloud computing networks requires planning and strategy to be successful. Companies need to devote just as much energy toward securing their cloud as they do securing their data center, buildings, people, and information.

Security risks, threats, and breaches can come in so many forms and from so many places that many companies take a comprehensive approach to security management. Many companies will focus on the broad range of potential vulnerabilities to its data center as well as ways to safeguard sensitive corporate, customer, and partner information, including using built-in applications and data level protections. Even with all that, it's not always enough.

In general, follow these steps to reduce the risk of suffering security breaches:

- Authenticate all people accessing the network.

- Frame all access permissions so users have access only to the applications and data that they've been granted specific permission to access.

- Authenticate all software running on any computer — and all changes to such software.

  This includes software or services running in the cloud.

  Your cloud provider needs to automate and authenticate software patches and configuration changes, as well as manage security patches in a proactive way. After all, many service outages come from configuration mistakes.

- Formalize the process of requesting permission to access data or applications.

  This applies to your own internal systems and the services that require you to put your data into the cloud.

- Monitor all network activity and log all unusual activity.

  Deploy intruder-detection technology. Even if your cloud services provider enables you to monitor activities on its environment, you should have an independent view.

Even when cloud operators have good security (physical, network, OS, application infrastructure), it is your company's responsibility to protect and secure your applications and information.

- Log all user activity and program activity and analyze it for unexpected behavior.

Nearly 70 percent of security breaches are caused by insiders (or by people getting help from insiders). Insiders rarely get caught.

- Encrypt, up to the point of use, all valuable data that needs extra protection.

- Regularly check the network for vulnerabilities in all software exposed to the Internet or any external users.

Given the importance of security in the cloud environment, you might assume that a major cloud services provider would have a set of comprehensive service level agreements for its customers. In fact, many of the standard agreements are intended to protect the service provider — not the customer.

References

- 9-cloud-computing-security-risks-every-company-faces, cloud-security: skyhighnetworks.com, Retrieved 14 June, 2019

- Security-as-a-service-secaas, cyber-edu: forcepoint.com, Retrieved 02 February, 2019

- Cyber-security-in-cloud-computing-this-is-how-it-should-be: opendatasecurity.io, Retrieved 22 June, 2019

- How-to-reduce-security-breaches-in-cloud-computing-networks, networking, programming: dummies.com, Retrieved 31 August, 2019

Cloud Computing Technologies

Cloud Computing Technologies refer to the hardware, software and infrastructure which enable the delivery of cloud computing services. Cloud computing and IOT, cloud radio access networks, hybrid cloud computing, multi-cloud, serverless computing, etc. are some technologies that fall under its domain. All these cloud computing technologies have been carefully analyzed in this chapter.

Virtualization in Cloud Computing

Virtualization is basically making a virtual image or "version" of something such as server, operating system, storage devices or network resources so that they can be used on multiple machines at the same time.

The main aim of virtualization is to manage the workload by transforming traditional computing to make it more scalable, efficient and economical. Virtualization can be applied to a wide range such as operating system virtualization, hardware-level virtualization and server virtualization.

Virtualization technology is hardware reducing cost saving and energy saving technology that is rapidly transforming the fundamental way of computing.

Architecture of Virtualized Technology

In cloud computing space/memory is virtually allocated to the users in the servers which requires a host (platform) on which hypervisor (software which interacts with the hardware) runs. The virtualization model is consisting of cloud users, service models, virtualized models and its host software and as well as their hardware. Virtualization software makes it possible to run multiple operating systems and multiple applications on the same server at the same time," said Mike Adams, director of product marketing at VMware, a pioneer in virtualization and cloud software and services. It is based on three service models that are SAAS (software as a service), PAAS (platform as a service) and IAAS (infrastructure as a service). SAAS provides applications to the cloud users to full fill their needs and demands. PAAS provides the cloud users a common platform on which they can execute their applications and IAAS provides the security and hardware to maintain the cloud resources The basic idea is to share large pools of resources like compute cycles or virtual CPUs (VCPUs), storage, software services etc.

Host: For virtualization the hypervisor software runs on a virtualization platform i.e. is host.

Hypervisor: The software program which handles the virtual machine to work under the virtually simulated environment is called hypervisor.

Traditional Servers and Virtual Servers

It plays a very important infrastructure in the cloud computing technology. It receives the requests sent by they cloud users and formulates it and also performs various tasks.

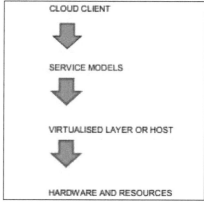

Basic architecture.

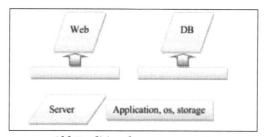

Old Traditional server concept.

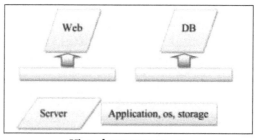

Virtual server concept.

Basic Traditional Servers

Traditionally the servers that were used has a lost of disadvantages and were not at all cost effective. "These servers are maintained by system administrator, normally these servers are described as combined unit that consist of operating system, the hardware, the storage and the application". In traditional server if the storage becomes full then it has to be replaced by a new server.

- Merits

  - Things are easily deployed in them.

  - Easy to maintain backup.

  - Application can be run virtually with traditional servers.

- Demerits

  - Hardware maintenance is very cost effective.

  - Duplication is very difficult.

  - Physical infrastructure cannot be updated.

  - Redundancy implementation is very difficult.

Virtual Server

"Virtual server seeks to encapsulate the server software away from the hardware the virtual server consists of the operating system (os), storage and application". By maintaining virtual server we can reduce the service provided by the cloud provider.

- Merits

  - IT pool maintenance.

  - High availability of hardware.

  - Deployment of servers in virtually based environment.

Advancement for Real World

There are many positive and negative effects of virtualization technology on the environment as well as the business and IT field.

Temperature

Virtualization technology is based on the group of hardware machines due to which a large amount of heat is released when they are used. So to overcome this problem special cooling mechanism should be employed to cool them and rise its performance.

Energy Consumption

With virtualization the power consumption due to machines has reduced as the number of hardware machines has been reduced which makes this technology more efficient and eco friendly.

Redundancy

Redundancy is basically the repetition of data which is mainly encountered when the systems don't shares a common storage and different memory storages are created. Due to the large number of data centres the fault tolerance is very high due to which redundancy is reduced.

Types of Virtualization

In cloud computing the virtualization can be done in two ways either by storage virtualization or by software virtualization.

- Storage virtualization: The storage available is virtualized to get large virtual storage access and it is further used for allocating memory to the cloud clients.

- Software virtualization: software built by the company can be used by a large number of systems at the same time with the help of virtualization. A virtual layer is created on which the software is installed and used.

Why Virtualization?

With the help of virtualization we can increase the use of resources available to us in many to get more benefits.

We should virtualize because of the following reasons:

- Isolation among users: one user should be isolated from the other users so that he/she may not get information about the others user's data and usage and cannot even access other's data.

- Resource sharing: a big resource can be fragmented into multiple virtual resources so that it can be used by multiple users using virtualization technique.

- Dynamical resources: reallocation of resources such as storage and computational resources is very difficult but if they are virtualised then they can be easily re-allocated.

- Aggregation of resources: the small resources available can be increased at a large extent with the help of virtualization.

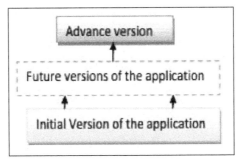

Upgradable Model.

Benefits of Virtualization Technology

- Virtualization is one of the cost-saving, hardware-reducing and energy-saving techniques.

- It helps to make cloud computing more efficient and eco-friendly.

- A big step towards new technology making life easier and better.

- Isolation.

- Resource sharing.

- Aggregation of resources.

- Dynamical resource.

Cloud Computing and IOT

Countless business opportunities are in the fire hose of IoT (Internet of Things) data due to the connected products. Yet what matters behind the millions of connected apps, devices, and sites are "customers". Therefore, it is very crucial to give customers the best experience and it can only be possible via IoT Cloud. It is the only platform where you put your IoT data and help you serve your customers better.

Role of Cloud Computing in the Internet of Things

Both Cloud computing and the IoT have a complimentary relationship. The IoT generates massive amounts of data whereas cloud computing ads in offering a pathway for that data to travel to its destination, thus helping to increase efficiency in our work. There is no need for you to guess your infrastructure capacity needs. Cloud computing increases speed and agility while making resources available to developers. You can save money on operating data centers and can deploy your applications worldwide in a matter of minutes.

Fog Computing – The Next Evolution of Cloud Computing

The next in the world of cloud computing is Fog computing. Many IoT devices don't have their own computing power. Fog computing typically provides a better way to collect and process data from these devices than the cloud does. Instead of storing data at the cloud or at a remote data center, fog computing provides a way to gather and process data at local computing devices.

Fog computing is also known as Edge Computing. In this model, sensors and other connected devices send data to a nearby edge computing device like a gateway (switch or router).

Today we expect everything to be connected, right from our refrigerator to the car. But do you know that they all will communicate with the cloud server.

This was the reason why companies had already manufactured smart devices with storages that are instantly upgradable and have a long term value. But do you know that there are disadvantages of the connectivity too. And the major one is the security issue. Although it is going to take a few close calls for the industry to wake up and understand that anything connected must come with well-defined and well-implemented security.

With the growth in cloud-based services for devices we shall also witness growth in compute and storage services to support these devices. There shall be upgrades in communications networks, including higher-speed cellular systems that will rival the pace of home networks.

You can see the number of devices connected to your Wi-Fi hub at home. As IOT services is progressing, we can see the evidence that we're undergoing a major change in terms of technology. However, we must know that change cannot happen without the use of IoT cloud services.

Cloud Radio Access Networks

The cloud radio access network (C-RAN) is one of the most efficient, low-cost, and energy-efficient radio access techniques proposed as a potential candidate for the implementation of next-generation (NGN) mobile base stations (BSs). A high-performance C-RAN requires an exceptional broadband radio frequency (RF) front end that cannot be guaranteed without remarkable antenna elements.

Mobile data traffic has grown 4000-fold over the past 10 years, and it is projected to grow by more than 500 times over the next few years. To cope with this large demand for mobile services, the mobile communication industry is currently developing fifth-generation (5G) mobile communication systems with the objective of providing pervasive, ubiquitous, always-connected broadband data communication. Many issues must be addressed to ensure 5G networks' superior performance, such as higher energy efficiency, higher system spectral efficiency, broadened network coverage, user coverage in hot spot and crowded areas, low latency, and better quality of service (QoS). Many key enabling technologies have been suggested for 5G, including millimetric wave transmission, massive multiple-input multiple-output (MIMO) networks, small cellular cells, heterogeneous network architectures, cloud radio access networks (C-RANs), and cognitive radio.

Cell densification (i.e., adding more cellular cells to the network) is proposed to increase the capacity, coverage area, and spectral efficiency of 5G networks. However, a major drawback of cell densification is the signal interference between adjacent base stations (BSs), which may diminish the capacity gain. Considering the issues and challenges related to the cell densification in next-generation (NGN) mobile networks, mobile operators have proposed a cost-effective and energy-efficient solution that can provide optimized performance suitable for gigabits per second (Gbps) networks: the C-RAN.

The architecture for a general C-RAN system is shown in Figure. In a C-RAN, the baseband units (BBUs), which consume high power, are separated from the radio access units (also called remote radio heads (RRHs)). The idea in C-RANs is to move the BBUs to a central location (data center) and connect it to the radio access units via optical fibers. At a remote site, the radio access unit (RRH) consisting of the antennas and radio frequency (RF) front end performs digital processing, digital-to-analog conversion, analog-to-digital conversion, power amplification, and signal filtering. Moving the BBUs to a central location improves energy efficiency, since all the baseband processing are done at the central location, called the cloud. Furthermore, the C-RAN network architecture enables inter-BS operations. Coordinated multipoint processing (CoMP) techniques can mitigate the interference between BSs and provide better management and coordination. In addition, CoMP minimizes energy consumption in MIMO systems by enabling coordinated multipoint concepts.

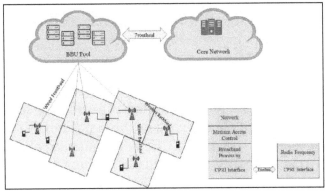

Architecture for general C-RAN system.

The performance of a 5G RAN strongly relies on an efficient RF front-end transceiver section. In addition to the amplifiers' nonlinearity, in-phase and quadrature-phase imbalance, imperfect timing causing synchronization problems, and channel interference issues, the efficiency of the RF front end is strongly affected by the antenna design, RF impairments, antennas' special dispersion causing signal distortion, mutual cou-pling, and broadband antennas' nonlinear characteristics. Since wireless transmission involves antennas at both user terminals and the BSs, considerable attention is required in the designing and characterization of the antennas to achieve 5G networks' objectives.

State-of-the-art Antennas

In addition to the massive bandwidth of the antenna elements required for the implementation of NGN communication networks, several other key parameters such as gain, polarization purity, radiation efficiency, radiation patterns stability over the wide bandwidth, and minimum dispersion to the input signal are required to satisfy the systems' specifications. Antennas are classified into various types based on their key parameters/characteristics and targeted applications. In order to fulfill the ever-growing demand for wireless high-data-rate applications, ultra-wideband (UWB) technology has been considered a comprehensive solution for RF front-end design to enhance channel capacity. UWB technology has drawn considerable attention, especially since the US Federal communication commission (FCC) authorized the use of the 3.1–10.6-GHz frequency band for commercial communication applications in 2002. Therefore, due to its huge bandwidth and unique feature of spectrum sharing, UWB can be considered one of the leading technologies for the implementation of NGN radio access networks, including the C-RAN.

Recent UWB antenna designs have focused on low cost, small size, and low-profile planar technology because of their ease of fabrication and their ability to be integrated with other components. The planar circuit development technique has brought monopole antennas with different shapes (polygonal, rectangular, triangular, square, trapezoidal, pentagonal, and hexagonal), circular, elliptical, etc.), which have been proposed as suitable candidates for UWB antenna systems. Mainly, the printed antennas consist of the planar radiator and ground plane etched oppositely onto the dielectric substrate of the printed circuit boards (PCBs). In some configurations, the ground plane may be coplanar with the radiator. The radiators can also be fed by a microstrip line or coaxial cable.

Numerous microstrip UWB antenna designs have been proposed. For instance, a patch antenna has been designed as a rectangular radiator with two steps, a single slot on the patch, and a partial ground plane etched on the opposite side of the dielectric substrate. It provides a bandwidth of 3.2–12 GHz and a quasi-omni-directional radiation pattern. Moreover, a clover-shaped microstrip patch antenna has been designed with a partial ground plane and a coaxial probe feed. The measured bandwidth of the antenna is 8.25 GHz with a gain of 3.20–4.00 dBi. In addition, it provides a stable radiation pattern over the entire operational bandwidth. Another design is a printed circular disc monopole antenna fed by a microstrip line. The matching impedance bandwidth is from 2.78 to 9.78 GHz with an omni-directional radiation pattern, and it is suitable for integration with PCBs. In addition, several elliptical shaped-based antennas have been designed. For example, three printed antennas have been designed starting from the elliptical shape, namely the elliptical patch antenna, its crescent-shaped variant, and the semielliptical patch.

Another type of printed antenna is the UWB-printed antenna fed by a coplanar wave-guide (CPW). For example, one trapezoidal design and its modified form cover the entire UWB band (3.1–10.6 GHz) and have a notch for the IEEE 802.11a frequency band (5.15–5.825 GHz). The frequency notch function is obtained by inserting different slot shapes into the antenna. The notch frequency can be adjusted by varying the slot's length. The antennas show good radiation patterns as well as good gain flatness except in the IEEE 802.11a frequency band. Another kind of radiating element considered suitable for phased arrays is the class of Vivaldi antennas, also known as quasi-end-fire nonresonant radiator or tapered slot antennas (TSAs). However, the element is normally fabricated by cutting a notch in a metal plate and backed by a quarter-wave cavity behind the feed point to improve its forward gain. A few examples of designed and fabricated UWB monopole and directional antennas are shown in Figure.

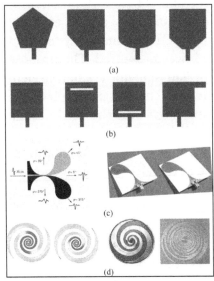

Different types of UWB antennas (a) conical antennas,
(b) planar monopoles, (c) planar monopoles with band stop filters,
(d) Vivaldi antennas and (e) spiral antennas.

The next generation of ongoing wireless revolution with the growing demand of wireless facilities in mobiles, the millimeter-wave (MMW) frequency band appears to be a strong candidate for future radio access technologies. In addition to UWB, MMW technology (30–300 GHz) allows the developing of miniaturized and compact antenna sensors to be used in the RF front end, thus reducing the overall size of the system. Compared to lower frequency signals, MMW signals can propagate over shorter distances due to their larger attenuation. Therefore, the development of MMW antennas with high gain performance for wireless access networks has attracted the interest of many researchers. In order to improve the spectral efficiency and exploit the benefits of spatial multiplexing, MMW antennas are expected to be used for large-scale MIMO (i.e., massive MIMO) systems. Therefore, it is important that improving a single parameter of an individual antenna will significantly improve the overall performance of a MIMO system, since each branch of the MIMO system will find at least one of them. The following are some well-known architectures and packaging techniques for improving the performance of MMW radios in terms of bandwidth, gain, and directivity.

Vettikalladi et al. explained the significance of the addition of a superstrate on an aperture-coupled antenna at MMW frequencies. It can be seen that with the addition of a superstrate, the bandwidth is noted to be BW = 58.7–62.7 GHz (i.e., 6.7%) with a maximum gain of 14.9 dBi. The patch and horn were designed separately and then assembled together. The horn antenna had a reflection coefficient of less than –10 dB and a port isolation greater than 30 dB over 14.6–15.2 GHz and a gain of 12.34 dBi and 10-dB beamwidths of 87° and 88° at 14.9 GHz. The final structure had a gain of 12.34 dBi. It is found by measurement that by using a superstrate above the aperture antenna, we can improve the gain up to 13.1 dBi with a wide bandwidth of 15% and an estimated efficiency of 79%. This good result is higher than that of a classical 2 × 2 array, on an RT Duroid substrate, with a gain of 12 dBi and an efficiency of 60%., a new concept of a directive planar waveguide (WG) antenna array for the next generation of point-to-point E-band communication was presented. The proposed antenna consisted of two major parts: first, the array of Gaussian horn radiating elements, and second, the mixed feeding rectangular WG network. The design adopted microstrip/conical horn hybrid technology for a 6-dB enhancement over the conventional circular patch antenna. A novel micromachining approach for realizing 60-GHz foam aperture-coupled antennas was presented in Ref. The foam is indeed an ideal antenna substrate, as its electrical properties are close to those of the air. High-gain compact stacked multilayered Yagi designs were proposed and demonstrated in the V-band. This novel design showed for the first time an antenna array of Yagi elements in an MMW-stacked structure. The measured Yagi antenna attained an 11-dBi gain over a 4.2% bandwidth with a size of 6.5 × 6.5 × 3.4 mm². Efficient and high-gain aperture-coupled patch antenna arrays with superstrates at 60 GHz were studied and presented. The maximum measured gain of a 2 × 2 superstrate antenna array was 16 dBi with an efficiency of 63%, 4 dB higher than that of a classical 2 × 2 array at 60 GHz.

In order to meet recent requirements of designing large-scale MIMO wireless communication systems, conformal antenna technology enables the development of compact antenna arrays. Moreover, to create high-capacity MMW-MIMO systems, conformal antenna structures can be integrated with modern beam-switching technology, resulting in a data rate of several gigabytes. In cases in which the line-of-sight link is blocked, beam-switching technology allows the dynamic control of the antenna's main beam in order to find the received signal with the highest power. Recently, a beam-switching conformal antenna array system operating at the 60-GHz mm-wave frequency band offering 1.5-GHz bandwidth was reported However, the size of the developed switched beam array system was 31 × 46.4 mm² rounded around a cylinder with a radius of 25 mm. Second, the simulations resulted in a gain value of 16.6 dBi.

Design of Planar Antennas for C-RANs

Among various devices, C-RANs have a good number of highly efficient antennas integrated with their RF front ends. In order to make these antennas more adaptable and fulfill the telecom vendors' requirements, they are expected to operate in one of the future proposed 5G bands: (i) UWB (3–12 GHz), (ii) 28/38 GHz, or (iii) 57–64 GHz suggested for system design and implementation. we will design, model, and optimize state-of-the-art antenna elements operating over the proposed frequency bands that can be considered suitable candidates for the implementation of a C-RAN's RF front end. The proposed antennas are designed to be efficient, moderate in size, low-profile (i.e., can be implemented using conventional fabrication processes), and cost-effective. In addition, the designed antennas' key parameters such as reflection coefficient, gain, radiation pattern, dispersion effect, radiation efficiency, and pattern stability are calculated and optimized to achieve the C-RAN's high data rate requirements.

UWB Antenna Element

We present antipodal tapered slot antennas (ATSAs) with elliptical strips termination modified with elliptical-shaped edge corrugations. The proposed corrugated antenna uses elliptical slots loading to improve the gain by up to 1.9 dB over an operational bandwidth of 0.8–12 GHz. It also improves the front-to-back lobe ratio. The designed ATSA exhibits minimum distortion to ultra-short pulses of 50 ps covering the 3–12-GHz frequency band.

Antenna Design

The antenna element shown in Figure is a traveling wave ATSA developed on Rogers 5880 substrate having dielectric constant $\varepsilon_r = 2.2$ and thickness $h = 1.574$ mm. The size of each antenna is 160 × 120 mm².

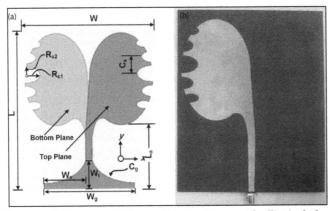

Layout diagram of (a) antipodal tapered slot antenna with elliptical-shaped edge corrugation (ATSA-EC) and (b) photograph of fabricated antenna.

The ATSA-EC contains strip conductors on both sides of the substrate. In order to have impedance matching over a bandwidth of more than 10:1. The exponential taper C_g is used for the ground in order to achieve the broadband microstrip to parallel plate transition. The tapered curve C_g is defined as:

$$C_g = W_y - 1 + 0.1 W_y e^{\alpha W_x}$$

Where α is the rate of transition for the exponential curve defined as follows:

$$\alpha = \frac{1}{1.92 W_x} In\left(\frac{W_y + 0.1 W_t}{0.1 W_t}\right).$$

Where w_x is the x-directed length of the curve with w_y and w_t being the y-directed initial and final points, respectively. The variation of impedance bandwidth and radiation characteristics against different geometrical parameters of proposed ATSAs are analyzed by full-wave simulation software CST Microwave Studio. Table presents the geometry of the ATSA, which results in 182% impedance bandwidth with the required radiation performance.

R_1	R_2	D	w_y	w_x	w_t	w_o	w_1
32.5	42.25	65	8	43.85	35	5.95	6.12

Table. Optimized geometrical dimensions (mm) of ATSA.

In order to improve the radiation characteristics, elliptical edge corrugations are applied to the ATSA, as shown in Figure. At each edge of the antenna, unequal half-elliptical slots (UHESs) are loaded with the period C_s = 17 mm. The largest UHES having minor axis and major axis radii R_{s1} = 15 mm and R_{s2} = 8 mm, respectively, is placed at the center of the elliptical fin. Conversely, the major axis radii of the other UHESs are decreased linearly by the factor C_r = 0.7 having the constant ellipticity ratio e_r = 0.533 = R_{s2}/R_{s1}.

The photograph of the fabricated ATSAs is shown in Figure. The measured return loss of the fabricated ATSA-EC is compared with the simulation results, as shown in Figure. The simulation results are in good agreement with the measured performance. Generally, the radiation of an ATSA is a function of length, aperture width, and substrate thickness. The added inductance due to edge corrugation increases the electrical length of the antennas. The loading of the ATSA with UHES can suppress the surface current at both back edges, resulting in improved gain performance compared to un-slotted antenna gain. Similarly, the UHESs increase the effective length of the antenna, resulting in more directive beams in both the E- and H-planes. Figure presents the simulation results of the ATSAs' gain performance against various corrugation depths compared with un-corrugated ATSAs. The realized gain of the ATSA is found between 3 and 8.5 dBi over the 0.8–6 GHz frequency band. The edge corrugation arranges the current path to be parallel with the desired radiating current and opposite to the undesired surface current. The former enhances the gain, whereas the latter decreases the backward radiation. Therefore, the realized gain of the ATSA-EC is improved over the 0.8–6 GHz band by varying elliptical slots radii R_{S1} and R_{S2}. Comparatively, better gain improvement is found for the ellipticity ratio $e_r = R_{S2}/R_{S1}$ less than 0.35, as depicted in figure.

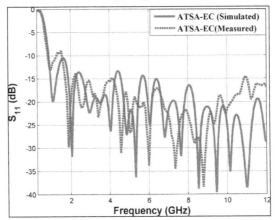

Measured return loss characteristics of fabricated ATSA-EC.

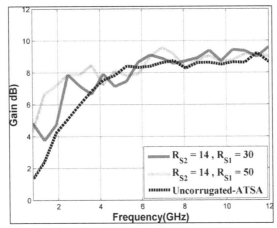

Simulated gain characteristics of ATSAs at
different edge corrugation values.

The simulated time domain response of ATSAs when excited with pass-band Gaussian pulses covering the complete spectrum of operating frequency is shown in Figure. The received pulses are obtained by placing an x-oriented E-field probe 10 m along the broadside direction of the antenna. The FWHM of the transmitted pulse is 50 ps, while the received pulses preserve the Gaussian shape having a maximum FWHM of 56 ps related to the ATSA-EC with R_{S1} = 30 mm and R_{S2} = 18 mm. The FWHM of the ATSA without corrugation and ATSA-EC with R_{S1} = 50 and R_{S2} = 14 are found to be 58 and 59 ps, respectively. The fidelity factor is calculated according to the following relation.

$$Fidelity = \max_{\tau} \frac{\int_{-\infty}^{\infty} S_t(t) S_r(t-\tau) dt}{\sqrt{\int_{-\infty}^{\infty} |S_t(t)|^2 dt |S_r(t-\tau)|^2 dt}}$$

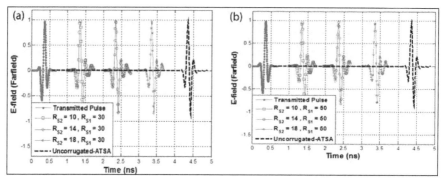

Simulated transmitted and received pulses on E-field probe
for different edge corrugation parameters.

Where $S_t(t)$ and $S_r(t)$ represent the transmitted and received time domain pulses, respectively. The fidelity factors for ATSA-EC at different edge corrugations are presented in Table.

$\dfrac{R_{S2}}{R_{S1}}$	$\dfrac{10}{30}$	$\dfrac{14}{30}$	$\dfrac{18}{30}$	$\dfrac{10}{30}$	$\dfrac{14}{30}$	$\dfrac{18}{50}$
Fidelity	0.89	0.88	0.87	0.91	0.92	0.9

Table. Calculated fidelity factor for ATSA-EC at different edge corrugation.

Compact Switched-beam MMW Conformal Antenna Array System

A compact (25 × 30-mm²) ATSA element is designed presenting the reflection coefficient value less than −10 dB over a wide spectrum covering the 14.8–40-GHz frequency band. The MIMO antenna system is comprised of four ATSAs. Antenna elements are placed 90° apart from each other over a small cylinder having a 12-mm radius. The conformal ATSAs are loaded with a dielectric lens for gain enhancement. The optimized dimensions of the dielectric lens are obtained by several full-wave simulations resulting in a gain value of more than 20 dBi from 24 to 40 GHz. The proposed system presents four orthogonal independent beams switched at the angle of ±14° along the coordinate axis.

Broadband MMW ATSA Design

The geometry of the ATSA antenna is shown in Figure. The antenna was designed on RT/duroid® 5880 laminate having a dielectric constant of $\varepsilon_r = 2.2$ and a thickness of 0.254 mm. The top and the bottom plane conductors form an antipodal feed arrangement, enabling the ATSA antenna to exhibit excellent broadband characteristics. The tapered ground plane is obtained by cutting a half-ellipse with the radii of the major axis and minor axis, r1 and r2, respectively. In order to reduce backward radiations, the linear corrugation is designed and optimized by executing several full-wave simulations using the CST Microwave Studio computer program. The optimized parameters of the ATSA are listed in table.

Parameter	W	L	Hf	Lf	lg	Wo	Wg	r1
Value (mm)	24	32	16	15	1.63	0.67	16	7.6
Parameter	l1	l2	l3	l4	w1	w2	ws	r2
Value (mm)	5.15	3.07	2.27	2.99	5	3	0.5	5.36

Table. Optimized dimensional parameters of the proposed antenna.

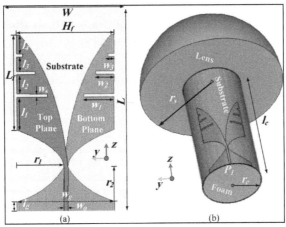

Geometry of ATSA, (a) rectangular configuration,
(b) lens-loaded conformal configuration.

The geometry of the proposed conformal ATSA is shown in Figure. The ATSA element is designed over a low-thickness flexible substrate, which allows us to round the antenna element over a cylindrical surface. We selected a cylinder of foam material to preserve the electrical characteristics of the designed antenna. The radius of the foam cylinder is 12 mm. In order to enhance the gain, the ATSA is loaded with a half-spherical dielectric lens with a relative permittivity of ε_r = 2.2 and optimized radius (rs) of 32 mm. The length (lc) of the conformal structure is the same as that of the nonconformal antenna, which is equal to 32 mm.

The ATSA of the conventional rectangular shape was first optimized to exhibit a –10 dB bandwidth over a wider frequency spectrum. In the conformal antenna design, the radius of the foam cylinder is optimized for a minimum realizable value without compromising the electrical performance of the original ATSA. Finally, a dielectric lens is introduced toward the end-fire direction of the conformal ATSA, and S-parameter values are calculated. The S-parameter curves of the ATSAs having rectangular, conformal, and lens-loaded conformal configurations are presented in Figure, showing S11 values less than –10 dB from the 14.8 to 40-GHz frequency band. All three curves presenting the reflection coefficient performance of different ATSA configurations are found to be in close agreement with each other. The rectangular-shaped ATSA radiates toward the end-fire direction with E- and H-plane pattern symmetry. Figure compare the normalized radiation patterns of ATSAs' rectangular, conformal, and lens-loaded configurations at 28 and 38 GHz, respectively. The conformal ATSA without a lens exhibits almost the same radiation pattern as the rectangular ATSA at both frequencies, except there is a shift of 4° in the H-plane pattern. The ATSA configurations without a lens present an average 3-dB beam-width of more than 40° in both planes. On the other hand, the lens-loaded ATSA finds a 14° shift in the H-plane beam with a 3-dB angular width of 12°. The introduction of the dielectric lens toward the end-fire direction enhances the gain of a conformal ATSA due to the focusing of the radiated field in space. The diameter of the dielectric lens is optimized by several full-wave simulations. The results presenting a parametric study of gain versus frequency against different diameters of dielectric lens are shown in Figure. A significant improvement (i.e., more than 10 dB) in gain parameters is observed by increasing the radius (r_s) of the dielectric lens up to 32 mm. Table presents the comparison of the radiation characteristics among the three configurations of the ATSA .

	Peak gain (dBi)	Radiation efficiency (%)
Element 1	6.06	97
Element 2	5.18	98
Element 3	5.50	97

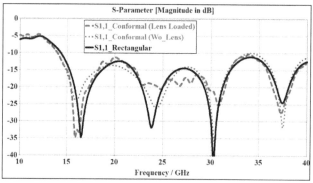

Reflection coefficient versus frequency of three different configurations of proposed ATSA.

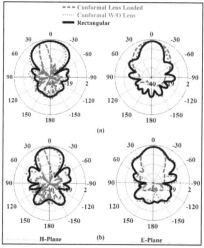

Copolarization radiation patterns in φ= 0° (H-plane) and φ = 90° (E-plane) cuts at (a) 28 GHz and (b) 38 GHz.

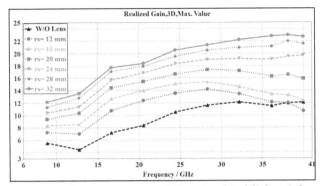

Gain versus frequency against different radii of dielectric lens
loaded toward end-fire direction of ATSA.

Four-element Beam-switched MIMO ATSA System

The geometry of the proposed conformal MIMO antenna system is shown in Figure. The four ATSA elements are placed along the ± x, y co-ordinate axis of a 12-mm-radius cylinder. The physical separation between the subsequent antenna elements is dc = 17 mm, which is 1.58 λ_0 at 28 GHz. The dimensions of conformal MIMO ATSAs are the same as mentioned previously. Antenna elements 1 and 2 are approximately perpendicular to each other, placed parallel to the yz-plane and xz-plane, respectively. Similarly, antenna elements 3 and 4 are placed opposite to antenna elements 1 and 2, respectively.

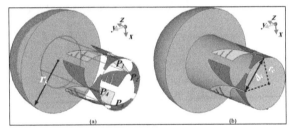

Geometry of four-element switched-beam MIMO antenna system,
(a) transparent view and (b) solid view.

The four-element conformal ATSAs loaded with a dielectric lens are simulated to calculate and analyze S-parameters using the full-wave simulation program CST Microwave Studio. The proposed conformal configuration of ATSAs does not affect the impedance bandwidth of the original design, since the mutual coupling between the antenna elements is below −20 dB over the complete spectrum, as shown in Figure. The minimum values of the reflection coefficient and mutual coupling values are below −10 and −20 dB, respectively, from 14.8 to 40 GHz. Moreover, better isolations are achieved between antenna elements 1 and 3. Considering the frequencies 28 and 38 GHz proposed for 5G wireless communications, the designed switched-beam AT-SAs exhibit excellent S-parameter performance at those particular frequencies. Due to the symmetry of the designed configuration, only the S-parameter results for ATSA 1 are presented. The radiation performance of the proposed antenna configuration is calculated by exciting the particular element and terminating the other element with 50-Ω matched loads. Consider the proposed conformal configuration where antenna 1 and antenna 3 are placed opposite to each other at the −ve and +ve x-axis, respectively. Similarly, antenna 1 and antenna 3 are placed at the −ve and +ve y-axis, respectively. Since the dielectric lens is placed off-center with respect to each antenna element, exciting antenna 1 enables the focusing of electromagnetic energy toward the +ve x-axis and vice versa. The same phenomenon is observed between antenna 2 and antenna 4. The calculated H-plane and E-plane radiation patterns with their respective excitations at different ports are shown in Figure. For the excitation of antenna 2 and antenna 4, the H-plane pattern is calculated by taking theta (θ) cut at the $\varphi = [90]^o$ plane. Antenna 2 and antenna 4 find beams switched at $\theta = [12]^o$ and $\theta = [-12]^o$, respectively. Similarly, the same radiation pattern results for antenna 1 and antenna 3 in the H-plane are observed at $\varphi = 0^o$ cut. The E-plane radiation pattern is calculated by taking phi (φ) cut at $\theta = [12]^o$. It is worth noticing that the consecutive excitation of each individual port can result in four orthogonal switched beams placed 90° apart from each other.

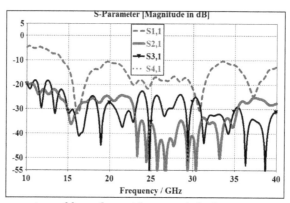

S-parameters of four-element beam-switched antenna system.

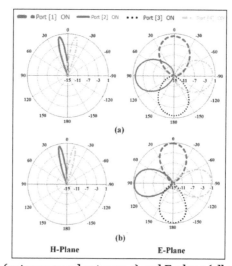

H-plane (antenna 2 and antenna 4) and E-plane (all antennas) switched beam radiation patterns at (a) 28 GHz and (b) 38 GHz. Beam switches at each co-ordinate axis (± x, y) displaced by 12° in H-plane.

60-GHz Radio or MMW Antenna Array for Cloud Computing

A simulated design of an MMW and array or 60-GHz radio band is presented for a cloud computing architecture. The design achieves the minimum requirements for the 60-GHz radio in terms of wide bandwidth (7 GHz at least, i.e., 57–64 GHz) and high gains (~8 dBi). The proposed antenna design is based on the aperture coupling technique that alleviates the problem of feedline and conductor losses while working at higher frequencies. The design consists of a multilayer structure with an aperture-coupled microstrip patch and a surface-mounted horn integrated on an FR4 substrate. The proposed antenna contributes an impedance bandwidth of 10.58% (58.9–65.25 GHz). The overall antenna gain and directivity are about 11.78 and 12.51 dBi, respectively. The antenna occupies an area of 7.14 mm × 7.14 mm × 4 mm with an estimated efficiency of 82%. In order to make the antenna more directive and to further increase the gain, a 2 × 2 and 4 × 4 array structure with a corporate feed network is introduced as well. The side lobe levels of the array designs are minimized, and the back radiations are reduced by utilizing a reflector at a λ/4 distance from the corporate feed network. The 2 × 2 array structure resulted in an improved gain of 15.3 dB with an efficiency of 83%, while the 4 × 4 array structure provided further gain improvement of 18.07 dB with 68.3% efficiency. The proposed design is modeled in CST Microwave Studio, and its results are verified using HFSS.

Wideband and High-gain Aperture-coupled Microstrip Patch Antenna (ACMPA) with Mounted Horn for MMW Communication

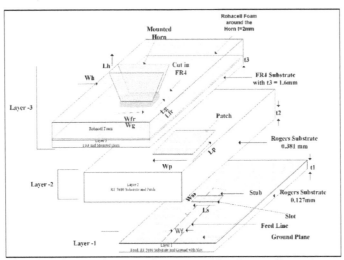

3D exploded view of proposed ACMPA with relevant dimensions.

The geometry of the single-element multilayer ACMPA integrated with a mounted horn antenna on an FR4 substrate is shown in Figure. The 3D exploded view shows the entire multilayer structure with relevant parameters. For the first and second layers, RT/duroid 5880 Laminate having dielectric constant $\varepsilon_r = 2.2$ and loss tangent 0.003 is used, while the third layer has an FR4 substrate with a dielectric constant of 4.3. A Rohacell foam is also placed on top of the FR4 substrate to assist the mounted horn antenna. The optimized dimensions of the horn antenna can be obtained from the guidelines listed in Ref. The conducting materials for the substrate have copper as an element with a thickness of t = 0.0175 mm.

Antenna design simulation tools were used to optimize and verify the proposed ACM-PA design. The return loss S11 parameters below the −10 dB resonance and the gain of the antenna are shown in Figure. The antenna achieves an impedance of 10.58% (58.9–65.25 GHz) with a gain and efficiency of 11.78 dB and 88%, respectively. Substrate and metallic losses were taken into account during simulations. Figure show the E-plane and H-plane radiation patterns, simulated in CST and HFSS, of the proposed antenna, for the frequencies at 59, 62, and 65 GHz, respectively. Thus, for the multilayer structure at 62 GHz, the E-plane has a side lobe of level −5 dB, half-power beamwidth of 31°, and back radiation of −18.3 dB. The H-plane radiation pattern at 62 GHz has a side lobe of −13.2, half-power beamwidth of 69.8°, back radiation of −17dB, and cross-polarization level of >−30 dB.

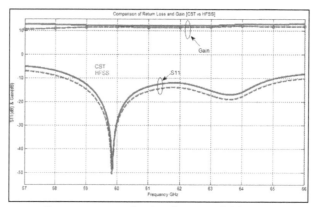

S-parameters and gain of proposed ACMPA.

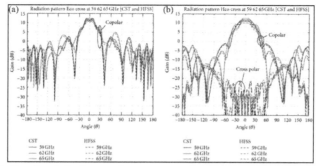

(a) Simulated E-plane radiation pattern at 59, 62, and 65 GHz and
(b) simulated H-plane radiation pattern at 59, 62, and 65 GHz.

2 × 2 and 4 × 4 ACMPA Array Design

MMWs or 60-GHz radio bands offer wide bandwidth and higher gains for short-range communications. In order to fulfill these requirements, especially that of higher gain, the proposed ACMPA was optimized in terms of arrays (i.e., 2 × 2 and 4 × 4). Two factors are important when designing arrays: (1) array factor and (2) feeding network impedances. The theory behind the antenna array factor was utilized as explained in Ref., where each antenna element is treated as an individual isotropic point source. Energy contributions from each point source are derived in the far field expressed as array factor (AF). For the feed network, one can select either single feed or parallel/ corporate feed depending on the design requirements. For our proposed design, since we are working at higher (i.e., 60 GHz) bands, we opted for the corporate feed network, as it would suppress further losses encountered during analysis. A general 2 × 2 and 4 × 4 corporate feed network is shown in Figure with relevant impedances. Corporate feed networks are in general very versatile, as they offer power splits of 2n (i.e., n = 2, 4, 8, 16, 32, etc.) and control to the designer in terms of amplitude and phase selection of the individual feed element and its power division among the transmission lines. It is ideal for scanning phased arrays, shaped-beam arrays, and multibeam arrays. The length and width of the transmission lines can be varied as per the requirement of the power division. The feed network consists of a 50-Ω transmission line and a 70.7-Ω quarter-wavelength transformer matched to a primary 50-Ω feeding line.

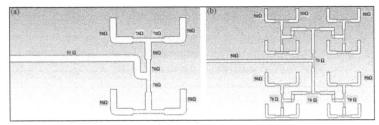

Corporate feed network (a) 2 × 2 array and (b) 4 × 4 array.

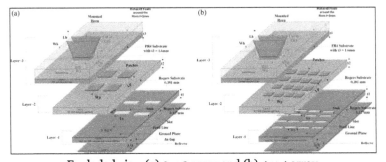

Exploded view (a) 2 × 2 array and (b) 4 × 4 array.

The E-plane and H-Plane radiation patterns for the 2 × 2 array and 4 × 4 arrays are shown in Figures. For the 2 × 2 array, it is observed that the E-plane at 62 GHz has a side lobe of level −13.7 dB, half-power beamwidth of 22.1°, and back radiation of −25.3 dB. The H-plane radiation pattern at 62 GHz has a side lobe of −9.1 dB, half-power beamwidth of 22.2°, back radiation of −21.8 dB, and cross-polarization level of >−30 dB. For the 4 × 4 array, the E-plane at 62 GHz has a side lobe of level −11.8 dB, half-power beamwidth of 13.6°, and back radiation of −23.07 dB. The H-plane radiation pattern at 62 GHz has a side lobe of −12.4, half-power beamwidth of 16.1°, and back radiation of −23.07 dB. Table shows the comparison of the improved gain from a single element to 2 × 2 and 4 × 4 arrays.

Array/parameters	Single element	2 × 2 array	4 × 4 array
Bandwidth (%)	10.58	10.55	10.51
Gain (dB)	11.78	15.3	18.07
Efficiency (%)	88	83	68.3

Table. Simulated results of single element, 2 × 2 and 4 × 4 array.

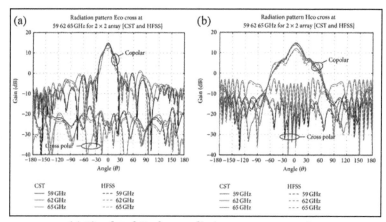

(a) Simulated E-plane radiation pattern at 59, 62,
and 65 GHz and (b) simulated H-plane radiation
pattern at 59, 62, and 65 GHz.

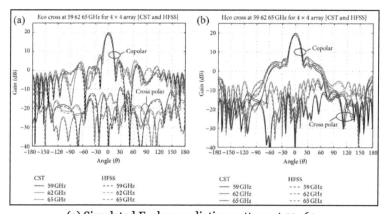

(a) Simulated E-plane radiation pattern at 59, 62,
and 65 GHz and (b) simulated H-plane radiation
pattern at 59, 62, and 65 GHz.

Hybrid Cloud Computing

In a hybrid cloud computing environment, an organization provides and manages in-house resources and accesses resources in a public cloud. One or several touch points exist between the private cloud and public cloud environments. The services and data from both clouds combine to create a unified and well-managed computing environment.

Components of a Hybrid Cloud

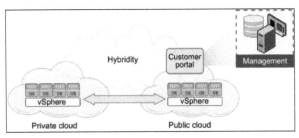

In their private clouds, customers manage their business workloads using virtualized, pooled compute resources. Virtual Private Cloud OnDemand, managed by VMware, exists in the public cloud and exposes infrastructure capabilities through a Web UI and publically available APIs. Together, customers' on-premises private clouds and the VMware public cloud provide hybrid cloud functionality—the ability to extend private cloud resources to the public cloud. In a hybrid cloud environment, computing resources and business processes are designed to connect customers' private clouds and the public cloud as though they are a single environment for each customer.

Hybrid Cloud Characteristics

Not all companies that use some public and some private cloud services have a hybrid cloud. A hybrid cloud environment is not an environment where a few developers in a company use a public cloud service to prototype a new application that is completely disconnected from their private cloud or on-premises data center.

A hybrid cloud is an environment where the private and public cloud services are used together to create value. Hybrid cloud computing began as a way to take advantage of the ability to move workloads between private and public clouds. At different times of the month or year, certain workload requirements might need extra capacity. In many cases, it was the idea that customers owned the applications and rented the capacity spikes.

Customers built virtual private clouds for numerous reasons; for example, to handle dynamic scaling requirements, to run workloads at lower costs, or to run workloads for limited time periods. The resources ran in the public cloud but linked back to resources in their private clouds through VPN or other private connections. Their workloads ran where it made the most sense but required visibility back to resources in their private clouds, for example, to allow for authentication of users or archive data at set intervals into secure storage.

Hybrid Cloud Interconnection between Private and Public Clouds

Over time, the characteristics of hybrid clouds have evolved. Today, hybrid cloud computing exists as a private cloud and multi-public clouds. A customer leverages resources whether they are public and public, multi-public, private and public, or any combination, and has a single way to orchestrate and provide services to their business based on a multitude of criteria (cost, location, performance, or availability).

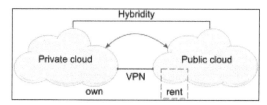

For example, a customer might need to keep legacy applications private but look to moving new applications public to take advantage of geography, time zone, or for legal reasons. For example, in 3, public cloud "Public - West" might be in a required geographical location.

Multiple Public Clouds with Single Point of View

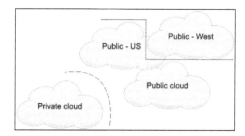

Customers approach their hybrid cloud strategy by looking at all resources across all clouds. They want a dashboard way of managing cloud resources whether they are private or public. In this environment, customers do not think in terms of moving resources between public and private clouds, but rather as operating them in environments that best solve their business needs to give them business advantages.

Hybrid Cloud Architecture

Hybrid User Interface

Varying user group workload interacts asynchronously with an application hosted in an elastic environment while the rest of the application resides in a static environment. An application responds to user groups with different workload behavior. One user group presents a static workload, while the other user group presents periodic, once-in-a-lifetime, unpredictable, or continuously changing workloads. Since user group size and workload behavior is unpredictable, this interface ensures that unexpected peak workloads do not affect application performance while each user group is handled by the most suitable environment. The user interface component serving varying workload users is hosted in an elastic cloud environment. Other application components that are in a static environment. The user interface in the elastic cloud is integrated with the rest of the application in a decoupled manner using messaging to ensure loose coupling.

Hybrid Processing

Processing functionality with the varying workload is in an elastic cloud while the remainder of the application is in a static environment. A distributed application provides processing functions with different workload behavior. The user group accessing the application is predictable in size but accesses the functions differently. Although most functions are used equally and experience static workload, some processing components experience periodic, unpredictable, or continuously changing workloads. The processing components with varying workloads are provisioned in an elastic cloud. Loose coupling is ensured by asynchronously exchanging information between the hosting environments via messages.

Hybrid Data

Data of varying size is in an elastic cloud while the rest of an application is in a static environment. A distributed application handles data with drastically varying size. Large amounts of data may be periodically generated and then deleted, data may increase and decrease randomly, or data may display a general increase or decrease. During these changes, the user number and application accesses can be static resulting in a static workload on the other application components. Elastic cloud storage offerings handle data with varying size that are unsuitable for static environment hosting. Data is accessed either by data access components hosted in the static environment or by data access components in the elastic environment.

Hybrid Backup

For disaster recovery, data is periodically extracted from an application and archived in an elastic cloud. Requirements regarding business resiliency and business continuity are challenging. There are also laws and regulations that make businesses liable to archive data for audits over very long periods of time. A distributed application is in a local static environment. Data handled by stateful components is extracted periodically and replicated to cloud storage.

Hybrid Backend

Backend functionality is made up of data-intensive processing and data storage with varying workloads is hosted in an elastic cloud while all other components reside in a static data center. A distributed application provides processing with different workload behaviors. Support for a mainly static workload needs to available, but some processing components experience periodic, unpredictable, or continuously changing workloads. Application components that have varying workloads should be in an elastic environment.

These components, however, need to access large amounts of data during execution making them very dependent on availability and timely access to data. The processing components with varying workloads are in an elastic cloud together with the data accessed during operation. Asynchronous messages exchanged from the static environment are used to trigger the processing components in the elastic cloud through via message-oriented middleware message queues. A static environment data access component ensures that data required by elastic processing components is in storage offerings The data location may then be passed to the elastic processing components via messages. Data not required by the backend functionality may still be stored in stateful components in the static data center.

Hybrid Application Functions

Some application functions provided by user interfaces, processing, and data handling is experienced varying workload and is in an elastic cloud while other application functions of the same type are in a static environment. Distributed application components experience varying workloads on all layers of the application stack: user interface, processing, and data access. All components provide functionality to the application user group, but user groups access functionality differently. In addition to the workload requirements, other issues may limit the environments to which an application component may be provisioned. Application components are grouped based on similar requirements and are deployed into the best fitting environments. Components interdependencies are reduced by exchanging data with asynchronous messaging to ensure loose coupling. Depending on the function accessed, a load balancer seamlessly redirects user accesses to the different environments.

Hybrid Multimedia Web Application

Website content is primarily provided from a static environment. Multimedia files that cannot be cached efficiently are provided from a large distributed elastic environment for high-performance access. A distributed application provides website access to a globally distributed user group. While most of the website has static content, there is a significant amount of multimedia content that needs to be streamed to users. Static website content is in a static environment where users access it. The streaming content is in an elastic cloud environment where it is accessed from a user interface component. Static content is delivered to users' client software which references the multimedia content. Streaming content retrieval is often handled directly by the users' browser software.

Hybrid Development Environment

A runtime environment for production is replicated and mocked in an elastic environment for new applications development and testing. Applications have different runtime environment requirements during the development, testing, and production phases. During development, hardware requirements vary, so hardware resources need to be flexible and able to extend resources as necessary. During the test phase, diverse test systems are needed in order to verify proper application functionality on various operating systems or while being accessed with different client software. Large numbers of resources are also required for load tests. In production, other factors, such as security and availability are of greater importance than resource flexibility. The application production environment is simulated in the development and test environment using equivalent addressing, similar data, and equivalent functionality. Applications migration is ensured through the transformation of application components or the compatibility of runtimes. Some testing resources are exclusively provided in the development environment to verify the application behavior under different circumstances.

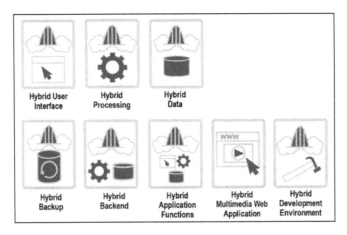

Each pattern employs certain characteristics and attributes. These help solution architects accurately visualize interoperability, and models, and compare the impact of economics, technology choices, and potential strategies. Pattern attributes and their associated metrics can also be used to models and test solutions using computing aided design tools. Aligning pattern characteristics, attributes, and metrics with organizational requirements and goals will normally lead to successful solution deployments.

Hybrid Cloud Management

Hybrid cloud management is the process of controlling an organization's multiple cloud infrastructure deployments. It is often implemented through dedicated third-party software which integrates the infrastructure from different cloud service vendors into a single management platform which allows administrators to view and control all assets from both the private and public cloud through a single UI.

In some cases, going pure public cloud or pure private cloud is not viable for some organizations, especially those that deal with sensitive data, so a hybrid solution has to be taken. Having two different infrastructures can be a hassle so a centralized management process has to be put in place that bridges the different platforms. Hybrid cloud management is both a process and a software platform which dictates the principles of how a hybrid cloud should be managed.

A hybrid cloud management solution is often offered by most vendors of cloud computing services which bridges their own infrastructure and services with that of other vendors to enable the organization to control both platform from a single user interface as if they were simply pieces of a whole. Since both private and public clouds are essentially offering the same technology, this is not really that difficult to implement in practice.

Through the management portal, an administrator is able to provision or decommission instances, assign content, and view performance characteristics.

Multi-cloud

Multi-cloud is a strategy where an organization leverages two or more cloud computing platforms to perform various tasks. Organizations that do not want to depend on a single cloud provider may choose to use resources from several providers to get the best benefits from each unique service.

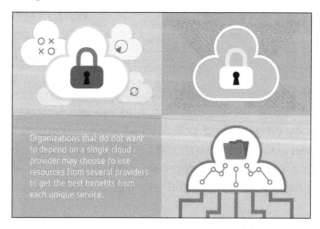

A multi-cloud solution may refer to the combination of software as a service (SaaS), platform as a service (PaaS) and infrastructure as a service (IaaS) models. It may also refer to the use of several private and public cloud solutions. Generally, IT professionals use the term to describe a strategy that employs several public cloud offerings.

Multi-cloud Strategy versus Hybrid Cloud

A hybrid cloud is not a multi-cloud, though a multi-cloud may include hybridization. Essentially, a hybrid cloud refers to a pairing of a private cloud and public cloud. Organization's leverage this model when they want to maintain the security and privacy of sensitive data within an on-site cloud solution - or within a privately hosted cloud. A hybrid solution relies on a private data center, yet leverages the advanced computing resources of a public solution.

Multi-cloud strategy can include the use of a hybrid environment but relies on more than one public cloud. The strategy may reduce the need for cloud migration, as some data can remain on the enterprise's servers. An organization could choose to store user data on site, leveraging one provider for IaaS and another for SaaS. Some cloud environments may be tailored for specific use cases, which prompts IT stakeholders to select specific cloud service providers for various business functions.

Why do Organizations adopt Multi-cloud Strategy?

Organizations choose multi-cloud strategies for a number of reasons. Some leaders want to avoid dependence on a single cloud provider, thereby reducing financial risk. Getting stuck with a single vendor could make it difficult for an organization to adopt a responsive strategy. Other organizations decide upon a multi-cloud strategy to mitigate the risk of a localized hardware failure. Such a failure in an on-site data center could push the entire enterprise offline. Multi-cloud greatly reduces the risk of catastrophic failure.

Multi-cloud can be an effective strategy for combating shadow IT. Shadow IT is technology used by individuals or groups within an organization that is not managed by the organization's IT department. This problem tends to arise when policy-compliant IT does not fully meet the needs of the organization. A multi-cloud environment allows groups to comply with IT policy while benefiting from a specific cloud technology.

IT stakeholders can manage a multi-cloud environment with tools offered by the cloud service providers or abstract away from the complexity by leveraging a cloud management platform. There is no singular best practice guideline for managing multi-cloud because each organization's use case will be unique.

Benefits of Multi-cloud

A multi-cloud strategy brings choices to an organization. With more options comes the ability to invest in digital transformation without getting locked into a single service or putting down a huge outlay of capital. Specific benefits of multi-cloud include:

ROI Optimization

A multi-cloud strategy allows stakeholders to pick and choose the specific solutions that work best for their organization. As diverse business needs arise, change and become more complex, the business can allocate resources for specific uses, maximize those resources and pay for only what they use.

Advanced Security

As with hybrid cloud, multi-cloud empowers organizations by maintaining strict security compliance while optimizing computing resources. Multi-cloud also reduces the risk that a distributed denial of service (DDoS) attack could take mission-critical applications offline. When even a single hour of downtime can cost an organization thousands, advanced security protocols pay for themselves.

Freedom of Choice

A single cloud provider may not be able to provide an organization with all of the computing services it requires. Many financial stakeholders may be wary of vendor lock-in, as well. If the business finds a better deal with another provider, it may prove difficult to move away from an architecture that is designed from the ground up for another provider's cloud environment.

Reliable Architecture

Utilizing multiple cloud solutions creates redundancies that reduce the risk of a single point of failure. Multi-cloud reduces the likelihood that a single service failure will take the entire enterprise offline. Adding hybridization adds another level of security by keeping sensitive data within a secure, local network.

Serverless Computing

Serverless computing is a method of providing backend services on an as-used basis. A Serverless provider allows users to write and deploy code without the hassle of worrying about the underlying infrastructure. A company that gets backend services from a serverless vendor is charged based on their computation and do not have to reserve and pay for a fixed amount of bandwidth or number of servers, as the service is auto-scaling. Note that although called serverless, physical servers are still used but developers do not need to be aware of them.

In the early days of the web, anyone who wanted to build a web application had to own the physical hardware required to run a server, which is a cumbersome and expensive undertaking.

Then came the cloud, where fixed numbers of servers or amounts of server space could be rented remotely. Developers and companies who rent these fixed units of server space generally over-purchase to ensure that a spike in traffic or activity wouldn't exceed their monthly limits and break their applications. This meant that much of the server space that was paid for usually went to waste. Cloud vendors have introduced auto-scaling models to address the issue, but even with auto-scaling an unwanted spike in activity, such as a DDoS Attack, could end up being very expensive.

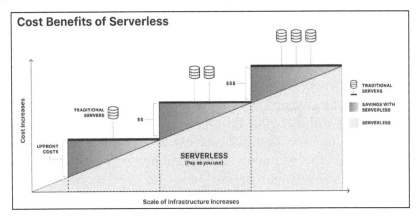

Serverless computing allows developers to purchase backend services on a flexible 'pay-as-you-go' basis, meaning that developers only have to pay for the services they use. This is like switching from a cell phone data plan with a monthly fixed limit, to one that only charges for each byte of data that actually gets used.

The term 'serverless' is somewhat misleading, as there are still servers providing these backend services, but all of the server space and infrastructure concerns are handled by the vendor. Serverless means that the developers can do their work without having to worry about servers at all.

What are Backend Services? What is the Difference between Frontend and Backend?

Application development is generally split into two realms: the frontend and the back-end. The frontend is the part of the application that users see and interact with, such as the visual layout. The backend is the part that the user doesn't see; this includes the server where the application's files live and the database where user data and business logic is persisted.

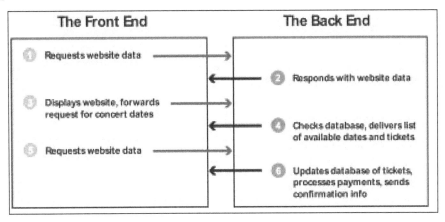

For example, let's imagine a website that sells concert tickets. When a user types a request into the browser window, the browser sends a request to the backend server, which responds with the website data. The user will then see the frontend of the website, which will include text, images, and form fields for the user to fill out. The user can then interact with one of the form fields on the frontend to search for their favorite musical act. When the user clicks on 'submit', this will trigger another request to the backend. The backend code checks its database to see if a performer with this name exists, and if so, when they will be playing next, and how many tickets are available. The backend will then pass that data back to the frontend, and the frontend will display the results in a way that makes sense to the user. Similarly, when the user creates an account and enters financial information to buy the tickets, another back-and-forth communication between the frontend and backend will occur.

What Kind of Backend Services can Serverless Computing Provide?

Most serverless providers offer database and storage services to their customers, and many also have Function-as-a-Service (FaaS) platforms, like Cloudflare Workers. These platforms can execute pieces of code on the edge without storing any data.

What are the Advantages of Serverless Computing?

- Lower costs: Serverless computing is generally very cost-effective, as traditional cloud providers of backend services (server allocation) often result in the user paying for unused space or idle CPU time.

- Simplified scalability: Developers using serverless architecture don't have to worry about policies to scale up their code. The serverless vendor handles all of the scaling on demand.

- Simplified backend code: With FaaS, developers can create simple functions that independently perform a single purpose, like making an API call.

- Quicker turnaround: Serverless architecture can significantly cut time to market. Instead of needing a complicated deploy process to roll out bug fixes and new features, developers can add and modify code on a piecemeal basis.

Why use Serverless Computing?

Serverless computing offers a number of advantages over traditional cloud-based or server-centric infrastructure. For many developers, serverless architectures offer greater scalability, more flexibility, and quicker time to release, all at a reduced cost. With serverless architectures, developers do not need to worry about purchasing, provisioning, and managing backend servers. However, serverless computing is not a magic bullet for all web application developers.

How does Serverless Computing Work?

Serverless computing is an architecture in which a vendor provides backend services as they are needed.

What are the Advantages of Serverless Computing?

No Server Management is Necessary

Although 'serverless' computing does actually take place on servers, developers never have to deal with the servers. They are managed by the vendor. This can reduce the investment necessary in DevOps, which lowers expenses, and it also frees up developers to create and expand their applications without being constrained by server capacity.

Developers are Only Charged for the Server Space they use, Reducing Cost

As in a 'pay-as-you-go' phone plan, developers are only charged for what they use. Code only runs when backend functions are needed by the serverless application, and the code automatically scales up as needed. Provisioning is dynamic, precise, and real-time. Some services are so exact that they break their charges down into 100-millisecond increments. In contrast, in a traditional 'server-full' architecture, developers have to project in advance how much server capacity they will need and then purchase that capacity, whether they end up using it or not.

Serverless Architectures are Inherently Scalable

Imagine if the post office could somehow magically add and decommission delivery trucks at will, increasing the size of its fleet as the amount of mail spikes and decreasing its fleet for times when fewer deliveries are necessary. That's essentially what serverless applications are able to do.

Applications built with a serverless infrastructure will scale automatically as the user base grows or usage increases. If a function needs to be run in multiple instances, the vendor's servers will start up, run, and end them as they are needed, often using containers (the functions start up more quickly if they have been run recently). As a result, a serverless application will be able to handle an unusually high number of requests just as well as it can process a single request from a single user. A traditionally structured application with a fixed amount of server space can be overwhelmed by a sudden increase in usage.

Quick Deployments and Updates are Possible

Using a serverless infrastructure, there is no need to upload code to servers or do any backend configuration in order to release a working version of an application. Developers can very quickly upload bits of code and release a new product. They can upload code all at once or one function at a time, since the application is not a single monolithic stack but rather a collection of functions provisioned by the vendor.

This also makes it possible to quickly update, patch, fix, or add new features to an application. It is not necessary to make changes to the whole application; instead, developers can update the application one function at a time.

Code can Run Closer to the End user, Decreasing Latency

Because the application is not hosted on an origin server, its code can be run from anywhere. It is therefore possible, depending on the vendor used, to run application functions on servers that are close to the end user. This reduces latency because requests from the user no longer have to travel all the way to an origin server. Cloudflare Workers enables this kind of serverless latency reduction.

What are the Disadvantages of Serverless Computing?

Testing and Debugging become more Challenging

It is difficult to replicate the serverless environment in order to see how code will actually perform once deployed. Debugging is more complicated because developers do not have visibility into backend processes, and because the application is broken up into separate, smaller functions. The Cloudflare Workers Playground is a sandbox that helps reduce friction in testing and debugging.

Serverless Computing Introduces New Security Concerns

When vendors run the entire backend, it may not be possible to fully vet their security, which can especially be a problem for applications that handle personal or sensitive data.

Because companies are not assigned their own discrete physical servers, serverless providers will often be running code from several of their customers on a single server at any given time. This issue of sharing machinery with other parties is known as 'multitenancy' – think of several companies trying to lease and work in a single office at the same time. Multitenancy can affect application performance and, if the multi-tenant servers are not configured properly, could result in data exposure. Multitenancy has little to no impact for networks that sandbox functions correctly and have powerful enough infrastructure. For instance, Cloudflare runs a 15-Tbps network with enough excess capacity to mitigate service degradation, and all serverless functions hosted by Cloudflare run in their own sandbox (via the Chrome V8 engine).

Serverless Architectures are not Built for Long-running Processes

This limits the kinds of applications that can cost-effectively run in a serverless architecture. Because serverless providers charge for the amount of time code is running, it may cost more to run an application with long-running processes in a serverless infrastructure compared to a traditional one.

Performance may be affected

Because it's not constantly running, serverless code may need to 'boot up' when it is used. This startup time may degrade performance. However, if a piece of code is used regularly, the serverless provider will keep it ready to be activated – a request for this ready-to-go code is called a 'warm start.' A request for code that hasn't been used in a while is called a 'cold start.'

Cloudflare Workers largely avoids the cold-starting issue by using the Chrome V8 engine, which in most cases is able to start up and run JavaScript code in under 5 milliseconds. If the code is already running, the response time is under a millisecond.

Vendor Lock-in is a Risk

Allowing a vendor to provide all backend services for an application inevitably increases reliance on that vendor. Setting up a serverless architecture with one vendor can make it difficult to switch vendors if necessary, especially since each vendor offers slightly different features and workflows. (Cloudflare Workers are easier to migrate because they are written in JavaScript and written against the widely used service workers API.)

Who should use a Serverless Architecture?

Developers who want to decrease their go-to-market time and build lightweight, flexible applications that can be expanded or updated quickly may benefit greatly from serverless computing.

Serverless architectures will reduce costs for applications that see inconsistent usage, with peak periods alternating with times of little to no traffic. For such applications, purchasing a server or a block of servers that are constantly running and always available, even when unused, may be a waste of resources. A serverless setup will respond instantly when needed and will not incur costs when at rest.

Also, developers who want to push some or all of their application functions close to end users for reduced latency will require at least a partially serverless architecture, since doing so necessitates moving some processes out of the origin server.

When should Developers Avoid using a Serverless Architecture?

There are cases when it makes more sense, both from a cost perspective and from a system architecture perspective, to use dedicated servers that are either self-managed or offered as a service. For instance, large applications with a fairly constant, predictable workload may require a traditional setup, and in such cases the traditional setup is probably less expensive.

Additionally, it may be prohibitively difficult to migrate legacy applications to a new infrastructure with an entirely different architecture.

How does Cloudflare Help Developers Build Serverless Architectures?

Cloudflare Workers is a product that enables developers to write JavaScript functions and deploy them at the edge of the Cloudflare network. This makes it possible to run application code in a serverless architecture as close to the end user as possible, minimizing latency.

References

- Virtualization-in-cloud-computing-2165-7866-1000136: longdom.org, Retrieved 28 March, 2019

- State-of-the-art-antenna-technology-for-cloud-radio-access-networks-c-rans, cloud-computing-architecture-and-applications, books: intechopen.com, Retrieved 21 June, 2019

- Hybrid-cloud-architecture-concepts, cloud-infrastructure: networkcomputing.com, Retrieved 25 May, 2019

- Hybrid-cloud-management-30474: techopedia.com, Retrieved 10 August, 2019

- What-is-multi-cloud, glossary: citrix.com, Retrieved 27 March, 2019

- What-is-serverless, learning, serverless: cloudflare.com, Retrieved 12 June, 2019

Applications of Cloud Computing

There are various applications of cloud computing in biomedical sciences, business operations, education, transportation systems, manufacturing industry, etc. This chapter closely examines these key applications of cloud computing to provide an extensive understanding of the subject.

Cloud Applications for Energy Management

Energy management is the process of monitoring, controlling, and conserving energy. In smart grid, energy management is a major concern. It is needed for resource conservation, climate protection and cost saving without compromising work processes by optimally coordinating several energy sources. BEMS (Building Energy Management System) and HEMS (Home Energy Management System), dynamic pricing, and load shifting are different applications that are implemented by researchers in the past to address energy management.

Problems with Existing Approaches without Cloud

Demand Response (DR) refers to "changes in electric usage by end-use customers from their normal consumption patterns in response to changes in the price of electricity overtime, or to incentive payments designed to induce lower electricity use at times of high wholesale market prices or when system reliability is jeopardized". DR is achieved through the application of a variety of DR resource types, including distributed generation, dispatchable load, storage and other resources that may contribute to modify the power supplied by the main grid. In the conventional smart grid architecture (without cloud), several problems, as detailed below, are addressed by researchers:

- Master-Slave architected (without clouds) could cause Cyber-attacks (Distributed Denial of Service (DDoS)).

- Any failure in Master-Slave architecture could lead to a system failure, which does not exist in cloud computing.

- Can serve for limited number of users (customers) due to limited server capacity.

- Serving of such large number of the customer will be challenging because of limited memory and storage.

- Management, as well as stability issues, will be required.

Solution Concept with Cloud Applications

For many years, researchers proposed several solution concepts for demand response and micro-grid management.

Kim et al. proposed the concept of Cloud-Based Demand Response (CDR) for fast response times in large scale deployment. In the concept of CDR, the Energy Management System (EMS) and smart meters will be the slaves while master will be the utility. The data-centric communication, publisher/subscriber will be used by the CDR, whereby two cloud-based demand models are suggested (a) data-centric communication and (b) topic-based group communication rather than typical IPcentric communication. Overhead problems, such as implementation cost, and the selection of appropriate strategy, exists in the demand response model that occurs in the private cloud when the size of the network is small.

Ming Chen et al. analyzed the necessity and feasibility of cloud computing technology in power dispatching and presented the Deployment Method of power dispatching automation system based on cloud computing. Easy standardization of power dispatching technique; rapid delivery of advanced functions; and significant improvement reliability of IT infrastructures can be achieved by means of cloud computing technology. It reduces administrative costs, and it solves the contradiction between hierarchical management and "integrated construction" in energy sector.

Zhang Liang proposed the concept of cloud dispatching, a kind of cloud computing-based overall framework of intelligent dispatching center. The cloud computing-based layered architecture includes Physical Resource Layer- physical hardware, platform resources and application systems such as SCADA, EMS, TMR, WARMS, Virtual Resource Layer - map physical resources in various types into virtual resources, Cloud Service layer - packages virtual resources into services, that are posted to the clouds, Cloud Management Layer - provides integrated management of cloud services for users, and Cloud Access Layer - the way user access cloud dispatching. It integrates the existing resources demands among various dispatching centers, reduces the system construction and expansion cost and improves overall dispatching business ability.

The smart grid infrastructure needs to be deployed globally. In order to balance the real-time demand and supply curves, rapid integration and analyzation of information that streams from multiple smart meters simultaneously is required that necessitates the scalable software platform. Yang et al. proposed that cloud platforms are well suited to support huge data and computationally-intensive, always-on applications. To build a software infrastructure to support such dynamic and always-on applications, scalable requirements of resources are offered by the cloud applications. In these environments, cloud platforms serve as essential components due to the various benefits they offer, as mentioned below:

- Cloud acts elastically to avoid costly capital investment by the utility during the peak hours.

- Customers can be benefited from the real-time information by sharing the real-time energy usage and pricing information.

- Some data can be shared with a third party by using cloud services, after meeting the data privacy policies for developing intelligent applications to customize consumer needs.

In order to take decisions at different instances, implementation of specialized data abstraction for data streams generated from the different components is required for real-time monitoring. On the other hand, third-party vendors are allowed to participate in such real-time monitoring system that necessitates defining an effective privacy policy as a security mechanism.

Virtualization is one of the most efficient techniques for cost reduction, resource optimization, and server management. Cloud computing can be implemented in the form of different strategies of the micro-grids. Researchers proposed a framework for integrating cloud computing applications for micro-grid management in the form of different modules such as infrastructure, power management, and service. The infrastructure and power management modules are used for task scheduling and micro-grid power management respectively. The different operators publish their service description using the service module. With the implementation of cloud computing, the external computing devices can be integrated with the internal ones. Thus, the number of supported customers increases as suggested by Rajeev and Ashok. In such a manner, integrating virtual energy sources with the existing energy storage devices and the energy exchange mechanism can be achieved among the micro-grids to meet the energy requirements from consumers.

Dynamic pricing implementation can be used to address energy management. Xuan Li and Lo proposed two smart grid related issues: (a) peak demand and (b) dynamic pricing. Requests from customers, which are to be executed, based on the priority, available resources, and other applicable constraints, are scheduled with the integration of cloud. During peak hours, the messages from smart meters are more than those in the nonpeak hours. In such a scenario, incoming jobs from users are scheduled according to their priority, available resources, and applicable constraints. With the integration of dynamic bandwidth allotment mechanism using cloud application, these issues can be addressed conveniently. During the peak-hour, the allotted bandwidth is higher than that in the nonpeak hour, in order to serve all the incoming jobs simultaneously.

Cloud-based services are used for communication and management schemes in the smart grid by Ji et al., while providing the facility of power monitoring and early-warning system as well. In such a scenario, the real-time support is provided by using enterprise service bus (ESB) and serviceoriented architecture (SOA). On-demand, efficient, flexible, and scalable smart grid power monitoring system can be built by this approach. Standard Web services, service finding, service registry, interfaces, and service access are implemented into a single cloud application using SOA, as the SOA relies on publishing applications as a service. Smart grid energy management can be performed using the ESB architecture, which includes activities such as security management, task management, and resource management, with the implementation of cloud applications.

The Energy Service Interface (ESI) interconnects internal customer energy resources and external systems. Eun-Kyu Lee et al. built an ESI test-bed which includes ESI, a demand response service server, and customer energy resources. A demand response client module is implemented by ESI. The customer energy data are represented by XML format and web service interfaces are implemented for inter-domain communications. An additional test-bed, in which the ESI is deployed on a public cloud. The two test-beds are deployed to verify that the ESI plays the service "prosumer" in a practical manner for a couple of energy service scenarios. The Energy Service Interface (ESI) interconnects internal customer energy resources and external systems.

The trend of the power grid to shift to the Smart Grid leads to the enormous pool of computing and massive data storage requirements. To overcome these demands of cloud computing, highly distributed and scalable computing resources, to host the smart grid applications was proposed. Bitzer and Gebretsadik discussed the feasibility of handling the monitoring of renewable energy in smart grid on cloud computing framework by a Lab-demonstrator. The Lab-demonstration set up considers the power system and the cloud computing domains. The distributed energy resources and the local SCADA control are considered as the power system domain whereas the cloud computing domain contains a specific cloud computing provider. Generation plants can be monitored and controlled by the local SCADA software running on the local computer. Through web-based SCADA monitoring and controlling of the plants can be done from anywhere.

Jinsung Byun et al. proposed intelligent cloud home energy management system (iCHEMS) to address inefficient home energy management systems due to intermittent energy generation by renewable energy. In iCHEMS, a household appliance is assigned with dynamic priority according to its type and current status. The use of household appliances is scheduled based on the assigned priority and renewable energy capability. To enhance utilization of computing and renewable energy system resources, iCHEMS exploits cloud computing. Energy distribution, situation-based energy management, and user-centric energy management are services provided by cloud resources. With the help of cloud computing, the proposed system reduces the high cost, required to implement smart green home and average total power consumption.

Aras Sheikhi et al. proposed a model for utilizing the cloud computing technology in the smart grid domain and explores how cloud computing plays an effective role in DSM (Demand Side Management) game among a group of Smart Energy Hubs (S.E.). Interaction between the utility company and demand response realizing functions, the amount of loads per customer are to be reduced and at which incentive price, are performed on the cloud. In this model, to reach an optimal DSM, based on the game theoretic approach, load profiles of S.E. Hubs are communicated to the CC (Cloud Computing) where each S.E. Hub attempts to minimize its own energy cost in response to the aggregated information on the actions of the other users. The result of the game, Nash Equilibrium (NE), leads to a proper strategy for each S.E. Hub to minimize their energy bill. The DSM game reduces the PAR (Peak to average ratio) in the electricity grid and the daily energy charges of each S.E. Hub can be significantly reduced.

Researchers proposed a dynamic load-shifting program, makes use of real-time data, in a cloud computing framework to address the forecasting and operational challenges issues, which are to be met when implementing effective renewable energy program. A new dynamic renewable factor, a reference parameter (captures and represents the dynamics in the pricing and shifting strategy) in the algorithm, is proposed to facilitate on-time incentive based load shifting program. With the help of cloud-based infrastructure, the widely distributed renewable energy sources operations are coordinated by the utility at a minimal cost. In addition improved utilization renewable sources, reduction in the peak demand at domestic level, additional household annual bill savings are the benefits of dynamic shifting program.

Smart grids with the usage of information technologies enable efficient power grid. To cope with the huge amount of data and daily fluctuations by the smart meters the underlying infrastructure must be (i) massively scalable and (ii) elastic. Cloud computing is a cost-efficient alternative to dedicated data centers. Martin et al. explored the combination of an elastic Event Stream Processing (ESP) system named Stream Mine3G and cloud technologies in the context of energy forecasting. ESP aim at processing high volume streams of data by processing data on-the-fly instead of storing it first. StreamMine3G, scalable and elastic ESP, is equipped with a resource manager, acquires and releases virtual machines, enables load shifting from overloaded nodes to less loaded ones through migration of stateful and stateless operators. The elasticity properties of ESP system was showcased by performing several experiments on deployed StreamMine3G at Amazon EC2.

Neeraj Kumar et al. proposed a context-aware layered architecture for demand side management using vehicular cyber–physical system (VCPS) with cloud support. With the integration of vehicles with cloud computing, storage, sensing, software, platform, and Network-as-a-Service (NaaS) are offered to the clients. Bayesian coalition game concept and learning automata, an intelligent context-aware data collection and processing, are used. In this scheme, players are the mobile vehicles, which can sense the SG environment and collect information from it. Alert generation and information dissemination are the actions performed by the players in the game. The player's action probability vector is updated based on the feedback from the environment to the players. Reduction in the energy shortage and information processing delay, the increase in energy sold back to the grid are achieved in the proposed scheme.

The importance of BEMS (Building Information Management System) is increasing as Smart Grid spreads. BEMS of each entity is improved to provide high-quality services. The number of the entity increases according to the coverage area of a building. Insung Hong et al. proposed the Cloud computing-based BEMS to lessen the burden of each entity by a System Manager, a centralized server. To monitor power consumption and environmental information, sensor entities with 8-bit microcontroller and ZigBee and Low-cost power are used. The BEMS consists of three the Power Monitoring Entity (PME) - monitor and control device's power consumption, Environmental Information Entity (EIE) - collect environmental information, and System Manager - collect and manage data and provide services to users. This system reduces each entity's cost and hardware specification.

Effective DEM depends on load and renewable production forecasting that leads to large volumes of data generated by a vast number of smart meters. In order to optimize the smart grid operations, DEM requires high performance computing, efficient data network management, robust data analytics, and cloud computing techniques; the cloud computing model meets these requirements. In Literature, approaches have been developed to increase the energy efficiency of High Performance Computing (HPC) data centers, such as the cooperation with the SG in, energy conscious scheduling in. Most of smart grid applications, such as advanced metering infrastructure, SCADA, and energy management can be facilitated by the available cloud service models, namely software as a service, platform as a service, and infrastructure as a service.

Cloud based Economic Power Dispatching

Smart grids needs to be equipped with an integrated solution to the problem of modern energy delivery network that enables two-way energy and communication with the customers. To manage large amounts of data, cloud computing is the best way for smart grids due to its scalable, economical, and flexible characteristics. We propose a cloud based dispatching model in the smart grid domain. The prime responsibility of the Electric Utilities is to meet the customers' requirements at all times with quality and quantity as agreed. It matches the power generation by the utilities against the customers' power demand at all times. As the consumers' demand changes at every instant, the power generation by the Utilities should match with the consumers' demand. In reality, the power generation can't be adjusted at every instance; hence the generation is adjusted normally at 20 minutes interval. The matching of power generation against the consumers' demand is known as Power Dispatching (Hongseok Kim et al., and Palanichamy et al.). In cloud based economic power dispatching model, the utility and customers interact through the cloud, and the functions for cost optimization are performed in the cloud. From utility's perspective, cloud appears to be an information system, which takes an input from utility (e.g., Power demand, weather data, fuel cost etc.), processes the information, and gives an output to utility and customers (e.g., generations of the individual plants, total production cost etc.). It is worth pointing out that the Cloud network performs the power dispatching job as per the instruction of the Electric Utilities since the decision authority is the Utility. For its services, the Cloud gets it service charges from the Utilities. This arrangement is economical for the Utilities since they need not invest on communication and computing facilities.

Reasons to use Cloud based Energy Management Software System

Accessibility

Cloud-based systems allow users to access information with greater flexibility. By utilizing a cloud based system, users can store information from many different data acquisition systems and access and analyze this information from different sites with one application. In fact, such a system allows for easier portfolio management as it is possible to view all managed sites at once. Because managers are able to access information remotely, this also reduces on-site maintenance to only when absolutely necessary, saving time and cost in manual maintenance.

Cost Reduction in Development

Cost reduction proves to be one of the greatest benefits of cloud-based energy management systems as it allows companies to curb costs for the development of local infrastructure. Innovation of the software as needed is crucial to remain competitive. Because these systems are generally sold as a service, the consumer does not need to take care of maintenance and updating of the database and infrastructure which again reduces wasted time and money that could be spent on implementing energy and money saving practices based on the data received. Clients also only need to pay for what they use thereby reducing excessive overhead cost. The flexibility of cloud-based services also allow for minimal sunk costs as needs of the company may change.

Cost Reduction in Man Power Resource Allocation

Not only do cloud services minimize costs of software development and maintenance but also direct monetary costs, the cost of time, and spent resources on maintaining in-house IT professionals and infrastructure on gathering, storing and analyzing energy data. This proves most beneficial for sectors that do not or cannot prioritize in-house energy management software experts.

Elasticity

Cloud-based systems allow for greater deployment flexibility, meaning that it is easy to either upgrade or downgrade resources which proves a great advantage for energy management systems compared to owned infrastructure. This allows the consumer to reduce or increase site data acquisition and maintenance much easier as demand dictates. For energy management specialists and consultants, this proves especially beneficial as clients change, more sites are easily implemented into the system for better-facilitated management.

Access to Data Anywhere, Anytime and on Any Device

A major selling factor for cloud-based services, especially for energy management is that users can access their data, dashboard and any analytics from any device around the world. For example, when looking at energy analytics for a building, an energy manager or consultant does not need to be in the building, or even in the office to get live updates on energy use or waste. With access to information from portable devices, this flexibility allows for a competitive edge for users.

Boost User Experience

Allowing customers to engage independently with the ever-innovating cloud-based software boosts the user experience. Customers being able to alter the use of the software to their needs without having to develop the platform differently on their own is crucial to support a changing market. The ability to also interact easily with energy data on a constantly updating system is crucial to a better understanding and use of that data.

Disaster Recovery

Every business possesses sensitive, important information that is crucial to business operations and must be protected. Cloud-based services are the simplest way to keep information backed up and safe. Specifically, it is cited that small businesses are twice as likely as larger companies to implement cloud-based backup and recovery solutions. This solution saves time and large up-front investments. With cloud-based energy management software, energy data and savings analysis is securely maintained and updated without much work from the customer.

Ease of Collaboration

By promoting accessibility, cloud-based services allow for analysis and access to data around the world. Especially beneficial for energy consultants or energy managers for large corporations, because the information is connected to one online system, it is possible to support either many clients at once or support many branches of one client from around the world. Consultants and managers can easily present this information from this one source across many platforms to optimize client service.

Enhances a Competitive Edge

Taking the first step towards cloud-based energy management software, and cloud-based services, in general, allow for a competitive edge in the market as a differentiating feature that can benefit the company. Cloud-based software can allow even small and medium-size businesses to act faster than larger, more established companies. For consultancy firms and utility companies especially, by using cloud-based services, they are able to offer clients quick response analytics and advice creating a better client relationship.

White Label Capabilities

Again, this aspect emphasizes the flexibility of potential cloud-based service systems. White label services indicate that the site can look like it is managed by the host company such as a consultancy firm to its clients. In order to increase brand awareness and differentiate your company especially for consultancy firms, this feature of certain cloud services allows for seamless integration with a company. The term white label can encompass many features, from the color theme, the URLs, the logos, the reports etc. For example, the white label services offered by Wattics are a premier differentiator of its cloud-based energy management software that allows white label services including but not limited to company colours, contact details, notifications sent from company email addresses and log in from company websites.

These top ten reasons why cloud-based energy management software provides more efficient and cheaper tools for energy management on any scale are important to understand for any professional looking to take their business to the next step with efficient energy management.

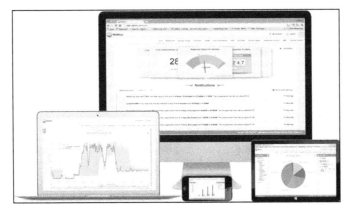

Cloud Computing in the Manufacturing Industry

Customer demands are shifting constantly. That means shorter product cycles and time to market schedules. Not only do you need to be efficient and ensure the highest quality but you also need to be fast and responsive.

On-premise and even hosted (private cloud) platforms cannot keep up with the ever-increasing complexity and demands of modern manufacturing. Your employees and supply chain participants (customers and suppliers) need timely and controlled access to your business and operations data for more-informed decision making—anywhere, from any device. True cloud platforms give you that connectivity.

Often, your IT team ends up spending most of their time ensuring that all users are on the correct version just to be able to use the functionality. As a result, your operations teams don't have the visibility or control needed to turn on a dime. And your business teams can't get insight to measure performance or act on changing demand. True cloud platforms are always current—there's no version control issues—so you can focus on optimizing your business instead of on IT maintenance.

Operating with a single source of truth, which is an inherent benefit of cloud systems, eliminates disparate tools and data silos so the entire business knows what happening at any given time. No more manual input or delayed syncing up of data needed. If you need to know whether products are within quality or customer specifications, you simply login and find out in the "manufacturing moment." And you reduce the amount of errors, bottlenecks, and mundane tasks in streamlining processes and workflows.

Investing in a cloud platform is not simply a technology decision—it's a business strategy—one that gives you the agility, speed, and insight you need. With cloud manufacturing, you're able to quickly and easily turn on new facilities and support market fluctuations because the onus is on the cloud provider to manage scalability. Not on you. Your cloud service provider is responsible for a secure, reliable, available, and scalable service—their incentives are aligned with yours. Their success depends on yours.

- Over 90 percent of global enterprises report using cloud computing in some part of their business.

- 66 percent of manufacturing enterprises from 17 countries reported using a cloud implementation.

- Cloud-hosted services are expected to account for nearly half of all organization-level software usage among manufacturers by 2023.

- 46 percent of respondents to a 2012 SCM World Survey contended that cloud computing contributed to greater supply chain collaboration, and leads to problems being solved twice as fast.

Cloud computing is transforming virtually every facet of modern manufacturing. Whether it's how you operate, integrate into supply chains, design and make products, or how your customers use the products. Cloud computing is helping manufacturers like you to innovate, reduce costs, and increase your competitiveness. The question is not "should we" go to the cloud but "how soon can we get on the cloud," because your competition may already be there.

Benefits of Cloud Computing for Manufacturers

Today, manufacturing companies the world over are faced with a clear choice: either be part of the technological revolution and embrace new developments such as cloud technology or risk behind left behind and losing business to more technologically-advanced competitors. The good news is that there are a vast range of areas in which businesses can implement cloud technology to benefit employees and optimize production across the sector as a whole.

Opportunities for Upskilling

In order to succeed in the long-term, a business needs to take care of its workforce. Fears surrounding the notion that AI and cloud computing could render some jobs obsolete can be allayed by helping ambitious employees to develop their skill set. Training your team to work with, rather than against, emerging technologies is the best way to continue driving your business forward while boosting employee morale and loyalty levels.

Migrating to the cloud can also free up valuable time that would otherwise be spent on manual processes, using it to work on higher-value tasks that have a greater impact on the wider business.

Maximize Efficiency

Effective implementation of cloud computing goes beyond connecting your PLCs and various tech on the shop floor—it means being able to connect your shop floor to the rest of the business. With a single manufacturing system of record on hand, employees, suppliers, and partners can refer to one source for accurate information, ensuring increased consistency and great efficiency when serving customers.

Efficiency is about accomplishing more with fewer resources, without compromising on quality. For sustained growth, manufacturers must drive efficiency both for its own operations, and for its clients. The way to do that is through the cloud.

The manufacturing cloud significantly decreases time-to-market. Cloud-based solutions are generally more straightforward than their traditional on-premise counterparts, making implementation easier and thereby saving both time and money.

Embracing cloud computing also allows manufacturing teams to focus their energies on core business functions. Such an approach transfers responsibility for the operation and maintenance of IT infrastructure to the cloud provider, cutting down running costs and freeing up internal resources to focus on driving value, rather than upkeeping systems. That means manufacturers can priorities core business functions.

Manage Energy Data more Effectively

When it comes to industry, the European Union's Energy Efficiency Directive tends to dominate the discussion. Without the resources necessary to get a comprehensive view of consumption levels, carrying out a worthwhile evaluation of your company's energy efficiency is essentially impossible. To properly navigate through the massive amounts of data extracted from the shop floor and translate that into something that makes sense, many manufacturers deploy energy data management systems or 'EDMS'.

EDMS are set up locally and embedded into a company's existing infrastructure, and can be moved into the cloud. The primary benefit of cloud-based EDMS is that it facilitates business-wide collation and analysis of energy data.

On-demand Delivery

90% of manufacturing companies use cloud-based productivity apps, while 70% felt that working in the cloud maximized their ability to effectively meet customer demand. Why?

For on-demand delivery to be possible, an clear view of that demand is necessary. Smart, cloud-driving manufacturing software can go through order history at different times of the year and use that to create a forecast. The forecast then becomes the basis for demand and capacity planning—where any gaps can be identified and shared across the business for departments to plan and adjust their strategies as necessary.

Minimize Costs

Cloud computing can minimize costs across procurement and operations, saving manufacturing teams money on software, hardware, and infrastructure. This frees up capital, creating more budget for other areas of the business.

When you work with cloud providers such as Amazon Web Services (AWS) or Azure, you only pay for the resources you need, exactly when you need them. In terms of operating costs, using a cloud provider completely eliminates costs associated with the operation, maintenance, and administration of hardware and software.

Cloud Computing for Intelligent Transportation System

Intelligent transportation clouds could provide Services such as autonomy, mobility, decision support and the standard development Environment for traffic management strategies, and so on. With mobile agent technology, an urban-traffic management system based on Agent-Based Distributed and Adaptive Platforms for Transportation Systems (Adapts) is both feasible and effective. However, the large-scale use of mobile agents will lead to the emergence of a complex, powerful organization layer that requires enormous computing and power resources.

IBM introduces urban traffic management system in the year of 1956. Today, transportation research and development is no longer a field dominated by civil, mechanical, operations research, and other traditional engineering and management disciplines. Rather, computer sciences, control, communication, the Internet, and methods developed in artificial intelligence (AI), computational intelligence, web sciences, and many other emerging information sciences and engineering areas have formed the core of new ITS technology and become integral and important parts of modern transportation engineering. Cloud computing control the traffic allocation process provides optimal solution with five stages specification. In the first phase, computers were huge and costly, so mainframes were usually shared by many terminals. In the 1960s, the whole traffic management system shared the resources of one computer in a centralized model. Introduction of large-scale integrated circuits and the miniaturization of computer technology, the IT industry welcomed the second transformation in computing paradigm. In this paradigm, microcomputer was powerful enough to handle a single user's computing requirements. At that time, the same technology leads to the appearance of the traffic signal controller. Each TSC had enough independent computing and storage capacity to control one period, researchers optimized the control modes and parameters of offline to improve control. Traffic management systems in this phase, such as transyt, consisted of numerous single control points.

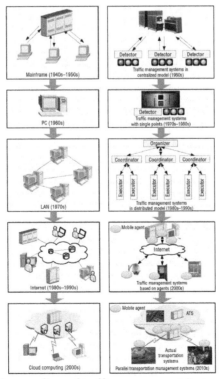

The paradigm of traffic management Systems.

In phase three, local area networks (lans) appeared to enable resource sharing and handle the increasingly complex requirements. One such lan, the ethernet, was invented in 1973 and has been widely used hierarchical model. Network communication enabled the layers to handle their own duties while cooperating with one another. In the following internet era, users have been able to retrieve data from remote sites and process them locally, but this wasted a lot of precious network bandwidth. Agent-based computing and mobile agents were proposed to handle this vexing problem. Only requiring a runtime environment, mobile agents can run computations near data to improve performance by reducing communication time and costs. This computing paradigm soon drew much attention in the transportation field. From multi-agent systems and agent structure to ways of negotiating between agents to control agent strategies, all these fields have had varying degrees of success. Now, the it industry has ushered in the fifth computing paradigm cloud computing. Based on the internet, cloud computing provides on demand computing capacity to individuals and businesses in the form of heterogeneous and autonomous services. With cloud computing, users do not need to be aware of or to understand the details of the infrastructure in the "clouds" they need only know what resources they need and how to obtain appropriate services and those resources, which shields the computational complexity of providing the required services. In recent years, the research and application of parallel transportation management systems (ptms), which consists of artificial systems, computational experiments, and parallel execution, has become a hot spot in the traffic research field. Here, the term parallel describes the parallel interaction between an actual transportation system and one or more of its corresponding artificial or virtual counterparts.

Agent Based Traffic Management System

Agent technology was used in traffic management systems as early as 1992, while multi-agent traffic management systems were presented later. However, all these systems focus on negotiation and collaboration between static agents for coordination and optimization. In 2004, mobile agent technology began to attract the attention of the transportation field. The characteristics of mobile agents—autonomous, mobile, and adaptive—make them suitable to handling the uncertainties and inconstant states in a dynamic environment. The mobile agent moves through the network to reach control devices and implements appropriate strategies in either autonomous or passive modes. In this way, traffic devices only need to provide an operating platform for mobile traffic agents working in dynamic environments, without having to contain every traffic strategies. This approach saves storage and computing capacity in physical control devices, which helps reduce their update and replacement rates. Moreover, when faced with the different requirements of dynamic traffic scenes, a multi-agent system taking advantage of mobile agents will perform better than any static agent system. In 2005, the Agent-Based Distributed and Adaptive Platforms for Transportation Systems (Adapts) was proposed as a hierarchical urban traffic- management system. The three layers in Adapts are organization, coordination, and execution, respectively. Mobile agents play a role as the carrier of the control strategies in the system. In the follow-up articles, both the architecture and the function static agents in each layer were also depicted in detail of mobile traffic control agents were defined clearly. What's more, a new traffic signal controller was designed to provide the runtime environment for mobile agent. Currently, Adapts is part of PtMS, which can take advantage of mobile traffic strategy agents to manage a road map. The organization layer, which is the core of our system, has four functions, agent-oriented task decomposition, agent scheduling, encapsulating traffic strategy, and agent management. The organization layer consists of a management agent (MA), three databases (control strategy, typical traffic scenes, and traffic strategy agent), and an artificial transportation system.

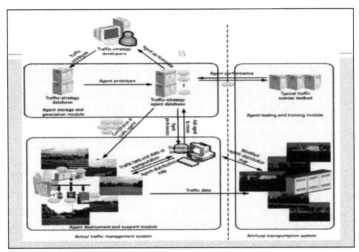

Organizational layers of Agent based Distributed Transportation System.

As one traffic strategy has been proposed, the strategy code is saved in the traffic strategy database. Then, according to the agent's prototype, the traffic strategy will be encapsulated into a traffic strategy agent that is saved in the traffic strategy agent database. Also, the traffic strategy agent will be tested by the typical traffic scenes to review its performance. Typical traffic scenes, which are stored in a typical intersections database, can determine the performance of various agents. With the support of the three databases, the MA embodies the organization layer's intelligence. The function of the agents' scheduling and agent-oriented task decomposition is based on the MA's knowledge base, which consists of the performances of different agents in various traffic scenes. If the urban management system cannot deal with a transportation scene with its existing agents, it will send a traffic task to the organization layer for help. The traffic task contains the information about the state of urban transportation, so a traffic task can be decomposed into a combination of several typical traffic scenes. With knowledge about the most appropriate traffic strategy agent to deal with any typical traffic scene, when the organization layer receives the traffic task, the MA will return a combination of agents and a map about the distribution of agents to solve it. This way, this system takes advantage of the strategy agent to manage a road map. Lastly, we set up an ATS to test performance of the urban-traffic management system based on the map showing the distribution of agents. ATS is modelled from the bottom up, and it mirrors the real urban transportation environment. because the speed of the computational experiments is faster than the real world, if the performance is unsatisfactory, the agent-distribution map in both systems will be modified.

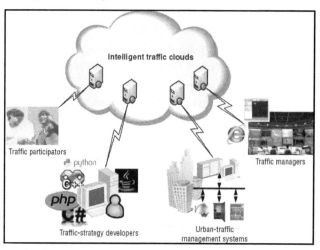

Cloud computing for urban traffic management system.

New Challenges

We need to send the agent-distribution map and the relevant agents to ATS for experimental evaluation, so we can test the cost of this operation during the runtime of Adapts. In our test bed, traffic-control agents must communicate with ATS to get traffic detection data and send back lamp control data. Both running load and communication volumes increase with the number of intersections. If the time to complete the experimental evaluation exceeds a certain threshold, the experimental results become meaningless and useless. As a result, the carry capacity for experimental evaluation of one PC is limited. In our test, we used a 2.66-GHz PC with a 1-Gbyte memory to run both ATS and Adapts. The experiment took 3,600 seconds in real time. The number of intersections we tested increased from two to 20. When the number of traffic-control agents is 20, the experiment takes 1,130 seconds. If we set the time threshold to 600 seconds, the maximum number of intersections in one experiment is only 12. This is insufficient to handle model major urban areas such as Beijing, where the central area within the Second Ring Road intersection contains up to 119 intersections. scale of several hundreds of intersections. Furthermore, a complete urban traffic management system also requires traffic control, detection, guidance, monitoring, and emergency subsystems. To handle the different states in a traffic environment, an urban-traffic management system must provide appropriate traffic strategy agents. And to handle performance improvements and the addition of new subsystems, new traffic strategies must be introduced continually. So future urban-traffic management systems must generate, store, manage, test, optimize, and effectively use a large number of mobile agents. Moreover, they need a decision-support system to communicate with traffic managers. A comprehensive, powerful decision-support system with a friendly human-computer interface is an inevitable trend in the development of urban-traffic management systems. Thus, future systems must have the following capabilities. Computing Power the more typical traffic scenes used to test a traffic-strategy agent, the more detailed the learning about the advantages and disadvantages of different traffic strategy agents will be.

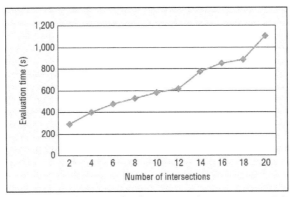

Time required ATS and Adapts experiments on one PC.

In this case, the initial agent-distribution map will be more accurate. To achieve this superior performance, however, testing a large amount of typical traffic scenes requires enormous computing resources. Researchers have developed many traffic strategies based on AI. Some of them such as neural networks consume a lot of computing resources for training in order to achieve satisfactory performance. However, if a traffic strategy trains on actuator, the actuator's limited computing power and inconstant traffic scene will damage the performance of the traffic AI agent. As a result, the whole system's performance will deteriorate. If the traffic AI agent is trained before moving it to the actuator, however, it can better serve the traffic management system. Rational traffic decisions and distributions of agents need the support of ATS, which primarily use agent oriented programming technology. Agents themselves can be humans, vehicles, and so on. To ensure ATS mirrors real urban transportation, we need large computing resources to run many agents.

Storage

Vast amounts of traffic data such as the configuration of traffic scenes, regulations, and information of different types of agents in ATS need vast amounts of storage. Similarly, numerous traffic strategy agents and relative information such as control performances about agents under different traffic scenes also consume a lot of storage resources. Finally, the decision-support system requires vast amounts of data about the state of urban transportation. Two solutions can help fulfil these requirements:

- Equip all centres of urban-traffic management systems with a supercomputer.

- Use cloud computing technologies— such as Google's Map-Reduce, IBM's Blue Cloud, and Amazon's EC2—to construct intelligent traffic clouds to serve urban transportation.

The former both wastes social resources and risks insufficient capacity in the future. On the contrary, the latter takes advantage of the infinite scalability of cloud computing to dynamically satisfy the needs of several urban-traffic systems at the time. This way we can make full use of existing cheap servers and minimize the upfront investment of an entire system.

Intelligent Traffic Clouds

Urban-traffic management systems using intelligent traffic clouds have overcome the issues we've described. With the support of cloud computing technologies, it will go far beyond than any other multi agent traffic management systems, addressing issues such as infinite system scalability, an appropriate agent management scheme, reducing the upfront investment and risk for users, and minimizing the total cost of ownership.

Prototype

Urban-traffic management systems based on cloud computing has two roles: service provider and customer. All the service providers such as the test bed of typical traffic scenes, ATS, traffic strategy database, and traffic strategy agent database are all veiled in the systems core: intelligent traffic clouds. The clouds customers such as the urban-traffic management systems and traffic participants exist outside the cloud. The intelligent traffic clouds could provide traffic strategy agents and agent-distribution maps to the traffic management systems, traffic-strategy performance to the traffic-strategy developer, and the state of urban traffic transportation and the effect of traffic decisions to the traffic managers. It could also deal with different customers' requests for services such as storage service for traffic data and strategies, mobile traffic-strategy agents, and so on. With the development of intelligent traffic clouds, numerous traffic management systems could connect and share the clouds' infinite capability, thus saving resources. Moreover, new traffic strategies can be transformed into mobile agents so such systems can continuously improve with the development of transportation science.

Intersection Manager Price Update

Input: Different kinds of traffic loads, costs and demand.

- We are taking the different numbers of driver agents.

- One driver agent supply the traffic loads to another agent.

- All the agents will be working intersection operation with the intersection manager.

- Intersection manager control the excess load allocation process.

- Excess numbers of requests can be handled with updated cost.

- We are updating the route and provide the new route identification.

- Apply the assumption function and increases the driver agent's creation process, create the new agents prototype.

- Apply the transportation from one driver agent to another driver agent.

- Numbers of requests are travel till for finding the desired route identification process.

- According to capacity provide the sufficient agents.

- It can works on decision making strategies for getting the good densities specification process.

- Provides transportation with minimization cost specifications.

Output: Equilibrium results identification.

Here, artificial systems serve mainly as a platform for conducting computational experiments or for systematic, continuous application of computer simulation programs to analyze and predict behaviors of actual systems in different situations. In addition, we can use this mode to estimate, evaluate, and validate the performance of proposed solutions for online and offline decision making.

Architecture

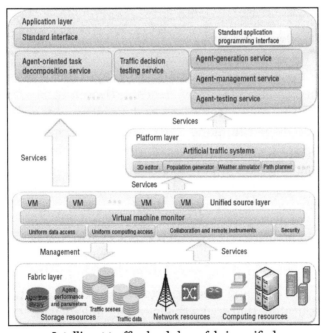

Intelligent traffic clouds have fabric, unified
source layer, platform and application layers.

According to the basic structure of cloud computing, an intelligent traffic clouds have four architecture layers: application, platform, unified source, and fabric. Figure shows the relationship between the layers and the function of each layer. The application layer contains all applications that run in the clouds. It supports applications such as agent generation, agent management, agent testing, agent optimization, agent oriented task decomposition, and traffic decision support. The clouds provide all the services to custoers through a standard interface. The platform layer is made of ATS, provided platform as a service. This layer contains a population synthesizer, weather simulator, path planner, 3D game engine, and so on to provide services to upper traffic applications and agent development.

The unified source layer governs the raw hardware level resource in the fabric layer to provide infrastructure as a service. It uses virtualization technologies such as virtual machines to hide the physical characteristics of resources from users to ensure the safety of data and equipment. It also provides a unified access interface for the upper and reasonable distribute computing resources. All those will help solve information silo problems in urban traffic and help fully mine useful information in the traffic data. Lastly, the fabric layer contains the raw hardware level resources such as computing, storage, and network resources. The intelligent traffic clouds use these distributed resources to cater the peak demand of urban-traffic management systems, support the running of agents and ATS test beds, and efficiently store traffic strategy agents and their performances.

Application of Cloud Computing in Education

Education system is mainly moving around the books, exams, marks and grades, where the creative learning lies far miles away. Teachers/Dosen teaches within the syllabus, students studies that part only, gives exams and it's all over! But change is occurred by creative thinking, and deeper thinking. That only occurs when you take your learning seriously but not the exams. So how do you improve it? Technology can be used as primary key in this situation. Now-a-days situation is changed, in many schools and colleges, the internet facility is available and even teachers use power-point presentation for teaching that improves easy understanding.

Cloud computing can be proved the boon in this scenario. Using Cloud Computing we can access any file or any document or even videos from any corner of the world. So it helps to give the basic lessons to those students who cannot afford it. Using the cloud computing, we can give easy and creative learning experience to the people and make the country more educated, that's why this new technology is used in worldwide now-a-days.

Cloud computing is a network of computing resources—located just about anywhere—that can be shared. Thus by implementing cloud computing technology we can overcome all these short comes and maintain a centralized system where all the authorities can check the education system from each and every aspects and continue monitor and guide the system. They not only check the needs of the institutions but also ensure that quality education is provide to every student and also his attendance, class performances etc can be effectively maintained without worrying for the infrastructure issue.

The cloud helps ensure that students, teachers/dosen, faculty, parents, and staff have on-demand access to critical information using any device from anywhere. Both public and private institutions can use the cloud to deliver better services, even as they work with fewer resources.

Present Education System

Most of the private educational institutions have become highly dependent on information technology to service their requirements. These services are increasingly provided using Internet technologies to faculty and students and accessed from web browsers. The services are offered cheaply or freely to education, often with much higher availability than can be provided by the educational institution.

Are we therefore facing a future where the majority of educational services will be hosted in the cloud and institutions no longer host their own data centers with expensive hardware, power bills, staff salaries and computing resources which are rarely fully utilized? This policy brief has analysed some of the emerging benefits and challenges of cloud computing for the educational sector. But in most of the government schools and colleges in Indonesia IT plays very limited role. Most of the work is done manually from attendance to classroom teaching to examination system.

Implementation of Cloud Technology in Education System

Cloud computing technology can provide solutions for the above mentioned problems in education system. Cloud computing enables users to control and access data via the Internet. The main users of a typical higher education cloud include students, Faculty, administrative staff, Examination Branch and Admission Branch as shown in Figure. All the main users of the institution are connected to the cloud .Separate login is provided for all the users for their respective work. Teachers can upload their class Tutorials, assignments, and tests on the cloud server which students will be able to access all the teaching material provided by the teachers via Internet using computers and other electronic devices both at home and college and 24 x 7. The education system will make it possible for teachers to identify problem areas in which students tend to make mistakes, by analyzing students' study records. In doing so, it will also allow teachers to improve teaching materials and methods.

This will not only make it possible for students to use online teaching materials during class but they will also be able to access these materials at home, using them to prepare for and review lessons. Utilization of cloud computing systems will reduce the cost of operation because servers and learning materials are shared with other colleges.

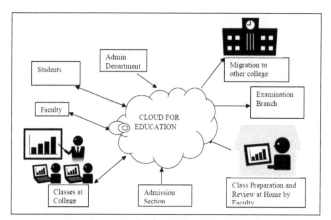

Services attached to Education Cloud.

In the traditional deployment model, all Information Technology resources are housed and managed in-house. Many aspects of these services and tools may be migrated to the cloud and consumed directly over the Internet either as fully functional applications (SaaS), development platforms (PaaS) or raw computing resources (IaaS). Figure shows how the different categories of university users may consume cloud services.

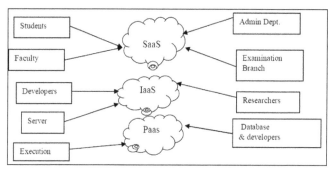

Users of an Education Cloud Computing System.

Benefits of cloud computing for institutions and students:

- Personalized learning: Cloud computing affords opportunities for greater student choice in learning. Using an Internet-connected device, students can access a wide array of resources and software tools that suit their learning styles and interests.

- Reduced costs: Cloud-based services can help institutes reduce costs and accelerate the use of new technologies to meet evolving educational needs. Students can use office applications for free without having to purchase, install and keep these applications up to date on their computers. It also provides the facility of Pay per use for some applications.

- Accessibility: Availability of the services is the most important and desired by the user using the education cloud. 24 x 7 is the availability that is needed by this system without failure. From anywhere one can login and access the information.

- Improved administrative efficiency of schools and universities: Colleges and the administrative staff can focus on the core functions of the institution instead of futile efforts on IT infrastructure and the applications set-up.

- No extra infrastructure: Colleges and governments are now free to focus on their goals that is making more research facilities available to the students and making the environment global in spite wasting time on worrying about the buildings, labs, teachers etc.

- Higher quality of education delivered anytime, anywhere: Courses with updated content can be delivered consistently across all locations.

- Standardisation of content: Courses delivered over cloud through a central location will lead to a standard content delivery to multiple remote virtual classrooms.

- Collaboration: Students and Colleges can collaborate on studies, projects using collaboration solutions.

- Agility to rollout new courses: Cloud-enabled technologies ensure rapid access to infrastructure services thereby rendering agility in rolling out newer products.

- Improved administrative efficiency of schools and universities: Teachers and the administrative staff can focus on the core functions of the institution instead of futile efforts on IT infrastructure and the applications set-up.

- Scalability: Scalable systems on cloud to provision big data platform for research and analysis.

- Go green: Education cloud will surely reduce the carbon footprint.

Considerations, Security Issues and Limitations

Table: Areas where cloud computing can have an impact.

Category	Description
Classroom Technology	
Engagement	• Centralised faculty assisted by local teachers • Students interaction with teachers, delivering lectures, presentations or response to polls and questions
Collaboration	• Students and teachers collaborating on projects by creating and sharing content • Communication by messaging or video
Mobility	• Extend classrooms and labs with mobile devices such as smartphones, • Tablets virtual desktop technologies facilitate remote access

Real-time assessment	• Adapting lessons based on observations of student interactions, notes taken • Content can be highlighted, annotated or updated via electronic media
Administrative Technologies	
CRM	• Student life-cycle management enables better management of recruitment and admissions, student financial aid and billing, student records and performance, transfers and alumni relationship
ERP	• Educational institutions manage internal and external resources including physical assets, financial and human resources
Business Intelligence	• Teachers and students use analytics in classrooms; evaluating and establishing curriculum
Smart campus	• Universities appear to be cities in themselves • The CIO is responsible for public safety, transportation, energy and water management, building maintenance, student services

Key Considerations

As barriers to technology adoption reduce and education industry looks to leverage technology to drive business advantage, following are the key questions to consider:

- Is there a business case for cloud?

- Which cloud service or deployment model is the most appropriate for my organisation?

- How can one profile, prioritise and architect services to migrate to cloud?

- How can cloud help me as I plan for a technology refresh or data center expansion?

- How should I create my vendor selection process and structure contracts and SLAs?

Security Issues

In cloud computing we are saving our important and crucial data in one place and it will be easy for hack. Protection of data is a major security issue. Educational Institutions may consider that their data is more secure if it is hosted within the institution. Transferring data to a third party for hosting in a remote data Centre, not under the control of the institution on and the location of which may not be known presents a risk. Some cloud providers now provide guarantees in their contracts that personal data will only be stored in particular countries. It has been suggested that the provision of cloud services through a single provider is a single point of failure and that it would be better to contract more than one cloud provider in order to minimize risk. Another security issue is Unsolicited advertising in which cloud providers will target users with unsolicited email or advertising.

Limitations

Following are the limitations of the Cloud in the education:

- Though the initial cost the system is very low, maintenance cost of the system is high.

- The security of the cloud is also the important issue need to be considered. Less secured cloud can be attacked from outsiders easily.

- Not all applications support the cloud structure.

- Low internet speed is major issue in the rural areas, where internet service provider may or may not have station. So due to less internet speed, the system should not be prove effective.

- The major problem about rural areas is the load shedding or lack of electricity. Without electricity, this all system is just a big zero.

Business Applications of Cloud Computing

Today statistics confirm that almost 97% of large enterprises, but also medium and small businesses have already embraced the advantages that cloud computing offers to a customer. Now, after the executives adopted the technology, they are exploring the ways to use it, in order to strategize their business goals. But cloud computing has many options to offer different users.

What Type of Cloud Services to use?

Cloud computing provides users with access to data everywhere if there is only an internet connection. In the today's ever-changing business climate, it is critical that business owners and employees get the much needed information right when they need it, whether they're on their computers, tablets or mobile phones – or in the office, out in the field, or on the road. This is exactly the convenience that cloud computing offers.

Cloud computing, as a term, covers different types of cloud services: storage, backup, software as a service (SaaS) and cloud hosting. Each company uses the type of service it needs. However, there is also another classification. Business owners use three types of cloud services to store their data and provide services: public, private or hybrid.

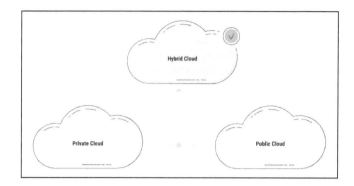

Public cloud: It is built on an external platform run by a cloud service provider. With this off-site service, users get their own cloud within a shared infrastructure. The provider offers everything from system resources to the security and maintenance of the cloud system. Everything is managed by an outside company specializing in cloud services. This type of cloud service is well suited to organizations that appreciate flexibility and cost-effectiveness.

Private cloud: This is a cloud platform built inside a company using the company's own hardware and software. A private cloud is managed by an internal IT team, so organizations have to build their own data centers, which makes it a costlier cloud option. However, this is the ideal solution for businesses that prefer an exclusive access and greater control over their cloud.

Hybrid cloud: A hybrid service unites both private and public clouds advantages. In a hybrid cloud system, an organization's own IT team manages the in-house cloud part, and the rest is done off-site. A hybrid cloud system is perfect for an organization that would rather manage all business-related data (such as customer files) in-house while storing the less-sensitive information with a third party.

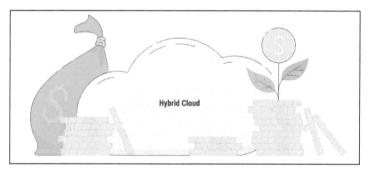

Despite all the benefits and advantages that cloud services offer, many business executives are having concerns about the safety of the cloud data. Cyber attacks are at an all-time high, and no business is completely safe. Companies are worried about their sensitive data and its vulnerability to unauthorized users in the cloud. While a public cloud is typically accessed with designated usernames and passwords, verifying the user identity itself remains a top concern. This is why the wide majority of big companies prefer private or hybrid clouds. Another solution would be to find the right cloud service provider, which can guarantee the safety of the information.

Accelerating Business Growth with Cloud Computing

The cloud technology journey began from a personal storage to an organization's storage system. The cloud itself gives small organizations the ability to grow quickly. This technology has many advantages like mobility, efficiency, cost-effectiveness, simplified collaboration, and high-speed connectivity.

The adoption of cloud services continues to rise and providers offer more and more options for small and big businesses. A good example is Cloud to Cloud Connectivity. Some businesses are not particularly fond of being tied to a single cloud provider, which is why multiple cloud providers are opening up the APIs on Platforms for connecting multiple solutions. Opening up APIs is necessary in order to synchronize the cross-functional process and data management, but it is also practical for integrating and connecting of systems and tools.

Reducing the costs is a good way to free more money and resources for achieving business goals. Instead of investing tens or hundreds of thousands of dollars upfront on servers and data centers, some of which a company might not even use, the company can leverage cloud computing resources to avoid the upfront capital expense of buying computer hardware. This is especially practical for start-ups, but also for small and medium businesses.

Most cloud providers maintain server availability over 99.9% and many of them have service level agreements that provide you with credits if their monthly uptime percentage drops below certain thresholds. The reason for this is that if one server fails, the applications hosted on that server can easily be transitioned to another available server. So, using a cloud for hosting websites or internet-stores is a better solution than maintaining in-house servers.

Cloud computing allows enterprises to obtain IT resources with minimal cost and time investment. This significantly shortens the time it takes to get a product to the market. Instead of provisioning servers, such enterprises focus on their business, deploy critical apps more quickly, delight the customers, and stay one step ahead of the competitors.

The cloud has transformed the way how corporations do business, securing for the users an increase in cost savings, efficiency, and agility.

Cloud Computing Implementation

From startups to large international businesses, many companies have already adopted cloud computing technologies to launch their applications, store their data, and automate processes. Yet, implementing a new type of technology requires training personnel and establishing an effective troubleshooting system.

A successful cloud computing implementation requires several important steps: a company should choose the could type, select the platform and service provider, determine the service level agreements, and solve all open questions before migrating data to the cloud. Sound decisions should take into account following three points:

Costs

Migration and overhead costs may vary widely depending on the target Cloud platform. This could skew the estimated cost savings. A cost analysis helps decide whether to go ahead with moving a particular application to the cloud or not, from a return on investment perspective. Estimated costs should include all capital expenditure, operational expenditure, and the overhead costs involved in migration.

Migration Strategy

Defining a migration strategy involves understanding the various migration options available, establishing business priorities, and evolving a strategy that offers a fine balance between costs and business priorities. On a basic level, enterprises have the two following options of a cloud infrastructure – private or public. The choice is driven by priorities such as business model and go-to-market strategy, and constrained by factors such as technical feasibility, security, and migration costs.

Data Migration

A provider must explain how data migration will be implemented. This is the single most important task of a cloud computing provider, because this will influence not only the future efficiency of an application but also the data security. A detailed plan with a corresponding time frame should be expected from the provider. This should be done to ensure proper migration without having to deal with future insecurities.

Creating and implementing a cloud strategy takes time, energy and effort. It is important to choose the right cloud strategy that would help the enterprise open up new market opportunities, grow the business and increase customer loyalty.

The Cloud is a globally growing platform. And one of the fundamental reasons responsible for its growth is its affordability. Cloud resources, offered by a computing service provider, significantly cut costs of purchasing expensive business systems and equipment.

Cloud Computing Applications for Biomedical Science

For certain types of biomedical applications, cloud computing has emerged as an alternative to locally maintained traditional computing approaches. Cloud computing offers users pay-as-you-go access to services such as hardware infrastructure, platforms, and software for solving common biomedical computational problems. Cloud computing services offer secure on-demand storage and analysis and are differentiated from traditional high-performance computing by their rapid availability and scalability of services. As such, cloud services are engineered to address big data problems and enhance the likelihood of data and analytics sharing, reproducibility, and reuse.

Progress in biomedical research is increasingly driven by insight gained through the analysis and interpretation of large and complex data sets. As the ability to generate and test hypotheses using high-throughput technologies has become technically more feasible and even commonplace, the challenge of gaining useful knowledge has shifted from the wet bench to include the computer. Desktop computers, high-performance workstations, and high-performance computing systems (HPC clusters) are currently the workhorses of the biomedical digital data research endeavor. Recently, however, cloud computing, enabled by the broad adoption and increasing capabilities of the internet and driven by market need, has emerged as a powerful, flexible, and scalable approach to disparate computational and data–intensive problems.

Cloud computing is a model for enabling convenient, on-demand network access to a shared pool of configurable computing resources (e.g., networks, servers, storage applications and services) that can be rapidly provisioned and released with minimal management effort or service provider interaction.

NIST categorizes clouds as one of 4 types: public, private, community, and hybrid. In a public cloud, the infrastructure exists on cloud provider premises and is managed by the cloud provider, whereas in a private cloud, the infrastructure can exist on or off the premises of the cloud provider but is managed by the private organization. Examples of public clouds include Amazon Web Services (AWS), Google Cloud Platform (GCP), and Microsoft Azure. A community cloud is a collaborative effort where infrastructure is shared between several organizations—a specific community—that have common requirements for security and compliance. For example, the Federal Risk and Authorization Management Program (FedRAMP) is a United States government-wide program that provides a standardized approach to security assessment, authorization, and continuous monitoring of information technology (IT) infrastructure. The AWS Gov-Cloud is an example of a FedRAMP-accredited resource that operates as a community cloud that addresses US government community needs. The JetStream Cloud serves as a community cloud serving the scientific community. A hybrid cloud is a composition of 2 or more distinct cloud infrastructures—private, community, public—that remain unique entities but are bound together in a way that enables portability of data and software applications.

Cloud types can use one or more cloud services—Software as a Service (SaaS), Platform as a Service (PaaS), and Infrastructure as a Service (IaaS). SaaS enables the consumer to use the cloud provider's applications (e.g., Google Docs) that are running on a cloud provider's infrastructure, whereas PaaS enables consumers to create or acquire applications and tools and to deploy them on the cloud provider's infrastructure. IaaS enables a consumer to provision processing, storage, networks, and other fundamental computing resources. Most public cloud providers like AWS, GCP, and Microsoft Azure provide IaaS, PaaS, and SaaS, and the customer can select the best applicable solution for their individual needs.

Cloud adoption, regardless of type, has varied in industry because of different levels of security and other features required for operation. Previously, both public and private clouds have been used more in unregulated industries and to a lesser extent in regulated industries, but this is changing. Federally funded scientific data sets are being made available in public clouds. For example, Human Microbiome Project (HMP) data, funded by the National Institutes of Health (NIH), is available on AWS simple storage service (S3), and more biomedical data sets are becoming available in the cloud. Research investigators can now request permission from NIH to transfer controlled-access genomic and associated phenotypic data obtained from NIH-designated data repositories to public or private cloud systems for data storage and analysis. Subject to appropriate access controls on human subjects' data, the NIH is committed to making public access to digital data a standard for all NIH-funded research.

Advances across the biological scales, from sequencing instruments to health monitoring devices, image collections to the expansion of electronic health record (EHR) platforms, will see a reduced cost in the acquisition of data. Estimates indicate that in 2016, the NIH alone was supporting 650 petabytes (PB) of data at various institutional repositories. Both volume and complexity of biomedical data will significantly increase in coming years, bringing challenges for storage, management, and preservation, suggesting an increased usage of cloud computing. Biomedical research can benefit from the growing number of cloud-based big data tools and platforms being developed and refined for other industries.

Adopting Cloud for Biomedical Work

Consider examples of how clouds and cloud services have been deployed in biomedical work. In genomics alone, usage ranges from single applications to complete virtual machines with multiple applications. Additional information on cloud resources in bio-informatics has been provided previously.

Individual Tools

BLAST is one of the most frequently used tools in bioinformatics research. A BLAST server image can be hosted on AWS, Azure, and GCP public clouds to allow users to run stand-alone searches with BLAST. Users can also submit searches using BLAST through the National Center for Biotechnology Information (NCBI) application programming interface (API) to run on AWS and Google Compute Engine. Additionally, the Microsoft Azure platform can be leveraged to execute large BLAST sequence matching tasks within reasonable time limits. Azure enables users to download sequence databases from NCBI, run different BLAST programs on a specified input against the sequence databases, and generate visualizations from the results for easy analysis. Azure also provides a way to create a web-based user interface for scheduling and tracking the BLAST match tasks, visualizing results, managing users, and performing basic tasks.

CloudAligner is a fast and full-featured MapReduce-based tool for sequence mapping, designed to be able to deal with long sequences, whereas CloudBurst can provide highly sensitive short read mapping with MapReduce. High-throughput sequencing analyses can be carried out by the Eoulsan package integrated in a cloud IaaS environment. For whole genome resequencing analysis, Crossbow is a scalable software pipeline. Crossbow combines Bowtie, an ultrafast and memory efficient short read aligner, and SoapSNP, a genotyper, in an automatic parallel pipeline that can run in the cloud.

Workflows and Platforms

Integration of genotype, phenotype, and clinical data is important for biomedical research. Biomedical platforms can provide an environment for establishing an end-to-end pipeline for data acquisition, storage, and analysis.

Galaxy, an open source, web-based platform, is used for data–intensive biomedical research. For large scale data analysis, Galaxy can be hosted in cloud IaaS. Reliable and highly scalable cloud-based workflow systems for next-generation sequencing analyses has been achieved by integrating the Galaxy workflow system with Globus Provision.

The Bionimbus Protected Data Cloud (BPDC) is a private cloud-based infrastructure for managing, analyzing, and sharing large amounts of genomics and phenotypic data in a secure environment, which was used for gene fusion studies. BPDC is primarily based on OpenStack, open source software that provides tools to build cloud platforms, with a service portal for a single point of entry and a single sign-on for various available BPDC resources. Using BPDC, data analysis for the acute myeloid leukemia (AML) resequencing project was rapidly performed to identify somatic variants expressed in adverse-risk primary AML samples.

Scalable and robust infrastructure for Next Generation Sequencing (NGS) analysis is needed for diagnostic work in clinical laboratories. CloudMan is available on the AWS cloud infrastructure. It has been used as a platform for distributing tools, data, and analysis results. Improvements in using CloudMan for genetic variant analysis has been carried out by reducing storage costs for clinical analysis work.

As part of the Pan Cancer Analysis of Whole Genomes (PCAWG), common patterns of mutation in over 2,800 cancer whole genome sequences were studied, which required significant scientific computing resources to investigate the role of the noncoding parts of the cancer genome and for comparing genomes of tumor and normal cells. The PCAWG data coordinating center currently lists collaborative agreements with cloud provider AWS and the Cancer Collaboratory, an academic compute cloud resource maintained by the Ontario Institute for Cancer Research and hosted at the Compute Canada facility.

Multiple academic resources were used to complete analysis of 1,827 samples taking over 6 months. This was supplemented by the use of cloud resources, where 500 samples were analyzed by AWS in 6 weeks. This showed that public cloud resources can be rapidly provisioned to quickly scale up a project if increased compute resources are needed. In this instance, AWS S3 data storage was used to scale from 600 terabytes to multiple PBs. Raw reads, genome alignments, metadata, and curated data can also be incrementally uploaded to AWS S3 for rapid access by the cancer research community. Data search and access tools are also available for other researchers to use or reuse. Sequence read-level data and germline data are maintained at the controlled tier of the cloud, and access to read data requires preapproval from the International Cancer Genome Consortium (ICGC) data access compliance office.

The National Cancer Institute (NCI) has funded 3 cloud pilots to provide genomic analysis, computational support, and access capabilities to the Cancer Genome Atlas (TCGA) data. The objective of the pilots was to develop a scalable platform to facilitate research collaboration and data reuse. All 3 cloud pilots have received authoritative and harmonized reference data sets from the cancer Genomic Data Commons (GDC) that have been analyzed using a common set of workflows against a reference genome (e.g., GRCh38). The Broad Institute pilot developed FireCloud using the elastic compute capacity of Google Cloud for large-scale data analysis, curation, storage, and data sharing. Users can also upload their own analysis methods and data to workspaces and/or use Broad Institute's best practice tools and pipelines on preloaded data. FireCloud uses the Workflow Description Language (WDL) to enable users to run scalable, reproducible workflows.

The Institute for Systems Biology (ISB) pilot leverages several services on the GCP. Researchers can use web-based software applications to interactively define and compare cohorts, examine the underlying molecular data for specific genes or pathways of interest, share insights with collaborators, and apply their individual software scripts and programs to various data sets.

The ISB Cancer Genome Cloud (CGC) has loaded processed data and TCGA project metadata into the BigQuery managed database service, enabling easy data mining and data warehouse approaches to be used on large-scale genomics data. The Seven Bridges Genomics (SBG) CGC offers both genomics SaaS and PaaS and uses AWS. The platform also enables researchers to collaborate on the analysis of large cancer genomics data sets in a secure, reproducible, and scalable manner. SGB CGC implements Common Work-Flow language to facilitate developers, analysts, and biologists to deploy, customize, and run reproducible analysis methods. Users may choose from over 200 tools and workflows covering many aspects of genomics data processing to apply to TCGA data or their own data sets.

Efforts are underway by the NIH Center for Excellence in Big Data Computing at the University of Illinois, Urbana-Champaign to construct a Knowledge Engine for Genomics (KnowEnG). The KnowEnG system is deployed on a public cloud infrastructure—currently AWS—to enable biomedical scientists to access data-mining, network-mining, and machine-learning algorithms that can aid in extracting knowledge from genomics data. A massive knowledge base of community data sets called the Knowledge Network is at the heart of the KnowEnG system, and data sets, even those in spreadsheets, can be brought to KnowEnG for analysis.

Commercial (AWS, Microsoft Azure) cloud-based platforms (e.g., DNAnexus) enables analyses of massive amounts of sequencing data integrated with phenotypic or clinical information. Also, the application of deep learning-based data analysis tools (e.g., Deep Variant) in conjunction with DNAnexus have been used to call genetic variants from next-generation sequencing data. Other bioinformatics platforms (e.g., DNAstack) use the GCP for providing processing capability for over a quarter of a million whole human genome sequences per year.

Healthcare

Cloud computing applications in healthcare include telemedicine/teleconsultation, medical imaging, public health, patient self-management, hospital management and information systems, therapy, and secondary use of data.

Real-time health monitoring for patients with chronic conditions who reside at considerable distances from their health service providers have difficulty in having their health conditions monitored. One poignant example are patients who suffer from cardiac arrhythmias requiring continuous episode detection and monitoring. Wearable sensors can be used for real-time electrocardiogram (ECG) monitoring, arrhythmia episode detection, and classification. Using AWS EC2, mobile computing technologies were integrated, and ECG monitoring capabilities were demonstrated for recording, analyzing, and visually displaying data from patients at remote locations. In addition, software tools that monitored and analyzed ECG data were made available via cloud SaaS for public use. Also, the Microsoft Azure platform has been implemented for a

12-lead ECG telemedicine service. For storage and retrieval of medical images, deployment of Picture Archive and Communication System modules were deployed in a public cloud. A review of publications on cloud computing in healthcare has pointed out that many healthcare-related publications have used the term "cloud" synonymously with "virtual machines" or "web-based tools", not consistent with characteristics that define cloud computing, models, and services. Several commercial vendors are interacting with hospitals and healthcare providers to establish healthcare services through cloud computing options.

General Purpose Tools

CloVR is a virtual machine that emulates a computer system, with preinstalled libraries and packages for biological data analysis. Similarly, Cloud BioLinux is a publicly available resource with virtual machine images and provides over 100 software packages for high-performance bioinformatics computing. Both (CloVR and BioLinux) virtual machine images are available for use within a cloud IaaS environment.

Cloud adoption can also include managed services that are designed for general Big Data problems. For example, each of the major public cloud providers offer a suite of services for machine learning and artificial intelligence, some of which are pretrained to solve common problems, (e.g., text-to-speech). Database systems such as Google BigQuery and Amazon Redshift combine the scalable and elastic nature of the cloud with tuned software and hardware solutions to deliver database capabilities and performance not easily achieved otherwise. For large, complex biomedical data sets, such databases can reduce management costs, ease database adoption, and facilitate analysis. Several big data applications used in biomedical research, such as the Apache Hadoop software library, are cloud based.

Developing a Cloud-based Digital Ecosystem for Biomedical Research

The examples introduced above, some ongoing for several years, illustrate a departure from the traditional approach to biomedical computing. The traditional approach has been to download data to local computing systems from public sites and then perform data processing, analysis, and visualization locally. The download time, cost, and redundancy involved for enhancing local computing capabilities to meet data intensive biomedical research needs (e.g., in sequencing and imaging) makes this approach worthy of re-evaluation.

Large-scale projects, like PCAWG introduced above, have shown the advantage of using resources, both local and public cloud, from various collaborating institutions. For institutions with established on-premises infrastructure (e.g., high-speed network infrastructure, secure data repositories), developing a cloud-based digital ecosystem with options to leverage any of the cloud types (public, hybrid) can be advantageous. Moreover, developing and utilizing a cloud-based ecosystem increases the likelihood of open science.

To promote knowledge discovery and innovation, open data and analytics should be findable, accessible, interoperable, and reusable (FAIR). The FAIR principles serve as a guide for data producers, stewards, and disseminators for enhancing reusability of data, inclusive of data algorithms, tools, and workflows that are essential for good data lifecycle management. A biomedical data ecosystem should have capabilities for indexing of data, metadata, software, and other digital objects—a hallmark of the NIH Big Data to Knowledge (BD2K) initiative.

Being FAIR is facilitated by an emerging paradigm for running complex, interrelated sets of software tools, like those used in genomics data processing, and involves packaging software using Linux container technologies, such as Docker, and then orchestrating "pipelines" using domain-specific workflow languages such as WDL and Common Workflow Language. Cloud providers also provide batch processing (e.g., AWS Batch) capabilities that automatically provision the optimal quantity and type of compute resources based on the volume and specific resource requirements of the batch jobs submitted, thereby significantly facilitating analysis at scale.

In Fig we illustrate integration of data producers, consumers, and repositories via a cloud-based platform for supporting the FAIR principles.

The core of a cloud-based platform should support the notion of a commons—a shared ecosystem maximizing access and reuse of biomedical research data and methods.

A cloud-based commons ecosystem can collocate computing capacity, storage resources, database, with informatics tools and applications for analyzing and sharing data by the research community. For multiple commons to interoperate with each other there are 6 essential requirements—permanent digital IDs, permanent metadata, APIs, data portability, data peering, and pay for compute.

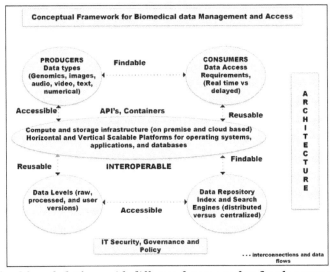

Conceptual cloud-based platform with different data types that flow between producers and consumers requiring variable data level needs.

Other features of the ecosystem include indexing and search capabilities similar to DataMed and a metalearning framework for ranking and selection of the best predictive algorithms. Many of the bioinformatics software tools have been successfully deployed in cloud environments and can be adapted to the commons ecosystem, including Apache Spark, a successor to Apache Hadoop and MapReduce for data analysis of Next Generation Sequencing Data. In addition, the data transfer and sharing component of the cloud-based commons ecosystem can include features discussed for the Globus Research Data Management Platform. We also envision cloud-based commons to be supported by techniques and methods that use a semantic data–driven discovery platform designed to continuously grow knowledge from a multitude of genomic, molecular, and clinical data.

Security is an integral part of a cloud commons architecture along with data policy, governance, and a business case for sustaining a biomedical digital ecosystem. For initial security controls assessment, guidance documents such as Federal Information Security Management Act (FISMA), NIST-800-53, and Federal Information Processing Standards (FIPS) can provide tools for an organizational assessment of risk and for validation purposes. Security in public cloud services is a shared responsibility, with the cloud provider providing security services and the end user maintaining responsibility for data and software that leverage those services. A wide range of issues involving ethical, legal, policy, and technical boundaries influence data privacy, all of which are dependent on the type of data being processed and supported.

A regular training program for data users of the cloud, especially for handling sensitive data (e.g., personally identifiable information) is important. The training should include methods for securing data that is moved to the cloud, and controlling access to the cloud resources, including virtual machines, containers, and cloud services that are involved for data life cycle management. Protecting access keys, using multifactor authentication, creating identity and access management user lists with controlled permissions, following the principle of least privilege—configured to perform actions that are needed for the users—are some of the recommended practices that can minimize security vulnerabilities that could arise from inexperienced cloud users and/or from malicious external entities.

Assessing risk is key to reliably determining the required level of protection needed for data in the cloud. A structured questionnaire approach developed as a Cloud Service Evaluation Model (CSEM) can be used to ascertain risks prior to migration of data to the cloud. Based on the results of risk assessment, a suitable cloud deployment model can be chosen to ensure compliance with internal policies, legal, and regulatory requirements, which, externally, differ in different parts of the world, potentially impacting the ubiquitous nature of cloud resources.

Striving towards open biomedical data has motivated an interest in improving data access while maintaining security and privacy. For example, a community-wide open competition for developing novel genomic data protection methods has shown the feasibility of secure data outsourcing and collaboration for cloud-based genomic data analysis. The findings from the work demonstrate that cryptographic techniques can support public cloud-based comparative analysis of human genomes. Recent work has shown that by using a hybrid cloud deployment model, 50%–70% of the read mapping task can be carried out accurately and efficiently in a public cloud.

In summary, a cloud-based ecosystem requires capability for interoperability between clouds, development of tools that can operate in multiple cloud environments and that can address the challenges of data protection, privacy, and legal constraints imposed by different countries.

Cloud Advantages and Disadvantages for Biomedical Projects

Cloud costs vary among biomedical projects and among vendors, so defining technical requirements for provisioning resources (e.g., amount of memory, disk storage, and CPU use) is an important first step in estimating costs. Remember the intent of commercial public cloud providers is to have you continue to use their cloud environment. For example, data may be free to upload but expensive to download, making adoption of commons approach in the cloud even more important for hosting large-scale biological data sets. This approach can meet community needs of data producers, consumers, and stewards to improve access and minimize the need for downloading sets to local institutions. To test this approach, NIH has initiated a data commons pilot by supporting the hosting of 3 important data sets, namely, Trans-Omics Precision Medicine initiative (TOPMed), Genotype Tissue Expression project (GTEx), and Alliance of Genomics Resource link, a consortium for Model Organism Databases (MODS) in the cloud.

Many cloud providers make available calculators for estimating approximate usage costs for their respective cloud services. Without any point of reference to start with, estimating costs may be challenging. Commercial public cloud providers generally offer free credit with new accounts, which may be sufficient to kickstart the planning and evaluation process. Cloud service charges are based on exact usage in small time increments, whereas on site compute costs are typically amortized over 3–5-year periods for systems that can be used for multiple projects. Though cost comparisons between local infrastructure and cloud approaches are frequently sought, in practice, such comparisons are often difficult to perform effectively due to the lack of good data for actual local costs. Moreover, funding models for cloud computing differ among institutions receiving the funds and the funders themselves. For example, use of cloud resources may be subject to institutional overhead, whereas on-site hardware may not. This is not the best use of taxpayer money, and funding agencies should review their policies with respect to cloud usage by institutions charging overhead. Given the growing competitiveness in the cloud market, cloud resources may be negotiable or available under special agreements for qualifying research and education projects.

Biomedical researchers in collaboration with IT professionals will need to determine the best way to leverage cloud resources for their individual projects. Computing costs for using on premise infrastructure requires determining the total cost of ownership (TCO). Both direct and indirect costs contribute towards TCO. Direct costs include hardware purchase costs, network services, data center, electricity, software licenses, and salaries. Indirect costs typically include technical support services, data management, and training. Indirect institutional costs vary significantly depending on the complexity of the project. Productivity is a consideration when assessing costs. For example, a whole genome pipeline in a cloud environment, once prototyped, can be scaled up for processing entire genomes with subsequent minimal human cost.

Using idle computing nodes in the cloud that are preemptible is one of the ways to reduce computing cost, but at the risk of increasing time to compute. For example, a recent report using the NCI cloud pilot ISB-CGC for quantification of transcript-expression levels for over 12,000 RNA-sequencing samples on 2 different cloud-based configurations, cluster-based versus pre-emptible, showed that the per sample cost when using the pre-emptible configuration was less than half the cost compared to the cluster-based method.

Other approaches have used linear programming methods to optimally bid on and deploy a combination of underutilized computing resources in genomics to minimize the cost of data analysis.

Cloud environments are pay-as-you-go, whereas research funding for computation is typically given at the beginning of an award and estimated on an annual basis. This can lead to a mismatch between the need for compute and the resources to meet that need. The NIH undertook a cloud credits pilot to assess an alternative funding model for cloud resources, details will be fully described in. Credits were awarded when needed as opposed to up front, thereby matching usage patterns. A simple application and review mechanism available to a funded investigator means credits can typically be awarded in weeks or less. The investigator can choose with which cloud provider to spend the credits, thereby driving competition into the marketplace and presumably increasing the amount of compute that can be performed on research monies.

Cloud credits have focused on incentivizing cloud usage; however, a challenge that remains to be addressed is longer term data sustainability in cloud environments. The cost for data management and storage for retaining all the data produced during a research program can be prohibitive as collections become large. One of the ways to proactively tackle this issue is by engaging data producers, consumers, and curators from the beginning of the research data lifecycle process for developing value-based models for data retention, which can be implemented via cloud storage. Based on usage patterns, a policy driven data migration to least expensive cloud storage pools can be adopted. Our perspective is that long-term retention of biomedical data is an excellent venue for public and private institutions to partner together, to explore ways for co-ownership to manage cost and policy that can continue to make research data accessible over time.

Cloud usage, from large-scale genomics analysis to remote monitoring of patients to molecular diagnostics work in clinical laboratories, has advantages but also potential drawbacks. A first step is the determination of what type of cloud environment best fits the application and then whether it represents a cost-effective solution. This introduction attempts to indicate what should be considered, what the options are, and what applications are already in use that may serve as references in making the best determination on how to proceed.

Cloud vendors provide multiple services for compute, storage, deployment of virtual machines, and access to various databases. Cloud vendors and third parties provide additional services to map users ranging from novices to experts. The ubiquitous nature of clouds raises questions regarding security and accessibility, particularly as it relates to geopolitical boundaries. Cost benefits of using clouds over other compute environments need to be carefully assessed as they relate to the size, complexity, and nature of the task. Clouds are termed elastic as they expand to embrace the compute needs of a task. For example, a simple, small prototype can be tested in a cloud environment and immediately scaled up to handle very large data. On the other hand, there is a cost associated with such usage, particularly in extricating the outcomes of the computation. Cloud vendors are seeking an all-in model. Once you commit to using their services, you continue to do so or pay a significant penalty. This, combined with being a pay-as-you-go model, has implications when mapped to the up-front funding models of typical grants. The idea of environments where multiple public cloud providers are used in a collective ecosystem is still mostly on the horizon. What is clear, however, is that clouds are a growing part of the biomedical computational ecosystem and are here to stay.

References

- Cloud-based-energy-management: wattics.com, Retrieved 19 May, 2019

- Cloud-computing-manufacturing-industry-don-t-get-left-behind, cloud-computing: industryweek.com, Retrieved 08 August, 2019

- Benefits-of-cloud-computing-for-manufacturers: industrytoday.com, Retrieved 11 June, 2019

- Application-of-Cloud-Computing-in-Education-292607782: researchgate.net, Retrieved 21 July, 2019

- Business-applications-of-cloud-computing: computools.com, Retrieved 27 March, 2019

Permissions

All chapters in this book are published with permission under the Creative Commons Attribution Share Alike License or equivalent. Every chapter published in this book has been scrutinized by our experts. Their significance has been extensively debated. The topics covered herein carry significant information for a comprehensive understanding. They may even be implemented as practical applications or may be referred to as a beginning point for further studies.

We would like to thank the editorial team for lending their expertise to make the book truly unique. They have played a crucial role in the development of this book. Without their invaluable contributions this book wouldn't have been possible. They have made vital efforts to compile up to date information on the varied aspects of this subject to make this book a valuable addition to the collection of many professionals and students.

This book was conceptualized with the vision of imparting up-to-date and integrated information in this field. To ensure the same, a matchless editorial board was set up. Every individual on the board went through rigorous rounds of assessment to prove their worth. After which they invested a large part of their time researching and compiling the most relevant data for our readers.

The editorial board has been involved in producing this book since its inception. They have spent rigorous hours researching and exploring the diverse topics which have resulted in the successful publishing of this book. They have passed on their knowledge of decades through this book. To expedite this challenging task, the publisher supported the team at every step. A small team of assistant editors was also appointed to further simplify the editing procedure and attain best results for the readers.

Apart from the editorial board, the designing team has also invested a significant amount of their time in understanding the subject and creating the most relevant covers. They scrutinized every image to scout for the most suitable representation of the subject and create an appropriate cover for the book.

The publishing team has been an ardent support to the editorial, designing and production team. Their endless efforts to recruit the best for this project, has resulted in the accomplishment of this book. They are a veteran in the field of academics and their pool of knowledge is as vast as their experience in printing. Their expertise and guidance has proved useful at every step. Their uncompromising quality standards have made this book an exceptional effort. Their encouragement from time to time has been an inspiration for everyone.

The publisher and the editorial board hope that this book will prove to be a valuable piece of knowledge for students, practitioners and scholars across the globe.

Index

A

Amazon Web Services, 55, 76, 93, 95, 105, 198, 215
Api Gateway, 82, 84-85
Appneta, 24
Asynchronous Messaging, 86, 176
Azure Load Balancer, 99

B

Back End Architecture, 47-48
Basic Traditional Servers, 152
Big Data, 54-56, 89, 106, 209, 215-216, 219-221

C

Cisco Intercloud Fabric, 76
Cloud Backup, 73, 75
Cloud Based Energy Management, 193
Cloud Bursting, 61, 67, 75-77
Cloud Computing Architecture, 45-47, 52, 169
Cloud Computing Networking, 61-62, 64, 68
Cloud Data Management, 36
Cloud Infrastructure, 10, 31, 36, 38, 41, 45, 52, 63-64, 87-90, 100, 113-115, 140-142, 177, 214, 218-219
Cloud Load Balancer, 95
Cloud Monitoring, 1, 20-24, 115
Cloud Platform, 38-41, 48, 52, 54-56, 105, 130, 196, 212, 214-215
Cloud Radio Access Networks, 151, 156-157
Cloud Runtime, 47-48
Cloud Service Evaluation Model, 222
Cloud Sql, 55-56
Cloud Storage, 41, 48, 55-56, 72-75, 89, 92, 108, 125, 127-128, 130-131, 134-135, 144, 175, 224
Cloud-based Demand Response, 188
Cloudbim, 38
Community Cloud, 50, 59, 215-216
Configuration Management, 17, 108
Cpouta, 107, 109
Cyber Security, 7, 10, 145, 147-148

D

Data Concealment, 127
Data Confidentiality, 124-128

Data Integrity, 124, 126, 131, 134, 136-137
Data Loss Prevention, 146
Database Management, 71, 124, 131-132
Database Outsourcing, 131-133
Distributive Storage, 126

E

Exoprise, 20, 23

F

Fog Computing, 156
Function-as-a-service, 182

G

Google Cloud Platform, 48, 54-56, 105, 215

H

High-performance Computing, 108, 215
Homomorphic Encryption, 125
Hybrid Cloud Architecture, 51, 174
Hybrid Cloud Computing, 151, 172-173
Hybrid Cloud Management, 177-178
Hybrid Clouds, 4, 23, 51, 173, 213

I

Infrastructure As A Service, 3-4, 88, 103-104, 107, 112, 115, 117, 151, 178, 192, 206, 216
Intelligent Traffic Clouds, 203-206
Internet Of Things, 7, 54, 155

L

Load Balancing, 55-56, 65, 92-97, 99, 105, 121

M

Microsoft Azure, 50, 55, 57, 76, 93, 99, 106, 215-217, 219
Microsoft Cloud Monitoring, 23
Mobile Cloud Computing, 1, 26, 28-30
Mobile Server Cloud Computing, 28
Mobile Service Clouds, 28
Monitoring As A Service, 103, 110, 113-114
Multi-cloud, 46, 151, 178-180, 186
Multiple-input Multiple-output, 157

N
Network-as-a-service, 191

O
Openstack, 24, 39, 107, 109, 217

P
Platform As A Service, 3-4, 89, 103-104, 112, 115-117, 151, 178, 192, 206, 216
Private Clouds, 11-12, 50, 58, 69, 88, 115, 173-174, 216
Public Cloud Architecture, 49-50
Public Clouds, 25, 49-50, 56, 173-174, 178, 212, 215-217

Q
Query Integrity Assurance, 131

S
Security As A Service, 126, 145-147
Serverless Computing, 151, 180-185

Servers, 1, 4, 6, 9, 14, 22, 36, 40, 43, 56, 61-62, 64-68, 70, 76, 86, 96, 100, 104, 111, 114, 120, 123, 128, 137, 142, 148, 153, 186, 204, 207, 213, 215
Simple Storage Services, 106
Software As A Service, 3, 21, 103-104, 112, 116-118, 120-121, 145, 151, 178, 192, 211, 216
Sustainable Cloud Computing, 1, 34, 42-43

V
Virtual Machine, 11, 35, 40, 54, 105, 107-110, 127, 152, 220
Virtual Network, 36, 63, 69, 107, 110
Virtual Server, 13, 90-91, 152-153
Vmware, 24, 48, 70, 77, 151, 173

W
Wan, 62-63, 72, 76-77, 90, 103, 105, 114
Web Services, 28, 42, 47, 55, 76, 93, 95, 103, 105, 190, 198, 215
Web-application-based Security, 131, 137

CPSIA information can be obtained
at www.ICGtesting.com
Printed in the USA
BVHW011453060222
628243BV00003B/46